T0319909

The Industrial Dynamics of
the New Digital Economy

This book is dedicated to
the memory of Keith Pavitt

The Industrial Dynamics of the New Digital Economy

Edited by

Jens Frøslev Christensen

Professor in Management of Technology,
Copenhagen Business School, Denmark

and

Peter Maskell

Professor of Business Economics,
Copenhagen Business School, Denmark

Edward Elgar

Cheltenham, UK • Northampton, MA, USA

Published by
Edward Elgar Publishing Limited
Glensanda House
Montpellier Parade
Cheltenham
Glos GL50 1UA
UK

Edward Elgar Publishing, Inc.
136 West Street
Suite 202
Northampton
Massachusetts 01060
USA

A catalogue record for this book
is available from the British Library

Library of Congress Cataloguing in Publication Data

The industrial dynamics of the new digital economy/edited by Jens Frøslev
    Christensen and Peter Maskell.
        p. cm.
    'Most of the chapters are based on papers presented in an earlier
    version at the DRUID Summer Conference 2002 in Copenhagen on
    "Industrial Dynamics of the New and Old Economy". Since its
    formation in 1995 DRUID – the Danish Research Unit for Industrial
    Dynamics – has organized biannual thematic conferences ...' – p. 2.
    Includes bibliographical references and index.
    1. Electronic commerce—Management—Congresses. 2. Business—
Data processing—Congresses. I. Frøslev Christensen, Jens. II. Maskell,
Peter.
HF5548.32.I53   2003
381'.1—dc21   2003051321

ISBN 1 84376 376 1

Printed and bound in Great Britain by MPG Books Ltd, Bodmin, Cornwall

Contents

Figures

Tables

ix

Contributors

Bo Carlsson
Department of Economics
Weatherhead School of Management
Case Western Reserve University

Dieter Ernst
Department of Economics
East-West Center
Honolulu, Hawaii, USA

Christopher Freeman
Science and Technology Policy Research (SPRU)
University of Sussex

Jens Frøslev Christensen
Department of Industrial Economics and Strategy (IVS)
Copenhagen Business School

Robert Inklaar
Faculty of Economics
University of Groningen
and the Conference Board

Martin Kenney
Department of Human and Community Development
University of California, Davis

Peter Maskell
Department of Industrial Economics and Strategy (IVS)
Copenhagen Business School

Robert H. McGuckin
Faculty of Economics
University of Groningen
and the Conference Board

Sandro Mendonça
DINÂMIA/ISCTE

Keith Pavitt
Science and Technology Policy Research (SPRU)
University of Sussex

W. Edward Steinmueller
Science and Technology Policy Research (SPRU)
University of Sussex

Nils Stieglitz
Philipps University Marburg

Bart van Ark
Faculty of Economics
University of Groningen
and the Conference Board

Foreword

Christopher Freeman

Keith Pavitt would have been proud that this intensely interesting book was dedicated to his memory. He would have been proud for many reasons. First of all, he always took a special delight in his participation in international projects and meetings. Ever since he started work in the OECD in the early 1960s, his approach to all his work was profoundly international in spirit. He took part in innumerable international seminars and conferences all over the world, but especially in Europe and the United States. The chapters in this book have been contributed by scholars from half a dozen different countries which certainly would have pleased him. When he left the OECD and came to work in SPRU, he did his best at all times to develop an international spirit in all our activities and to welcome colleagues from beyond our shores. He was at pains to overcome the narrower and more insular attitudes of people like me and was partly successful in this. SPRU soon had a majority of non-English graduate students and researchers and took part in numerous international projects thanks to the work of Keith Pavitt in Europe and Geoff Oldham in the developing countries. Even in sport, his internationalism came through. Whereas older nationalists like me clung to the idea that national and local teams should actually be representative of their countries and towns, Keith welcomed the French takeover of his beloved Arsenal, both at the level of management and of players, believing that traditional out-of-date attitudes could only be overcome by a strong injection of modern skills from overseas.

More seriously, he was deeply convinced that the method of international comparisons over time could be extremely fruitful in the study of the evolution of policies for science and technology. One of the reasons that he was willing to come and work in SPRU for nearly 40 years and for a much lower salary than in the OECD was that he believed that he would have the opportunity to study the changes in worldwide science and technology in depth over an extended period and to do so in industry and academia as well as in government. Together with colleagues like Pari Patel, he made extensive use of international statistics in such areas as patents and publications to illustrate the trends in scientific and technological activities. Several of the chapters in this volume illustrate some of the benefits of his approach, notably the chapter by

Sandro Mendonçã, as well as his own chapter. Keith Pavitt made especially valuable contributions to a taxonomy of industrial firms and to those processes of structural change which are exemplified in this book. They all illustrate the point that quantitative data illuminate policy problems only insofar as they are used within the framework of *qualitative* analysis and theory. Keith would have been especially glad that one of his last papers was a contribution to joint work with colleagues in AUC and in the Copenhagen Business School, which helped us all to understand the nature of the complex changes in technology and in the economy, which are transforming the so-called 'New Economy'. The experiences of Irving Fisher in the 1930s demonstrate how difficult and demanding this task can be.

I commend this book, in the spirit of Keith Pavitt, to all those who wish to understand, to appreciate and to criticize the 'New Economy' which now engulfs all our lives.

Introduction

Jens Frøslev Christensen and Peter Maskell

Since we entered the new millennium, the New Economy hype of the late 1990s has faded and proven to the world that whatever the New Economy may be about, it is not about eliminating cyclical dynamics in the economy. Only a few years ago the media got carried away with the prospects of ever-increasing returns. Now that the hype has subsided and the remaining Internet-related businesses have become mundane and 'normalized', the pendulum of popular interpretation has swung towards the other extreme: a 'nothing-has-changed' attitude.

The present book revisits the issue of the New Economy from a balanced perspective unembedded in any predominant and fashionable interpretation. The assembled authors are leading scholars of the implications of digital technologies and on the industrial and business dynamics of modern economies. Their contributions bring new knowledge and new perspectives to our understanding of the interplay between industrial dynamics and technical change.

One of the most striking general findings emerging from the studies presented in the book is related to the changes that have taken place within the Old Economy through exposure to and interaction with the New. While the digitization of existing processes may initially have been motivated by ideas of rationalization and cost-cutting, it has become evident that reaping the full benefits necessitates fundamental changes in procedures and organizational design. The effects have transcended the boundaries of the firm, as established channels of interaction with old partners have had to be reconfigured and the familiar division of labour rethought. Similarly, the entrepreneurial wave of the New Economy has challenged deep-rooted work practices of the Old while stimulating the imagination and promoting new schemes for profitable business.

Only slowly and reluctantly have the firms of the Old Economy responded to these novel challenges and picked up on the emerging opportunities. But gradually Information and Communication Technology (ICT) and other general-purpose technologies of the New Economy have started to seep into and help transform the Old. The real and long-term significance of the New Economy may actually be only loosely connected with the astonishing growth rates it reached on its own account in the glamorous heydays a few years back but is closely related to its broad and gradual impact on the innovation, productivity and organization of the vast industries of the Old Economy.

The book casts new light on these issues by presenting a series of empirical studies and theoretical reflections regarding central features of modern industrial dynamics. Most of the chapters are based on papers presented in an earlier version at the DRUID Summer Conference 2002 in Copenhagen on 'Industrial Dynamics of the New and Old Economy'. Since its formation in 1995 DRUID – the Danish Research Unit for Industrial Dynamics – has organized biannual thematic conferences, and the resources available through its homepage <www.druid.dk> have become prevalent within a truly global network of researchers. DRUID is anchored at Copenhagen Business School and Aalborg University and the summer conference in 2002 was organized in association with CISTEMA (Centre for Inter-disciplinary Studies in Technology Management), a research network based at Copenhagen Business School. The present book reflects a partnership between DRUID and CISTEMA. The individual contributions present new data, knowledge and interpretations of different aspects of the dynamics of the New Digital Economy. Taken together, they constitute a coherent framework for understanding recent processes of industrial dynamics and organization and thus for better differentiating new and emergent features of the increasingly digitally based network economy.

The book is structured into three parts, each representing a distinct analytical level: (1) the macro-economic and institutional level, (2) the corporate level and (3) the sectoral level. The first three chapters (by Bo Carlsson, Martin Kenney, and Bart van Ark, Robert Inklaar and Robert McGuckin) take an overall, macro-economic and institutional view on recent tendencies, especially in the US economy. The three subsequent chapters (by Keith Pavitt, Sandro Mendonça and Dieter Ernst) focus on the implications of digitization for the organization and strategies of the large industrial firm. Finally, the last three chapters (by Nils Stieglitz, Jens Frøslev Christensen and Edward Steinmueller) apply a sectoral view of the digital economy by studying the hand-held computer industry, Internet business services and the use of customer relations management (CRM) systems respectively.

The opening chapter by Bo Carlsson, 'The New Economy: what is new and what is not?' argues that the leap in productivity growth and several other economic indicators during the second part of the 1990s is consistent with the view that digitization of information and the Internet represents a form of general-purpose technology that is giving rise to a vast array of possible innovations and new combinations. Carlsson takes us back to ponder several historical cases of general-purpose technologies (transportation and communication technologies in the 19th century, the Corliss steam engine, and the electric motor) and shows that they have all led to higher efficiency and productivity in the economy as conventionally measured. However, perhaps the most important impacts of these technologies have been the mobilization of new combinations as reflected in innovation and entrepreneurship. After this historical journey, he provides examples of the massive and evolving impacts of digitization and the Internet on existing activities in existing industries (the oil industry), on restructuring of activities within industries (the banking industry, the automobile industry and the defence industry), on the market efficiency gains of the Internet, and on the new combinations leading to new products and industries. What is really new in the New Economy, according to Carlsson, is '... the Internet, [representing] a new level and form of connectivity among multiple heterogeneous ideas and actors, giving rise to a vast range of combinations'. Bo Carlsson concludes that so far, the New Economy has been largely a US phenomenon.

Martin Kenney's contribution, 'What goes up must come down: the political economy of the US Internet industry', sets out to analyse the specific features of the US innovation system that have given rise to the particularly strong entrepreneurial and innovative dynamics associated with the Internet. While Bo Carlsson views the Internet as a new general-purpose technology and focuses on the implications for traditional industries, Martin Kenney delivers a comprehensive historical analysis of the industrial and business dynamics of the Internet-related US economy. He provides evidence for his argument that certain characteristics of the US national system of innovation have proven particularly beneficial in mobilizing the commercial opportunities embedded in the originally university-based and government-funded Internet. Of particular importance for the rapid adoption and diffusion of the Internet in the US he points to the specific evolution in the economic organization of the telecommunication industry and to the particular modes of privatizing the Internet. Both contributed to the transformation of the Internet from a university- to a commercially-driven technology, in which university students and faculty played decisive roles. He demonstrates how Silicon Valley firms and venture capitalists were among the first to acknowledge and create the commercial opportunities surrounding the Internet. Hence, the regional core in the US innovation system once again demonstrated its ability to generate hyper-dynamic processes of technological and business experimentation, and US firms have captured and secured a leadership role in nearly every business area related to the Internet. To the question of what is new in the New Economy, Kenney hesitates to give a conclusive answer: '... if a New Economy refers to the implementation of a new communication system that allows the creation of new business models that may evolve so far as to change the organizational face of capitalism, then the question is still open'.

While Bo Carlsson's and Martin Kenney's chapters address the particularly powerful features of the US innovation system in stimulating the innovation and adoption of ICT technologies and especially the Internet, the chapter by Bart van Ark, Robert Inklaar and Robert McGuckin presents an analysis of the comparative dynamics of labour productivity performance during the 1990s between the United States and Europe and their association with ICT. The chapter examines international differences in labour productivity performance across ICT-producing industries, intensive ICT-using industries and less inten-sive ICT-users, with an additional breakdown into manufacturing and service industries. During the first half of the 1990s, aggregate productivity growth in Europe was considerably faster than in the United States, but since 1995, the picture has changed and the US has taken on the leading role. However, the chapter points out some important differences in comparative growth dynam-ics between industry groups. First, in the ICT-producing sector (including both manufacturing and service industries), computers and communication equip-ment have shown strong productivity growth and acceleration in virtually all countries. The contribution of these industries to aggregate productivity growth has been slightly higher in the US due to their larger size. Second, the key differences between Europe and the US have been found in the intensive ICT-using services, in which US productivity growth showed strong accelera-tion during the second half of the 1990s, whereas growth stalled in Europe. More specifically, the US showed rapid productivity expansion in retail and wholesale trade and securities, which account for much of the overall US-Europe gap since 1995. In contrast, in ICT-producing services the productivity growth in many European countries has been faster than in the US. This is mainly due to faster productivity growth in telecommunication services in Europe as a consequence of the rapid take-off of the market for wireless com-munication. The analysis moreover suggests that ICT diffusion in Europe is following similar industry patterns to those observed in the US, but at a con-siderably slower pace. This is consistent with Bo Carlsson's and Martin Kenney's assessment of the extremely powerful technology generating and adopting drivers in the US economy as compared to Europe.

After the initial focus on the aggregate features of the economy in Part I, the three subsequent chapters in Part II investigate the changing conditions for corporate dynamics in the New Digital Economy.

Keith Pavitt's chapter, 'What are advances in knowledge doing to the large industrial firm in the "new economy"?' engages in a dialogue with two of the major scholars of the theory and history of the modern firm, Edith Penrose and Alfred D. Chandler, with the objective of identifying new characteristics in the dynamics of the large firm. They are all concerned with the way in which the organization and practice of industrial firms since the industrial rev-olution have been conditioned by the production of technological knowledge.

Pavitt identifies two main characteristics of this process: (a) the continuous increase in specialization in production of both artefacts and knowledge and (b) the periodic waves of major innovations based on rapid improvements in specific technologies, the latest of which is ICT. He argues that this ongoing specialization in production and knowledge, when associated with the present wave of innovation in digital technologies, has increasingly disruptive effects on the large, integrated and diversifying manufacturing firm as described and analysed by Penrose and Chandler. These effects involve outsourcing an increasing share of product design and manufacture and an increasing focus on systems design and integration, including advanced applications of ICT. Thus, the historical tendencies towards vertical integration that Chandler analysed have been replaced by vertical disintegration or specialization. And earlier dynamics of product diversification in large firms, as analysed by Penrose, are confronted with increasing impediments. Whereas Penrose, like the late Schumpeter, saw the entrepreneurial function as a relatively manageable process, Pavitt argues that the experience of the past twenty years with the emergence of ICT suggests that this is not the case at all any more. The dynamics of technology have become more disruptive to the internal organization and routines of large firms. Moreover, specialization in knowledge production has increased the range of fields of knowledge, subsystems and components associated with the design and production of products. As a consequence, large firms have found it increasingly difficult to master fully the advances in all technological fields and to control the design and production of all subsystems and components. This process has led to increasing use of modular designs, and has driven the large firms to intensify their efforts to outsource and, partly as a consequence, to access external knowledge through networking. Pavitt envisions that these processes will lead to an increasing division of labour between system integration firms and manufacturing firms. However, he also points to limitations on the degree of possible vertical disintegration and argues that '[a]lthough vertically disintegrated, producers and designers are "relational" and not "arm's length"'. In this sense, the division of labour will remain incomplete and firms specializing in product development and systems integration will need to maintain competencies in related manufacturing, components, subsystems, logistics, etc. As a result, the former vertically integrated large manufacturing firms will be seen moving towards specializing within the 'skilled activities that manufacturing firms undertake, except manufacturing itself'.

Sandro Mendonça's contribution, 'News out of the old: the evolving technological incoherence of the world's largest companies' extends Pavitt's comprehensive analysis of the large industrial firm with an empirical study of the development of the technology portfolios of the large corporations during the 1980s and 1990s. The study builds on previous work on the multi-technology firm carried out by John Cantwell, Ove Granstrand, Keith Pavitt and others, which demonstrates how the corporate knowledge base became more complex during the twentieth century. The contemporary giants thus operated in an expanding range of technological areas, and in fact exhibited a much broader portfolio of technologies or competencies than of products. Using patent statistics, Mendonça is able to show how large companies are engaged in technology diversification that extends their technological capabilities to include 'New Economy' technologies, ICT, new materials and biotechnology. Most remarkable is the fact that this tendency is more pronounced for so-called nonspecialist sectors, that is, sectors that are not normally associated with these 'New Economy' technologies. With regard to ICT, Mendonça demonstrates that the growth in the volume of ICT patents originating in non-ICT sectors was much higher than the growth in patenting of typically ICT-producing sectors. In the words of Mendonça: '... cutting-edge technology capabilities in not only utilizing, but also generating ICT are of key importance for an increasing number of large corporations in almost all sectors'. Moreover there are clear empirical indications that ICT and materials technologies co-evolve with more traditional technologies, such as electrical and mechanical technologies, while biotechnology appears disconnected from the rest of the technology groups. One possible explanation of why the cluster of ICT-related technologies is increasingly developed, and not just utilized, by industries of the Old Economy is that '... ICT has the potential to "fuse" with many different technologies and that the resulting new technologies are likely to play a particular role in creating new areas of technological interconnectedness in the current paradigm'.

Dieter Ernst's chapter, 'Digital information systems and global flagship networks: how mobile is knowledge in the global network economy?' further extends Pavitt's study to include an analysis of the changing organization of international business. A central argument in Ernst's chapter is that two inter-related transformations may gradually reduce the constraints to international knowledge diffusion and exchange: the evolution of cross-border forms of corporate networking practices, especially as reflected in so-called global flagship networks (GFNs), and the increasing use of digital information systems. A defining characteristic of what Ernst terms 'the global network economy' is the transition from vertically integrated multinational corporations to GFNs, in which the flagships combine extensive outsourcing with integrative control mechanisms which are not based on ownership control. This shift in industrial organization of international business is, it is argued, driven by three inter-related factors: institutional changes since the 1970s towards liberalization in trade, capital flows, foreign direct investment policies and privatization; changes in competition and industrial organization; and the evolution of increasingly advanced digital information technologies. Two distinctive characteristics of GFNs are enhanced by these technologies: a rapid dispersion of value chain activities, and simultaneously, their integration into hierarchical networks. Thus, according to Ernst, these networks do not give rise to less hierarchical forms of organization than is the case with the 'multinational company' model. The counterpart of the global flagships is the myriad of local suppliers that join the flagship network. Since GFNs cannot work without substantial sharing of knowledge, local suppliers that manage to become integrated into such networks may benefit from virtual processes of learning and upgrading through knowledge exchange with the global flagships. Those suppliers who do not manage to get a foothold in such networks will tend to perish. A general implication of these dynamics is a reinforcement of the shift of manufacturing towards certain lower-wage countries that have invested in basic education and ICT infrastructures, a point also underlined in Pavitt's analysis.

The third part of the book contains three chapters, each dealing with particular dynamics of selected industries within The New Economy.

Nils Stieglitz's chapter, 'Digital dynamics and types of industry convergence: the evolution of the handheld computers market', raises the issue of industry and technology convergence. The first part of the chapter presents a typology of industry convergence involving the meeting of at least two industries through either technology-based convergence (technology substitution or integration) or product-based convergence (product substitution or product complementarity). Stieglitz's main proposition is that this typology of industry convergence 'allows the identification and disentanglement of different drivers of change in converging markets and provides a basic framework for analysing complex patterns of industry convergence'. Even if complex dynamics of industry convergence have always existed, such features have become reinforced in the increasingly digitalized economy. The second part of the chapter applies the typology to the case of the evolving handheld computer industry. It is shown that this industry initially emerged as the outcome of the dynamics of integration of a wide array of technologies developed in the consumer electronics, telecommunications and computer industries. Later in the development of this industry, convergence processes increasingly involved establishing product complementarity between handheld computers and online services mediated through new standards. More recently, dynamics towards product substitution between handheld computers and cell phones have encouraged product development in both the cellular phone industry and the handheld computer industry. This case illustrates a feature typical of industrial dynamics associated with digitization, namely that the rapid pace of technical development within the digital technology domains are constantly leading to the redrawing of industry boundaries, thus creating ongoing uncertainties about who your competitors, customers and suppliers are.

Jens Frøslev Christensen's contribution, 'Innovation, entrepreneurship and industrial dynamics in Internet services' takes its point of departure in Bo Carlsson's proposition (in the first chapter) that digitization and the Internet can be considered a general-purpose technology with particularly great impacts on service industries. In his analysis of the industrial dynamics of Internet services, Jens Frøslev Christensen identifies the structural and corporate patterns that within a period of just 6-7 years involved a massive wave of entrepreneurial and innovative entry, several boundary transformations as new types of Internet-related services emerged, as well as excessive cycles of mergers and acquisitions, alliance formations, divestitures and exits. While the early pioneers of the industry, the Web agencies, were *de novo* entrants, the later entrants (i.e. system developers, management consultants and system integrators) tended to be incumbent firms from other industries that have eventually come to be the predominant players in Internet services. The chapter confronts the empirical outline of this industry evolution with three 'old models' of industry dynamics that have proved particularly useful in understanding the dynamics of manufacturing industries (life cycle theory, organizational economics theory, and appropriability theory). It is shown that these frameworks also possess substantial explanatory power in understanding the dynamics of Internet services. However, contrary to most manufacturing sectors, this 'New Economy' sector has, like other Internet-related sectors, been subject to a much more rapid and turbulent development process which reflects '...the enormously wide applicability of Internet technology, its rapid diffusion..., the pre-existence of a huge installed base of PCs, and the enormous potential for innovation and entrepreneurship'. The analysis finally demonstrates the complex and dramatic prevalence of convergence dynamics for this sector.

Edward Steinmueller's contribution, 'Assessing European developments in electronic customer relation management in the wake of the dot.com bust', provides a thorough analysis of how European firms in important service sectors, such as finance, travel and retailing, have successfully engaged in electronic customer relation management (e-CRM) practices. Naive observers might have thought that the new opportunities to capture, retain, analyse and utilize digitized customer information would signal a return of sorts to the old personalized relationships between many businesses and customers that were 'disrupted' more than a century ago by the emergence of mass production and consumption. In the overly optimistic atmosphere of the early phase of e-CRM, the intermediate and intervening requirements for reaching the future were often perceived as mere 'details' that could be overcome quickly and effortlessly. This 'cognitive presbyopia' (seeing the distant future with a clear focus, while seeing the intervening events in a hazy or indistinct manner) gave way to a more sombre attitude when firms were confronted with the myriad of practical problems connected with identifying the needs of their specific customers and the way to meet them while creating new services. The reality is, Steinmueller shows, that few firms actually encourage close interactions between customers or emphasize the building of online communities. The study reported consists of 69 sample firms that have successfully engaged in specialized activities involving e-CRM. The practical problems of implementing the degree of integration suggested by the visionary proponents of e-CRM are plainly larger than most companies are willing to tackle at present. The Web-based applications of e-CRM are dominated by satisfying users' needs for information rather than interaction or transactions between companies and customers, and the principal value of the Internet is, Ed Steinmueller suggests, to 'extend and further articulate trends towards the "self service" economy in which customers produce services for themselves, principally the services involved in the informing and planning stages that occur prior to committing to a purchase transaction'.

Taken together, the chapters in this book combine to increase our understanding of how the industrial dynamics of the New Digital Economy unfold on the three levels of analysis investigated: the macro-economic, the corporate, and the sectoral level. The perspectives presented offer a wide-angled view on the topic in terms of geography and affiliation with contributions from many countries and different disciplines. Yet the stories told interact and reinforce each other. Observations made in one chapter are elaborated on in another, and the consequences of statements valid on one level of analysis are discussed when investigated on another in subsequent chapters. In this sense, the book reflects one of the most significant characteristics of the digital economy: the connectivity or inter-relatedness across traditional boundaries.

Co-ordinating a volume comprising nine chapters and eleven authors is never an easy task. We would like to thank Jill Archer for her sterling work in converting the multiple manuscript files into a coherent and readable form and preparing the final manuscript for press. In addition we would like to acknowledge the support provided by Jonas Kjær and Michael Olesen and in particular, Claus Fenger. Finally, thanks to Chris Freeman for kindly writing the foreword in memory of our dear colleague and mentor, Keith Pavitt.

PART I

1. The New Economy: What is New and What is Not?[1]

Bo Carlsson

1. INTRODUCTION

There is now mounting evidence that something new has happened in the United States economy during the last decade. The trend rate of non-farm labour productivity growth accelerated to 2.8 percent per year during 1995-1999 from 1.4 percent during 1972-1995 (US Department of Commerce, 2000, p. 1). There has been a similar acceleration in total factor productivity growth (TFP), not only in the computer sector but also more generally, especially in information technology (IT) intensive service industries (Baily and Lawrence, 2001). And while a five-year period is too short to render convincing evidence of a New Economy – there have been earlier periods with higher productivity growth than in the late 1990s – there are several indicators that something different happened during the US business expansion in the 1990s compared to those in the 1960s and 1980s: real GDP growth, real private investment, and real R&D expenditures accelerated as the business cycle grew older, while the rate of inflation declined and real profits continued to grow, in contrast to earlier cycles (US Department of Commerce, 2000, pp. 60-64).

There is also evidence of a wave of innovation manifested in a rise in Tobin's Q, a surge in R&D spending and the number of patents granted, a surge in production of IT, heightened competition in an increasingly deregulated economy facing strong international competition, a rising amount of R&D done in small companies, a rise in technology alliances and acquisitions, new forms of financing, and rapid growth of venture capital and the IPO market (Baily and Lawrence, 2001).[2]

Regardless of whether one regards such data as convincing evidence of a New Economy or simply as indicators of some interesting and possibly new patterns, the question is: what is the cause of the different behaviour of the US macro economy in the late 1990s compared to earlier periods? What is driving the observed changes?

In this chapter, I argue that the observed changes are at least consistent with the view that digitization of information, combined with the Internet, represents a form of general-purpose technology that is giving rise to a vast new array of possible combinations that we may refer to as the New Economy. The level of connectivity between actors and ideas is increasing dramatically. We have only begun to see the impact, and only part of it is measurable.

Interpreted in this way, the New Economy is about dynamics, not static efficiency. While economic growth can be described at the macro level, it can never be explained at that level. Economic growth results when a variety of actors create and use new technology. New technology is the result of new combinations of ideas. When connectivity increases, the number of possible new combinations also increases.

The chapter is organized as follows. The theoretical background is presented in the next section. This is followed by a brief review of historical examples of general-purpose technologies and their economic impact. Next, the effects of digitization and the Internet are reviewed: the productivity enhancement in traditional industries, the restructuring of economic activity within industries, the market efficiency effects, and the potential arising from entirely new products and industries. The chapter concludes with a brief summary.

2. THEORY

Schumpeter (1911) argued that economic growth is a result of innovations, i.e., new combinations of products, processes, markets, sources of supply, and organizations. The number of potential innovations is virtually unlimited. This means that at any moment only a small subset of all technical possibilities has been identified and only a yet smaller subset has been exploited commercially. Greater connectivity among actors and ideas creates more possible combinations through identification of existing opportunities and discovery of new ones. The economy is a system consisting of elements and connections. 'When connections change, so too does the structure of the system. When structure changes, the dynamic properties of the system change also. This changes the conditions under which connections exist; new ones may form, existing ones may fail or may even become strengthened' (Potts, 2001, p. 2).

Technological change occurs when the relationships among elements change or when new connections are established. Densely connected systems give rise to a large set of technical possibilities (a large state space), while more sparsely connected systems create fewer possibilities. 'In essence, the defining characteristic of the modern economy is extremely rapid technological, organizational and institutional change, all embedded within broader patterns of social change' (Potts, 2001, p. 4). This understanding of the modern economy is embedded in Eliasson's concept of the experimentally organized economy which incorporates a virtually unlimited set of technical possibilities as well as bounded cognition and rationality on the part of each actor. This combination makes it impossible to identify all possibilities (optimization is not possible); mistakes are therefore common; and more experiments lead to a larger number of technical possibilities (Eliasson and Eliasson, 1996).

Certain environments are more supportive of experimentation than others. It is useful to think of the business environment as an innovation system. While several types of innovation systems have been examined in the litera-ture, the notion of a technological system (Carlsson and Stankiewicz, 1991; Carlsson, 1995, 1997, 2002) has the advantage that it focuses on a particular technology or set of technologies and incorporates all the actors (not just those in the market), the networks through which they interact, and the institutional infrastructure. Thus, technological systems constitute frameworks that support the supply of innovations that give rise to new business opportunities. One of the functions of a technological system is to provide connections among vari-ous elements of the system.

There are three dimensions to technological systems: (1) a cognitive dimension, defining the clustering of technologies resulting in a new set of technological possibilities; this identifies the relevant knowledge base or 'design space' (see below) of the system, (2) an organizational and institution-al dimension, capturing the interactions in the network of actors engaged in the creation of these technologies, and (3) an economic dimension, consisting of the set of actors who convert technical possibilities into business opportuni-ties.

Technology can be interpreted as a set of combinatorial design spaces formed by clusters of complementary technical capabilities (Stankiewicz, 2002). A design space represents a small part of the opportunity set (the sum total of all technical possibilities). It may be thought of as a convenient way to group together the technical capabilities required for a particular type of eco-nomic activity. Design spaces undergo constant evolution.

There are three modes of technological growth (accumulation) in the design spaces: (1) expansion of the space through the addition of new capabil-ities; (2) progressive integration and structuring of the design spaces through the co-evolution of its various elements; and (3) accumulation of application-specific know-how linked to the evolutionary trajectories of particular arte-facts, such as, for instance, aircraft. Design spaces are potentially influenced by academic research (concepts, theories, research methods, and tools) and industrial R&D (increasing the absorptive capacity within the system).

If we apply the design space concept to economic activities involving digi-tization and the Internet, it is not hard to imagine that the Internet makes it easier than before to connect people, ideas and bodies of knowledge. This

makes it more likely that new capabilities will emerge and that previously separate activities will be connected, integrated and restructured. The search for
information and knowledge, and thereby their accumulation, is facilitated.
This will be illustrated later in this chapter.

When the design space changes, the elements of the organizational and
institutional dimension also change: individual actors, networks, organizations
such as universities, research institutes and public agencies, and institutions in
the form of regulations, standards, etc. For example, with the emergence of
biotechnology, the knowledge base of the pharmaceutical industry has shifted
from chemistry and chemical engineering towards biotechnology. The carriers
of this knowledge, their research tools and methods, and the organizations
with which they are associated are different from those in the conventional
pharmaceutical industry.

The greater the connectivity (density) of the design space (in both the cognitive and organizational dimension), the greater is the possibility of identification of technical possibilities (innovation) that can be converted into business opportunities. The role of entrepreneurs is to identify profitable innovations among all the technical possibilities and convert them into business
opportunities. In order to do so, entrepreneurs need support in the form of
venture capital (not just risk capital but also the business competence required
to develop suitable strategies as well as to identify and acquire key resources,
including personnel). To facilitate redeployment of resources and ownership
changes, well-functioning exit markets (such as an IPO market and an acquisi-
tion-friendly business climate) are needed. Collectively, competent customers,
innovators, entrepreneurs, venture capitalists, exit markets and industrialists
who take successful innovations to large-scale production may be referred to
as a competence bloc (Eliasson and Eliasson, 1996). Whereas the technological system is defined from the technology supply side, the competence bloc
constitutes the demand or market side.

In summary, then, the new connectivity through the Internet gives rise to a
massive increase in the number of new possible technical combinations. But
the conversion of new possibilities into profitable business opportunities is by
no means automatic. Only when the actors in the technological systems and
competence blocs interact with each other closely and frequently enough do
the new technical possibilities result in economic growth. The greater the
number and variety of actors with different beliefs and expectations, the
greater are the chances that new ideas will result in economic growth.
Institutions (such as markets and technological systems) reduce the costs of
making certain transactions by establishing powerful connections (Loasby,
2001, p. 407). Densely connected systems are more likely to absorb and
exploit new ideas than are more sparsely connected systems.

3. HISTORY

What historical evidence is there that new connections lead to economic growth? In this section I will discuss three examples of new technologies in the past that gave rise to new combinations, resulting in new business opportunities that were exploited by entrepreneurs and contributed to economic growth. Obviously, general-purpose technologies (GPTs) open up more new possibilities than more specific technologies. The more generally applicable are the technologies, the greater the economic growth potential. While the cost-saving potential of a GPT may be substantial, that is only a part, and not necessarily the most important part, of the contribution to economic growth:

> In our view a methodology that focuses on cost comparisons, and the concomitant cost-savings calculations, by and large misses the deeper point... [T]he impact of a general purpose technology on growth operates primarily through innovational complementarities and the positive loop that these set in motion, and not just through cost advantages. Regardless of the size of the cost savings that a new technology might bring about, if it does not prompt down-the-line innovations and related complementary investments across a wide range of user sectors, it will not propel long-term growth, and hence it will not qualify as a GPT. Conversely, a technology that does exhibit pervasive innovational complementarities may not result in significant cost savings vis a vis its closest substitute, but this latter fact would not necessarily hinder its role as a GPT. (Rosenberg and Trajtenberg, 2002, p. 9)

Transportation and Communication Technologies in the 19th Century

In *Scale and Scope,* Chandler (1990) argues that the emergence of steamships, the cable and the telegraph, and railroads raised the speed and dependability and significantly lowered the costs of transportation and communication. This created a vast new national market in the United States, making it possible in capital-intensive, process-oriented industries to take advantage of new and improved processes of production that for the first time in history enjoyed substantial economies of scale and scope. Large manufacturing units applying the new technologies could produce at much lower unit costs than could smaller units.

However, the conversion of the new opportunities into economic growth was by no means trivial or automatic:

> In order to benefit from the cost advantages of these new, high-volume technologies of production, entrepreneurs had to make three sets of interrelated investments. The first was an investment in production facilities large enough to exploit a technology's potential economies of scale or scope. The second was an investment in a

national and international marketing and distributing network, so that the volume of sales might keep pace with the new volume of production. Finally, to benefit fully from these two kinds of investment the entrepreneurs also had to invest in management: they had to recruit and train managers not only to administer the enlarged facilities and increased personnel in both production and distribution, but also to monitor and coordinate those two basic functional activities and to plan and allocate resources for future production and distribution. It was this three-pronged investment in production, distribution, and management that brought the modern industrial enterprise into being (Chandler, 1990, p. 8).

These large new industrial enterprises, particularly in the United States but also in other countries such as Britain and Germany, ushered in the industrial era and spearheaded economic growth for more than a century.

Chandler focuses on the large firms in capital-intensive, process-oriented industries, since they were the ones that made the three-pronged investment in production, marketing and distribution, and organization and management, thereby taking advantage of economies of scale and scope offered by technological change in production. While these firms were also among the main beneficiaries of the new and improved transportation and communication technologies, they were not the only beneficiaries. The railroads, the steamships, and the cable and telegraph influenced the nature and location of virtually all kinds of economic activity.

Thus, the innovations in transportation and communication involved general-purpose (enabling) technologies that made it possible for new combinations to be made throughout the economy, especially in certain capital-intensive industries. The new transportation and communication technologies made it possible to join together previously small regional markets into a single national market. The United States quickly became the largest national economy in the world. Rapid population growth (partly as a result of immigration) led to large investments in both infrastructure and manufacturing, enabling US firms in scale- and capital-intensive industries to take advantage of new technologies more rapidly than their European counterparts. All these factors created a more fertile environment for economic growth in the United States than elsewhere. As a result, the US benefited more than Britain and Germany from these innovations, even though Britain was more advanced and had a larger market until the late 19th century. The new technologies had a more transforming effect in America than in more densely populated Europe.

Corliss Steam Engine

The steam engine is widely regarded as the icon of the Industrial Revolution and a prime example of a general-purpose technology. Prior to steam engines, waterpower was the main source of energy for industrial activity, but it restricted the location of manufacturing to areas with a suitable topography and climate. Steam engines offered the possibility of relaxing this constraint, allowing industry to locate where key considerations such as access to markets for inputs and outputs directed. But even as late as 1870, the vast majority of steam engines used in the United States were quite small, with a capacity of only 5-25 horsepower (Rosenberg and Trajtenberg, 2002, p. 16). In the early 1850s, George Corliss of Providence, Rhode Island, invented a new type of steam engine that had much greater capacity than other engines and that also had an automatic variable cut-off mechanism. This meant that the speed of the engine was much more precisely controllable than in previous designs and led to substantial fuel savings.

The enhanced performance of the Corliss engine as well as its fuel efficiency helped tip the balance in favour of steam in the fierce contest with waterpower. Rosenberg and Trajtenberg (2002) show that the deployment of Corliss engines served as a catalyst for the massive relocation of industry away from rural areas and into large urban centres (especially in the north-eastern US), thus fuelling agglomeration economies, and attracting further population growth to the cities. Certainly, one of the advantages of being able to locate plants in large urban centres was to considerably increase the connectivity. This led to higher density of people and ideas, increasing the probability of new combinations and new connections.

The Dynamo (Electric Motor)

A third historical example of a general-purpose technology is the dynamo (electric motor) which has been studied in a series of papers by Paul David. Focusing primarily on the effects in manufacturing, David (1990) shows that the electric motor, in comparison with steam engines, provided savings in fuel input and greater efficiency (partly through more precise controllability). It also facilitated an improved plant layout in that individually powered machines could be placed within the factory to facilitate work and material flows rather than in the sequence dictated by a single power source. This led to savings in fixed capital (single-storey, lighter weight buildings); savings in operating capital due to better materials handling, flexible reconfiguration of machine placement; as well as more flexibility, more uptime, and less power consumption.

David found that 'approximately half of the 5 percentage point acceleration recorded in the aggregate TFP growth rate of the US manufacturing sector during 1919-29 (compared with 1909-19) is accounted for statistically simply by the growth in manufacturing secondary electric motor capacity during that decade' (David, 1990, p. 359).

While this is impressive enough, David also notes that the measured productivity improvement is only a part of the total contribution to the economy. Conventional productivity measures are especially problematic in accounting for new kinds of products. Better, more powerful machines with better controls presumably facilitated both improved products (better quality, more standardized output) and entirely new manufactured products. The introduction of the electric motor also helped to provide a better and safer working environment, better lighting, a cleaner workplace, and easier maintenance of machines. These effects are only partially reflected in measured productivity growth in the manufacturing sector.

If we extend the analysis to include not only manufacturing but also the total improvement in human well-being and economic welfare caused by electrification more generally, conventional measurement tools are even more deficient. The introduction of electric lighting and electric domestic appliances (e.g., refrigeration) permitted changes in lifestyle, improved the environment, and influenced how human beings spend their time and build their homes and cities. This created many new combinations in the form of new goods and services and increased variety. Almost none of this is captured in the productivity statistics.

It is also worth noting that it took several decades for the productivity improvements (as conventionally measured) to show up in the statistics. The reasons for this delay have to do with network externality effects (the building of transmission networks – power grid – was necessary). This required compatibility standards (e.g., the choice between AC and DC, and a common voltage) and the building of public infrastructure (including regulation). Another reason for the delay was the slow pace of factory electrification: the unprofitability of replacing still serviceable manufacturing plants and the resulting necessity of operating parallel systems for extended periods. As a result, the most rapid diffusion of the new technology occurred in the industries that happened to grow the most rapidly at the time (i.e., that were the least encumbered by previous investments): tobacco, fabricated metals, transportation equipment, electrical machinery.

Lessons from History: The Economic Impact of General-Purpose Technologies

This brief review of a few general-purpose technologies suggests that they have all led to higher efficiency and productivity in the economy as conventionally measured but also that the measured effects are only a part, and perhaps not even the most important part, of the contribution to economic well-being and long-run economic growth. The more generally applicable the technology, the greater are the systemic effects, and the greater is the number of possible new combinations it generates. The greater the connectivity, the greater are the dynamic effects.

In Chandler's *Scale and Scope* the main focus is on the creation of large enterprises in capital- and scale-intensive industries, even though the innovations that generated the process were general-purpose technologies (transportation and communication) with applications far beyond a subset of manufacturing industries. Rosenberg and Trajtenberg's study of the Corliss steam engine has a broader focus, as does David's study of the electric motor, even though in both of these cases the immediate effects in manufacturing were substantial. In the next section it will be argued that one of the most important current general-purpose technologies – digitization in combination with the Internet – has an even broader impact, though not any easier to measure.

4. THE NEW (DIGITAL) ECONOMY

In discussing the New (Digital) Economy, it is necessary to distinguish between information and knowledge. Information may be defined as a collection of data, whereas knowledge can be defined as a structure (theory or hypothesis) that makes it possible to organize and interpret information. Thus,

> In the *old economy*, information flow was physical: cash, checks, invoices, bills of lading, reports, face-to-face meetings, analog telephone calls or radio and television transmissions, blueprints, maps, photographs, musical scores, and direct mail advertisements.

> In the *new [digital] economy*, information in all its forms becomes digital – reduced to bits stored in computers and racing at the speed of light across networks... The new world of possibilities thereby created is as significant as the invention of language itself, the old paradigm on which all the physically based interactions occurred (Tapscott, 1995, p. 6)

Certainly information is not new, only the form in which it is gathered, manipulated, stored and transferred. Nor is knowledge new. In *Post-Capitalist Society*, Peter Drucker (1993) argues that knowledge has been at the core of economic activity since the industrial revolution: the essence of the change in economic activity during the period 1700 to 1850 was to convert practical experience into systematic, codified knowledge. Drucker argues further that the period 1850 to 1950 (the 'Productivity revolution') involved the application of knowledge to work (Taylorism), whereas he refers to the period from 1950 forward as the management revolution, characterized by the application of knowledge to knowledge. He concludes that

[k]nowledge is the only meaningful resource today. The traditional 'factors of production' – land (i.e. natural resources), labour and capital – have not disappeared. But they have become secondary. They can be obtained, and obtained easily, provided there is knowledge. And knowledge in this new meaning is knowledge as a utility, knowledge as the means to obtain social and economic results (Drucker, 1993, republished in Neef, 1998, pp. 29-30).

Therefore,

knowledge work – activities that involve complex problem identification, problem solution, or high-technology design and that result in innovative new products or services or create new ways of exploiting markets – has quickly become the focus for economic growth and individual and organizational prosperity' (Neef, 1998, p. 3).

In the long run, therefore, one would expect knowledge-intensive industries such as financial services, entertainment, health care, education and government to be those most transformed and benefiting the most from digitization and the Internet. In the medium term, the most visible effects may be seen in retailing, manufacturing and travel.

In order to examine the effects of digitization and the Internet, let us consider some examples in the following four categories of economic activity: (1) productivity enhancement in traditional industries, (2) restructuring at the industry level, (3) the creation of more efficient markets, and (4) the creation of new combinations that give rise to new products and new industries.

5. EFFECTS OF DIGITIZATION AND THE INTERNET IN EXISTING ACTIVITIES

The Oil Industry

The world has burned about 820 billion barrels of oil since the first strike at Oil Creek, Pennsylvania, in 1859, and 600 billion of those barrels – almost three quarters of the total – have been burned since 1973. Yet the world's proven oil reserves are about half again as large today as they were in the 1970s, and more than ten times as large as in 1950. Also, the average cost of finding new oil has fallen from $12-$16 a barrel in the 1970s and 1980s to $4-$8 today (Rauch, 2001).

What were the factors that made this possible? There are essentially six major developments:

1. Computers
The power of microprocessors increased by a factor of 7,000 between 1970 and 2000. Computing chores that took a week in the early 1970s now take a minute. The cost of storing one megabit of information, or enough for a 320-page book, fell from more than $5,000 in 1975 to 17 cents in 1999.

2. Seismic imaging
Knowing how fast sound travels, geologists can set off booms or pings and then analyse the returning echoes to infer the nature and location of the surface that has reflected them. For many years, the most that computers could handle was 2-dimensional imaging that showed vertical cross sections of rock. 3-dimensional imaging was first used commercially in 1975. It required enormous computer capability. Even a small 3-D survey might generate 200 gigabytes of data.

3. Combination of computers and 3-D seismic imaging
Between 1985 and 1995, the computing time needed to process a square kilometre's worth of data fell from 800 minutes to 10 minutes. From 1980 to 1990 the cost of analysing a 50-square-mile survey fell from $8 million to $1 million. Now it is more like $90,000.

4. Directional drilling
A directional well can run in any direction, approaching a reservoir from whichever angle geologists deem most promising. It can twist and turn to cut through any number of reservoirs. The effect was to bring all kinds of previously inaccessible or uneconomical reserves within reach. By the late 1980s, 3-D seismic imaging was revealing targets accurately enough to make directional drilling worth considering. The cost of horizontal drilling fell from 4-8 times that of vertical drilling in 1989 to less than double in 1993, while the productivity advantage of horizontal wells stayed constant at 2-5 times that of vertical wells.

5. Measurement-while-drilling
Before 1980, a driller would point his bit in the indicated direction, bore a few hundred feet, and stop. Then he would push an instrument down, take a picture of a compass, pull the instrument out, and check the location. Each survey could mean halting drilling for hours at a stretch (at a cost of around $4000/hour), and the results were approximate. In measurement-while-drilling, an instrument rides behind the drill bit, continually records the bit's location, and reports it back to the surface.

6. The Internet

Geologists and executives in the home office can now click on their Web browsers and see what the driller is seeing somewhere in the Gulf of Mexico, or in Prudhoe Bay, or in the North Sea. They can plug into the rig from laptops at the airport. They can instruct the rig to let them know by e-mail or pager when the hole reaches 20,000 feet, or when resistivity suggests oil, or when anything else of interest happens. Rigs can now talk to Palm Pilots. This makes it possible even in this capital-intensive industry to take advantage of short-run market changes and to reduce costs.

So, what's new in the oil industry? Higher-resolution (3-D) imaging increased the payoff for accurate drilling. This induced companies to invest in high-tech down-hole sensors. Powerful sensors increased the yields of directional drilling (i.e., resulted in faster, cheaper directional drilling), which led to higher payoffs to even higher resolution 3-D seismic imaging. None of these technologies were truly new, but they had co-evolved technologically to the point where they could be called new when they intersected with the proliferation of the Internet. They all involve digitization of information and the use of computers. What was really new was the way in which they developed simultaneously, energizing and reinforcing one another. The result is that even more than earlier, knowledge, not petroleum, is becoming the critical resource in the oil business. Though the supply of oil is 'fixed', the supply of knowledge is boundless (Rauch, 2001). Digitization of information that had occurred over decades made it possible to take advantage of the Internet. And the Internet made it possible to integrate decisions on where and when to drill into the overall management of the oil business.

Productivity Enhancement through Collaboration

Digitization and the Internet, in combination with new software, enable companies to collaborate with suppliers and customers in new ways and thereby to raise productivity. For example,

> In a March, 2002 poll conducted by the online newsletter of the National Association of Wholesaler-Distributors, readers were asked which of the following business strategies would have the biggest impact on them in the next three years: collaboration with supply chain partners (38 percent); new information technologies (26 percent); or network restructuring (five percent). Twenty-eight percent of respondents said that all three would impact their businesses (Tuttle, 2002, p. 59).

Accessing information and responding quickly to customers' needs are what drive the demand for Internet collaboration in the distribution industry. Using collaborative Web technology, distributors can become involved in designing and developing products more easily than in the past. Also, a distributor with direct supplier connections with a number of vendors can enable customers to check availability of needed items at these vendors and fill their orders immediately rather than having to wait while a salesperson calls each factory and then places an order. This can reduce the order cycle from days to minutes, and the software makes it possible to store information about the transactions which can be used later (Tuttle, 2002).

Similarly, Web technology makes it possible to bring together design engineers in collaborative systems to develop new products. An example is DaimlerChrysler's FastCar project. The company expects to develop the new car 40 percent faster through its new Web-based system than in a traditional system in which geographically dispersed engineers communicate via phone, fax and e-mail and where each proposed design change might require days or weeks. As a result, DaimlerChrysler expects to save billions of dollars off the cost of car development over the next few years (Moozakis, 2000). For similar reasons, General Motors can get a car into production in 18 months rather than the 42 months it took in the mid-1990s (Keenan et al., 2002).

Thus, digitization of information in conjunction with the Internet can reduce costs, increase productivity, and help producers respond more quickly to changing consumer demand. Through better connectivity, the design space becomes denser: more ideas are created, new ideas can be tried and implemented (or rejected) more quickly, and the knowledge base can expand through more experimentation. This reflects the supply side (the technological system) of the market for innovations. If the demand side responds appropriately – i.e., if the competence bloc succeeds in selecting and supporting viable new products – economic growth results.

Restructuring of Economic Activities within Industries

Many industries are beginning to confront the challenges and opportunities presented by the Internet. A few illustrative industry studies are now emerging. This section provides some examples from the banking and automobile industries.

The banking industry

A recent development in banking is the growth of vendors providing Web-based self-service technology. This changes the interaction between banks and their customers from bank customer facing staff (in particular, call centre agents) towards automated Internet-based channels, while maintaining a high level of service to the customer. This offers potential cost savings and efficiencies while theoretically improving customer service, with bank staff able to focus on higher-value and more customer-specific enquiries (Datamonitor, 2001).

On-line banking customers reduce costs for the banks because the majority of transactions by those customers are of the self-service type. Nevertheless, while it is likely that the Internet will continue to have a profound effect on the way banks do business in the future, it is much less clear whether the Net will create or destroy value for the banks, and what its overall impact on banking revenues is likely to be. As on-line banking becomes more common, it is likely to provide less strategic (competitive) advantage to individual banks, and the customers are likely to be the main beneficiaries.

The mortgage industry provides an example of restructuring of the financial services industry as a result of the Internet. The industry is changing as new Internet-based entrants identify niches and supply special services, bringing new value to customers, while outmoded traditional business models have disappeared. Among the reasons are:

1. The Internet aids cost reconfiguration: it facilitates cost control and process reconfiguration by work elimination, work shifting, work avoidance, and work sharing. Web-centric mortgage systems reduce employee training costs, are easier to navigate, and provide easier access to databases than conventional systems.
2. The Internet facilitates self-service: ubiquitous Internet access, coupled with real-time technologies, provides consumers with an opportunity to access and/or update information at any time, from anywhere. This reduces the demand for customer service departments. Consumers can also perform more complex interactions, such as calculating loan payoffs and determining how much additional payment to principal is required to qualify for mortgage insurance cancellation.
3. The Internet can enhance revenue by allowing service providers to cross-sell, refinance, and pursue other revenue-generating opportunities.
4. Asset/risk management is improved through Internet connectivity as information can be communicated, viewed and shared on an immediate, real-time basis (Thinakal, 2001).

In a recent paper, Autor, Levy and Murnane (2000) describe how a single technological innovation, the introduction of image processing of cheques, led to distinctly different changes in the structure of jobs in two departments of a large bank. In the deposit processing department, image processing led to the substitution of computers for high school educated labour in accomplishing core tasks and in greater specialization in the jobs that remained, raising the possibility of outsourcing and changes in the location of certain parts of the operation. In another department (exceptions processing), image processing led to the integration of tasks, with an associated increase in the demand for particular skills, and with an overall 28 percent reduction in labour input.

These examples from the banking industry suggest that digitization and the Internet are changing the locus and organization of banking services. They also suggest that the main beneficiaries are more likely to be the customers, not the banks.

The automobile industry

The automobile industry provides other examples. For instance, the major producers in the US automobile industry have joined together in Covisint, a business-to-business supply system, as well as other manufacturing systems and supply exchanges. Together with business-to-consumer ordering and purchase systems, such systems have the potential to improve efficiency in this otherwise traditional industry. Internet ordering by customers would greatly diminish the role of conventional dealers, who have thus far blunted its impact (Kwoka, 2001).

The e-business effects on consumer and supplier relationships in the US auto industry have also been studied by Helper and MacDuffie (2001). They find that although the impact of the Internet may be profound, it is by no means technically determined. It will depend on the extent to which complementary changes occur in the retail strategies of the auto producers (build-to-order, factory direct, and dealer direct), design strategy (modular or not, standardization or not), procurement strategy (voice vs. exit), technology strategy (incremental vs. radical technical change), and public policy (especially with respect to regulation).

The defence industry

The design and production of military aircraft provide another example of restructuring of economic activity due to collaboration via the Internet. While management experts have long talked about so-called virtual corporations (companies that focus on what they do best and farm out the rest to specialists), a new generation of Web-based collaboration technologies is making it easier for companies to work hand-in-hand with their partners to bring new products to the market much faster and more cheaply than previously. In designing and manufacturing the supersonic stealth fighter planes in the largest defence contract ever, Lockheed Martin Aeronautics Co. will engage in some intricate teamwork:

> More than 80 suppliers will be working at 187 locations to design and build components of the Joint Strike Fighter. It's up to the 75-member tech group at Lockheed's Aeronautics division to link them all together, as well as let the US Air Force, Navy, and Marines, Britain's Defense Ministry, and eight other US allies track progress

and make changes midstream if necessary. All told, people sitting at more than 40,000 computers will be collaborating with each other to get the first plane in the air in just four years – the same amount of time it took to get the much simpler F-16 from contract to delivery in the 1970s … Lockheed and its partners will be using a system of 90 Web software tools to share designs, track the exchange of documents, and keep an eye on progress against goals (Keenan et al., 2002).

The examples provided here are meant simply to illustrate the kinds of restructuring of economic activity that are likely to result from digitization and the Internet. There are not yet many studies on this topic – thus providing ample opportunities for further research. But there are many previous studies on structural change (reconfiguration of companies, restructuring of industries, increased role of small business, outsourcing, and alliances) that are suggestive and that could be reviewed from the standpoint of the role of digitization and the Internet. Another potentially fruitful avenue of research would be to examine the rapidly growing number of studies of innovation systems and industry clusters from a similar standpoint (such as the biotechnology-focused studies of Cooke (2001) and Carlsson (2002)).

The Market Efficiency Effects of the Internet

The market efficiency impact is the most heavily studied aspect of the Internet. Several studies of the efficiency effects of the Internet (see e.g., Smith, Bailey and Brynjolfsson, 2000) show that the main effects in the markets are to make it easier for buyers and sellers to compare prices, to cut out the middlemen between firms and customers, and to reduce transaction costs and barriers to entry. Thus, the Internet increases competition and improves the functioning of the price mechanism. In this sense, the most important immediate (and measurable) effect of the 'new' economy may be to make the 'old' economy more efficient. There is at least some evidence to bear out these claims. For example, Lehman Brothers (a financial services firm) reports that a transfer between bank accounts costs $1.27 if done by a bank teller, 27 cents via a cash machine (Automated Teller Machine (ATM)), but only 1 cent over the Internet. Similarly, it was reported in 1996 that the average cost to issue a ticket was $35-45 through traditional travel agents, less than $20 if the ticket was purchased directly through the airlines, $5-10 if the ticket was electronic, and only $2-5 if purchased on-line (Grant, 1996). These cost differentials are likely to have become even greater since then but are still illustrative. Recent actions by US airlines to stop paying commissions to independent travel agents and to encourage customers to use the Internet when purchasing tickets confirm these findings.

Litan and Rivlin (2001) have attempted to extrapolate judgmental estimates of the likely impact of the Internet at the industry level based on estimates by individual firms and analysts and then adding up the results to see what they imply for the overall economy. Their estimate shows a total annual cost saving of $100–$230 billion. This implies a total cost saving of about 1-2 percent which over five years translates into an annual contribution to productivity growth of 0.2-0.4 percent.

The sources of potential cost savings that they identify are reduced transaction costs, increased management efficiency, and increased competition leading to more transparent prices and broader markets. They conclude that the greatest impact may not be felt in e-commerce, but rather in a wide range of 'old economy' arenas, including health care and government, because of changes to the way information flows. Further, as a result of the Internet, there is considerable scope for management efficiencies in product development, supply-chain management, and a variety of other aspects of business performance, encouraged by enhanced competition. Finally, they conclude that much of the benefit from the Internet is likely to show up in improved consumer convenience and expanded choices, rather than in higher productivity and lower prices.

New Combinations: New Products and Industries

As has already been indicated, increased production and market efficiency and restructuring of economic activity are only the beginning; in the long term, the most important effects of digitization and the Internet are likely to come through entirely new products (goods and services). By definition, we do not know what these are. Nevertheless,

> ... a new economic theory is beginning to emerge, which suggests that the ability to exploit markets and to innovate... has replaced production efficiency (and therefore the concept of cost-reduction productivity) as the major driver of growth ...
> ... there are indications that domestic growth arises not through expansion or replenishment of market share (particularly in the near-saturation domestic market of developed economies), but through the introduction of entirely new technologies or problem-solving services that create new markets (Neef, 1998, p. 4).

A more thorough review of general-purpose technologies than that above, with particular attention to their broader impact on economic activity (not just productivity enhancement) is likely to yield insight as to the types of new economic activities generated in the past. Electrification, the automobile, commercial aviation, and television are examples of such technologies that have changed the way we live and organize our daily activities. It is hard to even imagine what life would be like without them. Digitization in combination with the Internet seems to have even broader applicability than previous general-purpose technologies, since it affects the service industries (e.g., health care, government and financial services) even more profoundly than the goods-producing industries, and since these service sectors represent over 75 percent of GDP[3] – in addition to the direct impact on consumers that we may never be able to measure.

6. CONCLUSION

So what is really new in the New Economy? Put briefly, the Internet, a new level and form of connectivity among multiple heterogeneous ideas and actors, giving rise to a vast new range of combinations. There are some measurable effects on productivity and efficiency, but the more important long-run effects are beyond measurement.

What is not new (but leveraged through the Internet) are digitization of information (this has been going on since the arrival of computers in the 1940s) and the Knowledge Economy (the economy has become more and more knowledge-intensive since the Industrial Revolution).

Thus far, the New Economy is largely a US phenomenon; at least as far as aggregate productivity growth is concerned (see van Ark et al., Chapter 3, this volume). Why has the United States economy grown faster than other advanced economies in the 1990s? Essentially because of a greater ability to absorb and support new business ideas, especially in the form of entrepreneurship (see Kenney, Chapter 2, this volume). Even though digitization in combination with the Internet (i.e., greater connectivity) creates new possibilities for all countries, the US is the greatest beneficiary thus far because of its greater ability to take advantage of the new possibilities: a more entrepreneurial culture, more venture capital, and better-functioning capital markets (especially for IPOs). Greater diversity and flexibility, more experimentation, and greater tolerance of failure have also played a role.

NOTES

1. I would like to thank Leonard Lane for valuable contributions and insightful comments on previous versions of this chapter.
2. Tobin's Q refers to the ratio between the market value of a firm's assets and their replacement value.
3. In 1999, transportation and public utilities, wholesale and retail trade, finance, insurance and real estate, services, and government represented 77 percent of US GDP (US Census Bureau, *Statistical Abstract of the United States*, 2001, p. 418).

REFERENCES

Autor, David H., Frank Levy and Richard J. Murnane (2000), 'Upstairs, Downstairs: Computer-Skill Complementarity and Computer-Labor Substitution on Two Floors of a Large Bank', National Bureau of Economic Research (NBER) Working Paper No. 7890.

Baily, Martin Neil and Robert Z. Lawrence (2001), 'Do We Have a New E-conomy?', *American Economic Review*, 91 (2), 308-12.

Carlsson, Bo and Rikard Stankiewicz (1991), 'On the Nature, Function, and Composition of Technological Systems', *Journal of Evolutionary Economics*, 1 (2), 93-118.

Carlsson, Bo (ed.) (1995), *Technological Systems and Economic Performance: The Case of Factory Automation*, Boston/Dordrecht/London: Kluwer Academic Publishers.

Carlsson, Bo (ed.) (1997), *Technological Systems and Industrial Dynamics*, Boston/Dordrecht/ London: Kluwer Academic Publishers.

Carlsson, Bo (ed.) (2002), *New Technological Systems in the Bio Industries – An International Study*, Boston/Dordrecht/London: Kluwer Academic Publishers.

Chandler, Alfred (1990), *Scale and Scope: The Dynamics of Industrial Capitalism*, Cambridge, MA: Harvard University Press.

Cooke, Philip (2001), 'New Economy Innovation Systems: Biotechnology in Europe and the USA', *Industry and Innovation*, 8 (3), 267-89.

Datamonitor (2001), 'Web-Based Self-Service in Banking: Taking the Pain out of Customer Service', August, http://www.datamonitor.com.

David, Paul (1990), 'The Dynamo and the Computer: An Historical Perspective on the Modern Productivity Paradox', *American Economic Review*, 80 (2), 355-61.

Drucker, Peter (1993), *Post-Capitalist Society*, New York: Harper Collins.

Eliasson, Gunnar and Åsa Eliasson (1996), 'The Biotechnological Competence Bloc', *Revue d'Economie Industrielle*, 78-4° Trimestre, 7-26.

Grant, J. Bellinda (1996), 'Trends in US Airline Ticket Distribution', *The McKinsey Quarterly*, No. 4.

Helper, Susan and John Paul MacDuffie (2001), 'E-volving the Auto Industry: E-business Effects on Consumer and Supplier Relationships', in BRIE-IGCC E-conomy Project, *Tracking a Transformation: E-Commerce and the Terms of Competition in Industries*, Washington, DC: Brookings Institution.

Keenan, F., S.E. Ante, B. Elgin, and S. Hamm (2002), 'The New Teamwork', *Business Week*, 18 February, p. EB12.

Kwoka, John. E., Jr. (2001), 'Automobiles: The Old Economy Collides with the New', *Review of Industrial Organization*, 19 (1), 55-69.

Litan, Robert E. and Alice M. Rivlin (2001), 'Projecting the Economic Impact of the Internet', *American Economic Review*, 91 (2), 313-17.

Loasby, Brian (2001), 'Time, Knowledge and evolutionary dynamics: why connections matter', *Journal of Evolutionary Economics*, 11 (4), 393-412.

Moozakis, Chuck (2000), 'Manufacturers Preach Teamwork – Producers of Customized Components Use Web to Design by Committee', *Internet Week*, 30 October, p. 83.

Neef, Dale (ed.) (1998), *The Knowledge Economy*, Boston: Butterworth-Heinemann.

Potts, Jason (2001), *The New Evolutionary Microeconomics: Complexity, Competence and Adaptive Behaviour*, Cheltenham, UK and Northampton, MA, USA: Edward Elgar.

Rauch, Jonathan (2001), 'The New Old Economy: Oil, Computers, and the Reinvention of the Earth', *The Atlantic Monthly*, January, 35-49.

Rosenberg, Nathan and Manuel Trajtenberg (2002), 'A General Purpose Technology at Work: The Corliss Steam Engine in the Late 19th Century US', National Bureau of Economic Research (NBER) Working Paper No. 8485, September.

Schumpeter, Joseph (1911) (English edition 1934), *The Theory of Economic Development*, Harvard Economic Studies, Vol. XLVI, Cambridge, MA: Harvard University Press.

Smith, Michael D., Joseph Bailey and Erik Brynjolfsson (2000), 'Understanding Digital Markets: Review and Assessment', in Erik Brynjolfsson and Brian Kahin (eds), *Understanding the Digital Economy: Data, Tools, and Research*, Cambridge, MA: MIT Press, pp. 99-136.

Stankiewicz, Rikard (2002), 'The Cognitive Dynamics of Biotechnology and the Evolution of Its Technological System', in Bo Carlsson (ed.), op. cit., pp. 35-52.

Tapscott, Don (1995), *Digital Economy. Promise and Peril in the Age of Networked Intelligence*, New York: McGraw-Hill.

Thinakal, Sadu (2001), 'Web-Centric Servicing Creates Mortgage Industry Value', *ABA Banking Journal*, 93 (10), 70.

Tuttle, Al (2002), 'E-Collaboration: Build Trust and Success', *Industrial Distribution*, 91 (6), June, 59.

US Census Bureau (2001), *Statistical Abstract of the United States*, 2001, p. 418.

US Department of Commerce (2000), *Digital Economy 2000*, http://www/esa/doc/gov/de2000.pdf, June.

2. What Goes Up Must Come Down: The Political Economy of the US Internet Industry

Martin Kenney

1. INTRODUCTION

The sheer magnitude of the Internet Bubble and subsequent technology stock market crash are a fascinating lens for examining the operation of the entrepreneurial portion of the US national system of innovation (NSI). The intense rapidity with which US firms commercialized the Internet and Worldwide Web (hereafter we refer to both as the 'Internet') is a prism for examining the creation of new economic spaces. If one includes the resulting crash, it also exposes some of the weaknesses of the US innovation system. This chapter draws upon the excellent work by Abbate (1999), Mowery and Simcoe (2002), and Berners-Lee (1999) which examines the pre- and early commercialization phases of the Internet. In building upon their work, we extend it in two ways. First, I situate the commercialization of the Internet in the US history of telecommunications deregulation and the entrepreneurial economy of US startup firms. Second, I describe the collapse of the Internet Bubble.

The Internet as a commercial proposition emerged during a period within which US industry was undergoing a profound rethinking of the firm's nature and competencies. Information technologies were one tool in a wave of restructuring, reengineering and reorganization. The firm was being reconceptualized as a 'modular' organization (Sturgeon, 2002). Moreover, there was a generalized belief that large firms were in danger of being outflanked by smaller, more entrepreneurial firms (Christensen, 1997). In this environment, the Internet and its perceived impact, driven by enormous hype, reached mythical dimensions, suggesting that it would change everything. Still, now that the hype has subsided, it is clear that in ten short years the Internet has become a significant artefact in both the office and home. There can be no doubt that it has opened what Schumpeter termed a 'new economic space'.

The Internet was commercialized during a period in which executives and management theorists were grappling with new ways of thinking about the firm. Firms were urged to consider their 'core competencies', while other management scholars were reconceptualizing the firm as a knowledge-based entity (Kogut and Zander, 1992; Nonaka and Takeuchi, 1995). The Internet, as an information technology-based medium that provided far richer and faster flows of information, resonated with these theoretical advances. Prior to the commercialization of the Internet, Reich (1991) reflected on the increased use of computers and involvement of managers in working with digital representations. He captured a movement to an information-based workplace in more popular terms when he wrote that 'symbolic analysts' were becoming the core of the US economy. In a more general way, Cohen et al. (2000) argued that the digital technologies were for the brain what, in an earlier time, the application of power and the removal of the tool from the workers' hands had been to physical production in a factory. Only rarely does a new technology emerge that can contribute, and even spark, both an intellectual reconsideration of the nature of the firm, the source of value creation, and the organization of an economy (Kenney and Curry, 2000).

The Internet evolved from a university-based, government-funded communication tool into a commercial system that many politicians, businesspersons, and academics believed would 'change everything.'[1] The readers will have to decide for themselves whether the Internet changed everything; certainly it has become a major new medium for communication and commerce. Carlsson, elsewhere in this book (Chapter 1), argues that the Internet is one of those general-purpose technologies that 'exhibit pervasive innovational complementarities' (Rosenberg and Trajtenberg, 2002). As Chandler (1990) observed was the case with the telegraphy and railway systems, such technologies can be inputs and catalysts, permitting actors to reorganize entire business systems. As an example, drawing upon the insights of Chandler and others, Fields (forthcoming) compares and contrasts the manner in which Dell Computer employed the Internet to reorganize its entire logistics systems to become the dominant PC manufacturer firm. The size and complexity of the US economy make it nearly impossible to grasp the dimensions of the commercialization process. National exceptionalism is a convenient argument, and evolutionary theory tells us that every NSI has a unique history of creating institutions differing from those in other nations. The US (or, at least, certain regions) has developed a powerful set of routines capable of encouraging the formation of new firms aimed at commercializing new technologies. In another venue, we argued that in the regions like Silicon Valley an entire sector or, what we term an 'Economy' had been formed, specializing in nurturing these firms (Kenney and von Burg, 1999).

The commercialization of the Internet is not the first example of this Economy creating new industries. For example, in the late 1970s and early 1980s, university-based biology research accompanied by enormous hype was converted into a biotechnology industry (Kenney, 1986). Also in this case, there was a bubble in biotechnology stocks that soon burst. The same institutions contributed to the rapid exploitation of the myriad possibilities that the Internet offered for commercial opportunity. With the benefit of hindsight, it is easy to conclude that some, if not most, of the investments made in attempting to commercialize the Internet were wasted. The more difficult question we will return to is whether, from a more distant perspective, these chaotic outbursts of new firm formations are wasteful.

This chapter is organized roughly in chronological order. The first section reviews the features of the macroeconomic environment that facilitated the rapid commercialization of the Internet. This section is wide-ranging as we discuss the peculiar configuration of the US telecommunications system, the diffusion of technologies necessary for Internet adoption, and the support system for entrepreneurship that facilitated its rapid commercialization. This is followed by a section that extends the research by Mowery and Simcoe (2002) on the diffusion of the Internet from the university to the larger economy and the reaction of various economic agents. Section 4 outlines the dimensions of the Internet Gold Rush and section 5 chronicles its subsequent collapse. The conclusion reflects upon the costs and benefits of the US innovation system with respect to the commercialization of the Internet.

2. THE MACROECONOMIC ENVIRONMENT

The governance system of the telecommunications industry was a critical backdrop for the trajectory and velocity of the Internet commercialization process. This section enumerates some basic aspects of the US political economy, arguing that they distinguish the US from other economies, and describes as well the commercialization process.

Despite the formation of the European Union, the US was (and remains) the largest single market united by common laws,[2] a common language, a common currency, and various features of a unified nation-state. A more prosaic, but nonetheless important, feature for the diffusion of the Internet was a well-developed telephone system with uniform rates and usage rules. Widespread credit card usage and the large number of US consumers comfortable in using their credit cards for telephone and catalogue sales meant that a payment system already existed.

At the technical level, during the entire period, the US had a larger installed base of computers than any other nation in the world. Though the US was often the leader in inventing new computational and communication devices, it was certainly not always the leader. However, the rapid adoption and large installed base created positive feedback loops, reinforcing the US advantage. Though IBM was a global colossus, US antitrust enforcement ensured a semblance of competition and fettered IBM's ability to throttle new entrants: witness Microsoft, DEC or Sun Microsystems. In most other nations, one national champion for computing and another for telecommunications equipment was chosen and subsidized by the national government; other entrants were discouraged. The evolution of the computer sector in the US was characterized by repeated waves of new entrants into the computing and data communications industry, whose innovations were more capable and/or less expensive than those of the dominant vendors in the previous generation. Thus, there was continuous turbulence – a feature not as common in Europe or Japan.

It was during the mid-1970s when personal computers and local area networking (LAN) systems emerged that the US became the leader in the development of what can be called distributed, networked computing. At each step of this evolution, US-based startups were the delivery mechanism for and the beneficiaries of the leaps in functionality caused by the creation of new evolutionary paths (Dosi, 1984; Garud and Karnoe, 2001). The rapid adoption and large installed base created positive feedback loops, as more Americans experimented with computers and networks, and therefore had greater opportunities to improve the technologies. Thus the computing and data networking systems evolved most rapidly in the US.

2.1 The US Telecommunications Industry

The distributed networked computing system articulated well with the relatively low-cost and open telecommunications system that had co-evolved with the US regulatory regime (Davies, 1994). Government policy toward AT&T, a private firm regulated by federal and various independent state regulatory commissions, differed markedly from those of other OECD nations where the telephone system was a government-operated monopoly (Fransman, 2001). The roots of this environment can be traced to a marketplace struggle during the first two decades of the twentieth century ending with the triumph of AT&T and the imposition of government regulation. Outcomes of this competition, the flat-rate price for local calls and 'universal service' became accepted norms and were enshrined in the regulatory structure (Lipartito, 1997; Kenney, 2003). This arrangement was stable for the next 50 years, despite the fact that telecommunications technology continually improved.

In the mid-1950s, AT&T owned and operated the entire phone system, from the consumer handsets to the network; it was a classic case of vertical integration. The US government had no vested interest in the system, however, and was committed to encouraging competition. The process by which the AT&T monopoly was opened to competition can be understood as a disintegration of the telecommunications infrastructure into independent market layers, whereby each layer was gradually opened to competition (Moore, 1996).

This gradual deregulation accelerated competition and innovation. This should not be attributed to far-sighted government regulators and legislators; rather, it was entrepreneurs who pressed for deregulation, which, to their credit, government regulators and the courts did not strongly resist. Because AT&T was not a government-owned monopoly, deregulation was much easier and more gradual. This progressive deregulation allowed new firms to emerge in every aspect of telecommunications. Repeatedly, the new entrants ignited cut-throat competition, by rapidly decreasing costs and/or increasing functionality. The outcome of this gradual deregulation was a low-cost, relatively open market within which entrepreneurs could experiment with new business opportunities.

Flat rate service has a particularly interesting history. After AT&T's victory, it no longer supported a flat rate for local calls and agitated for regulatory relief, as the rate encouraged wanton use of the telephone with no further compensation. In the 1970s and 1980s this fostered the growth of computer bulletin boards that operated over the phone lines. Here, flat rate service stimulated increased use of local phone lines for data communications, and created an enormous base of home users who would rapidly adopt the Internet (Jimeniz and Greenstein, 1998). These computer bulletin boards transformed into Internet service providers and thus integrated the home user into the Web. When considered as a totality, this section has demonstrated that the telecommunications infrastructure was sufficiently open so as not to provide an insurmountable obstacle, the technical infrastructure was in existence, and there was a latent market for greater data communications services.

3. FROM THE UNIVERSITY TO INDUSTRY

The ARPANet, established in 1969 as a US Department of Defense project for interlinking defence researchers at various universities and military research establishments, was the beginning of the Internet (Abbate, 1999; Mowery and Simcoe, 2002; Rogers, 1998). Due to increasing non-military related demand, it was transferred in 1985 to the National Science Foundation (NSF) and renamed the NSFNET. To further diffuse usage, the NSFNET was opened to all universities with the requirement that they must make a connection 'available to all qualified users on campus' (quoted in Leiner et al., 2000). This spread e-mail and file-sharing to the rest of academia, enlarging the installed base. In 1985, NSF also decreed that all NSF-related sites should use the TCP/IP protocol, which contributed to its establishment as the dominant data transmission protocol. Importantly, in the late 1980s, AT&T was uninterested in operating the NSF Internet backbones, creating an opportunity for startup Internet service providers such as UUNet and PSINet, both of which were funded by venture capitalists.

Even as the Internet grew, NSF began privatizing the NSFNET. In March 1991, some restrictions on commercial use were loosened. In September 1994, NSF announced its intention to discontinue subsidizing the Internet backbone effective in May 1995 (Ferguson, 1999; Howe, 2000). This privatization was significant, but was only related to infrastructure. The technological development that formed the basis of the Internet Bubble was the 1991 release of the Internet software and specifications by Timothy Berners-Lee of the CERN high-energy physics laboratory in Switzerland. These two unrelated developments combined to accelerate adoption and increase commercial interest. All the pieces were in place for what Usher (1954) termed a new synthesis.

In February 1993, Marc Andreessen and Eric Bina, working at the University of Illinois National Center for Supercomputer Applications, wrote the Mosaic Web browser for the Microsoft Windows platform. This user-friendly graphical browser simplified the use of the Internet. Moreover, by posting it on the Internet they made it freely available, and as a result millions of copies were downloaded in a few months. The rapid adoption of the Mosaic browser sparked consideration of the possible commercial potential of the Internet. The University of Illinois soon afterward licensed the Mosaic browser technology to the venture capital-funded firm Spyglass, and then later to Microsoft. The creation of Mosaic, the connection of commercially operated networks to the old NSF Internet, and the withdrawal of NSF, signalled the end of the precommercialization phase.

By early 1993, the technology was ready, and a few existing firms and several startups were experimenting with harnessing the technology for commercial purposes. And yet, industry and entrepreneurs were more interested in the implications of interactive television delivered through the cable system. In most respects, the Internet was still a university-driven technology, and for the users it was free. For businesspersons, the Internet was attractive, but it was difficult to decide whether there was a valid business model for its commercialization. The first significant report to the general public about the commercial implications of the Internet was the 8 December 1993 *New York Times* article by John Markoff (1993) entitled 'A Free and Simple Computer Link'. Markoff described how firms were putting documentation on-line, preparing on-line magazines, and thinking about advertising applications. On-line sales were not mentioned.

The single largest concentration of users (that is, expertise) was in the universities. Given this expertise, it is not surprising that universities were the source of several early startups. Computer science students and faculties formed the vanguard, but in the later Internet Bubble, students in other departments and, particularly, in business schools began launching e-commerce startups. The ensuing 'dot.com' fever made entrepreneurship an important career goal for students and faculties; many ventures were first conceived and then launched from campus. From 1997 to early 2000, the enthusiasm was giddy. The career goals for MBA students changed from joining investment banks or consulting firms to establishing or joining a startup. By 2002, the Internet frenzy had subsided, and the severe environment for entrepreneurship had decreased. However, from the NSI perspective the transference of knowledge and capabilities within the university to the commercial sector had been accomplished.

4. THE COMMERCIAL TIDAL WAVE

The commercialization process bore a certain resemblance to the Oklahoma Land Rush memorialized in the 1934 movie *Cimmaron* (Kenney and Curry, 1999).[3] The commercialization process was remarkable on many dimensions. The first dimension was its rapid diffusion and adoption. In 1992 it was largely confined to university applications, however its diffusion rate resembled an epidemic as the ranks of users exploded. By 2001 over 102 million US households representing 58 percent of the population had Internet access from their homes (Macaluso, 2001) and 28 percent of the population had access from their workplaces (Taylor, 2001). These early adopters were ideal potential customers as they had higher than average incomes, used credit cards, and had fewer security fears. And yet, for businesses the question was still how this new tool could be used.

The Internet is such a fascinating economic space, because of its breadth. In their organizational ecology of the Internet firms, Hunt and Aldrich (1998) include a range of firms from AT&T to startups such as Amazon.com. While we might exclude the traditional telecommunications service providers, an argument could be made for their inclusion. In some ways, as with other general-purpose technologies, it is possible to cast the net even further and include on-line activities of existing firms in a wide variety of industries. The multilevel aspect of the Internet, combined with the wide variety of applications, meant that there were an enormous number of commercial opportunities. Given potential capital gains there was an enormous burst of firm formations, both with and without venture capital funding. As with any new economic space, there was an enormous rush of entrants due to the low entry barriers (Utterback and Suarez, 1993).

4.1 Existing Firms and the Internet

The Internet had the potential to be a disruptive technology for existing businesses (Christensen, 1997). The first established firms to understand the implications of the Internet were Silicon Valley firms such as Cisco, Sun Microsystems, and Oracle; all of which had been financed by venture capitalists in the 1980s. This is not surprising, because they were infrastructure providers for organizations planning to utilize the Internet. In a sense, they resembled the merchants who supplied equipment to the miners in the Gold Rush. Cisco was particularly advantaged, since it produced the routers and switches that directed much of the Internet traffic (Mayer and Kenney, 2002). Sun, with its roots in the engineering and networking community, also experienced dramatic sales growth, as its servers became the standard for large Web sites. However, it was Oracle's database software that became the platform upon which most Web sites operated. These firms became critical Internet infrastructure firms.

Remarkably, it was not until 16 May 1995, with the release of Bill Gates's memo entitled 'The Internet Tidal Wave', that Microsoft demonstrated that it grasped the implications of the Internet (Ferguson, 1999). Given Microsoft's comparative tardiness, it is no surprise that in the period from 1995 to 1997 most non-technology firms were unaware of the impact that the Internet could potentially have on their businesses. IBM and Hewlett Packard were also slow to react, while DEC was very late. In DEC's case, this was particularly surprising because it owned Altavista, which was one of the most successful early search portals, and had been aware of the importance of the Internet in 1992 (Berners-Lee, 1999). Had DEC been more aggressive, it might have been able to create a successful portal and become a rival to startups such as Yahoo!

A comparison of two rival PC makers, Dell and Compaq, illustrates that management's awareness of the environment can affect technology adoption and competitive advantage. Dell rapidly transferred its build-to-order model to the Internet and was rewarded with lowered costs and increased sales. In contrast, Compaq, dependent as it was upon in-store retail channels for sales, found it difficult to convert its operations to the Internet. For Dell, the Internet became a powerful new competitive weapon, while for Compaq, the Internet proved to be a difficult medium to use effectively (Kenney and Curry, 2001; Fields, 2003). Although the Internet was a boom for many technology firms, it also created difficulties for firms that were ineffective in utilizing its potential.

For established firms, the Internet enabled the provision of new services to their customers, an opportunity to displace intermediaries, and/or a tool for transforming old business processes. Sales would only be the most visible use of the Internet. Easily as important was the adoption of Internet-enabled business process customer service, passive information provision, and software downloading; all of which decreased costs and/or assisted in customer retention.

As with so many technologies, the Internet contributed to a change in the relative power balance between links in the value chain. For example, the airlines have used the Internet as a tool for decreasing their commissions to travel agents. Prior to the advent of customer self-service on the Internet, when a customer reserved through a traditional travel agent, the airlines paid a commission of between 15-20 percent of the total ticket price to the travel agent. In contrast, when the customer reserves on the airline's Web site, the cost is between 3-5 percent of the ticket price. These enormous savings allowed airlines to reward customers for booking on-line, and the percentage of tickets reserved on-line grew rapidly (Global Aviation Associates, 2002).

Technology also has many unforeseen impacts. It has been suggested that, though the Internet has allowed airlines to save on reservations, it has also allowed consumers – especially business travellers – to compare prices more effectively, thereby resulting in losses in revenue that exceed the savings made.

During the early days of commercialization, the potential impacts of the Internet were not fully apparent. Not entirely surprisingly, firms like Dell, FedEx, and Southwest Airlines that were already exploiting new business models were the earliest to experiment with the Internet. In retail, the pioneers include catalogue-based firms such as REI, Eddie Bauer, and Land's End. In general, store-based retailers trailed the early adopters and established Web sites only after 1998. The response of manufacturers varied widely. For example, Cisco and Intel began on-line customer service in 1995 and 1996, respectively. Other firms were less aggressive, but by 2002, having a Web site and using the Internet as an intranet was nearly universal. Adoption was a learning-by-doing process, whereby adopters gradually evolved ever more applications, which gradually deepened the adoption of Internet technologies.

The safest generalizations that can be made about the established firms are that the more technologically sophisticated they were, the closer they were to computer networking, and the more entrepreneurial they were, the more rapidly they adopted and experimented with the Internet. However, many established firms were passive until startups actually entered their market, threatening to replace or disintermediate them (if they were retail operations) or reorganize the value chain (if they were manufacturers). Though, in nearly all cases, the startups were unable to dislodge the incumbents who were able to draw on a host of complementary assets (Teece, 1986), their threat forced them to experiment rapidly with the new medium.

4.2 The Startups

The role of startups in the commercialization of the Internet did not begin with the Internet. The Internet data communications firms, PSINet and UUNet, were funded by venture capitalists in the late 1980s, as was the dial-up message board firm, AOL.[4] Still, it is accurate to say that outside of these firms, there were few Internet startups and few investments until 1994. This was a function of the time it took for entrepreneurs to comprehend the opportunities that the Internet represented and the delay in convincing venture capitalists that the Internet presented an investment opportunity. However, the lag was not long – especially in Silicon Valley – and by early 1994, venture capitalists began receiving business plans from entrepreneurs with ideas for the commercial exploitation of the Internet. Given the greater venture capital resources and large numbers of entrepreneurs, Silicon Valley quickly became the centre for Internet startups (Kenney, 2003; Zook, 2002).

With the release of Mosaic, some existing small firms began developing software such as browsers and web-editing tools for use on the Internet. A few of these were funded by venture capitalists, but most were self-financed. Netscape was one of the earliest Internet startups dedicated to exploiting the Internet, that received venture capital. It was established in April 1994 by Jim Clark, an ex-Stanford professor and founder of Silicon Graphics Inc., and Marc Andreessen, a former student at the University of Illinois and leader of the team that created Mosaic. After hiring the others on the Mosaic team, they rewrote Mosaic and rapidly captured the browser market (Cusumano and Yoffie, 1998). Netscape had an initial stock offering in August 1995 at a price that gave it a valuation of nearly one billion USD. This alerted every venture capitalist and entrepreneur to the capital gains they might reap in the Internet field. By 9 March 2000, more than 370 self-identified Internet-related firms had gone public and their total valuation was $1.5 trillion, though they had only $40 billion in sales (Perkins, 2000).

As the number of users grew rapidly and new business ideas proliferated, the Internet became an economic space that continually expanded, providing further commercial opportunities. The greater the number of users, the more reason there was to create Web pages in order to increase content and reason to use the Internet. The result was a virtuous circle of increasing returns, or what has commonly been called 'Metcalfe's Law'. This provided opportunities for yet other startups to develop new software and Web-based services. For example, businesses could be built around searching and cataloguing other sites. There was an explosion of software tools firms, Web-hosting services, etc.[5] Each apparent success attracted more investors willing to fund entrepreneurs experimenting with yet other business models.

The rapidly growing user base, reinforced by the high valuations that Internet-related startups commanded in the stock market, unleashed a frenzy of venture investing. Naturally, this willingness to fund experiments encouraged ever more speculative experimentation. With public investors clamouring for shares in Internet firms, these experiments could be listed on the stock market for massive capital gains. Despite the scattered failures, the Internet sector burgeoned as more firms entered the space.

Investments in the pioneers returned excellent results as firms went public or were acquired. From 1995 to March 2000, the willingness of public markets to purchase the shares of newly formed Internet firms fluctuated, but in general the market was very positive and small firms were able to raise large amounts of capital. This illustrates how by mid-1999 there was what might be termed a full-scale investment panic as public investors drove the price of new issues skyward.[6] In 1999, the *average* return for early stage funds was 91.2 percent, the highest in history (NVCA, 2000a).[7] The returns for the most successful venture capital funds were astronomical. Table 2.1 shows that a number of funds had annual returns of 100 and even 400 percent per year. Rates of return of this magnitude, quite naturally, excite 'irrational exuberance' and excessive greed. This explains the increase in the amount of venture capital invested in Internet-related firms, which grew from a nearly negligible $12 million in the first quarter of 1995 to $31 billion in 1999 (NVCA, 2000b). In percentage terms, the increase was equally dramatic, growing from a negligible percentage in 1995 to over 60 percent of total investment in the fourth quarter of 1999 (NVCA, 2000b: 31).

Table 2.1   *The returns for selected venture capital funds raised during the Internet boom*

Firm	Date	Size (millions)	Annual IRR (%)
KPCB VII	1994	225	130
Benchmark	1995	101	236
Brentwood VII	1995	115	99
Matrix IV	1995	125	221
Accel V	1996	150	196
KPCB VIII	1996	299	350
Battery IV	1997	200	244
Benchmark II	1997	125	419

Source: Adapted from Lissom, 2002.

In this bubble, massive sums were committed to multiple firms intent on entering the same business segment, even when it was likely that only one firm could survive. Table 2.2 indicates the huge numbers of venture capital-funded startups in different segments. However, if these investments are thought of as being experiments, it means that the US launched an enormous number of experiments. This large number, even if accompanied by foolishness and stupidity, increased the probability of having made a correct investment; indeed, a few of these startups have become global leaders. Just as important, this feverish investment alerted established firms to the potential of the Internet and forced them to react. In effect, these investments both created new firms and changed the environmental conditions for established firms.

Table 2.2   Companies receiving venture capital funding, 1997-2000

Sector	Number of Companies	Representative Firms
Switches etc.	73	Ciena Networks
Data communication components	135	Optimight Comm.
Communications processors	84	Broadcom
Local area networks	92	Cascade Comm.
Wireless components	76	Metaware Comm.
Web aggregation, portals, exchanges	141	VerticalNet
E-commerce software	199	Kana Comm.
Internet communication & infra.	71	Akamai
Internet security/firewalls etc.	202	VeriSign
Software consulting services	134	CommerceOne

Source: Adapted from *Venture Economics*, April 2002.

The sheer diversity of Internet-based business activities is remarkable. Many of these businesses could not exist if it were not for the Internet. Cyberspace is being 'settled' and people are building economic activities. Some of these activities, like retail sales, are directly analogous to those in physical space, while others are unique to cyberspace. For example, portals and search engines such as Yahoo!, Excite (now part of Excite@home), and Google are only possible because of the Internet.

Portals are the central nodes through which Internet users pass on their way to other destinations. The dominant portals were established during the earliest days of commercialization. Due to the US head start, nearly all of the dominant global portals such as Yahoo!, Excite, Altavista, and Infoseek were US-based.[8] By 2002, Yahoo!, AOL, and MSN were the global leaders. The dominance of the US-based portals was predicated on a number of advantages. The precocity of the US market and its large size meant that the vast preponderance of sites were and continue to be in English. Not surprisingly, this is an advantage to the US portals, not only in terms of content, but also in terms of an ability to capture scale advantages. As David (1986) and Arthur (1994) predict, in the case of portals winner-takes-all economics seem to be operating.

Early entrance allowed these US firms to establish global brand names before other sites could compete in the English-language market. In other countries, indigenous portals had to defend their language market from the US portals, which already controlled the English-language traffic. The US portals also translated their sites into foreign languages, while leveraging their existing architecture, software, server farms and technical talent.

Another group of sites, such as eBay and the now defunct Napster, links users together. These sites are not based on direct sales; rather, their profits come from other revenue sources such as advertising, subscriptions, commissions, referral fees, etc. The most successful example is the auction site eBay. eBay was established in September 1995 and grew rapidly to become the largest Internet auction site with net revenues of $289 million in the third quarter of 2002 and an income of $61 million. On-line gaming is another application in which a firm provides a platform for gamers. What is remarkable is the sheer diversity of games, which range from fantasy sports and gigantic role-playing games to simple two person games like chess. There are also a myriad of community sites that provide platforms for Web pages, chat, and other interaction. For example, AsianAvenue.com provides a social interaction platform for Asian Americans.

Portals, auction sites, on-line gaming and social platforms are examples of activities that have no direct analogues off-line. These new activities are fascinating because they are not shifting existing commerce on-line; rather, they are the outcomes of the opening of a field for experimentation. These on-line-only applications show that despite the collapse of the Internet Bubble the technology has become a part of everyday life.

4.3 Software Tools and Internet Services

The early and rapid development of e-commerce, the large number of leading-edge users, and an already strong position in software provided significant advantages to US firms intent upon developing software tools for Internet users. As von Hippel (1988) pointed out, the needs of cutting-edge users can alert toolmakers to marketable improvements, or what could be termed 'learning from lead customers'. Further, the needs of customers such as Yahoo!, Amazon and/or eBay meant that software and services would be severely tested, thereby exposing limitations and problems. The intense competition among the users as they sought technological advantages meant that software innovators had a ready market. A symbiosis between software designers and leading-edge users developed, thus creating a virtuous circle in which improved tools accelerated the development of the Web sites and vice versa.

Rationalizing and transferring business processes and business-to-business (B-to-B) e-commerce to the Web-based protocols created significant new demand for software, and many startups were funded by venture capitalists to meet this new demand. Venture capital-funded startups such as CommerceOne, Ariba, E.piphany, and Kana Communications, to name only a few, became global competitors, and very often the US firms (which to a great extent had roots in Silicon Valley) were competing globally against each other. In the Internet services arena, US startups became global leaders in corporate web hosting. Other firms offered to manage corporate Web sites, e-mail, and a wide variety of other Internet-related functions. Other software firms such as Inktomi and Akamai developed software used for Internet infrastructure.

There were a number of *de novo* entrants initially, but later service entrants were actually incumbents in adjacent fields or firms that had previously offered a similar service without using the Internet. Christensen et al. (2003) show that as the Internet matured, other types of firms became significant players in Internet service provision. Some of these would be large European firms. However, US incumbent firms such as IBM Global Services, Accenture, etc. would be significant, not only due to their size, but also because they were able to draw upon the knowledge they had garnered in the US serving early adopters. It is quite possible that Internet service firms may disappear as an identifiable category and simply become part of the computing-related services industry, and the Internet will be a component of a larger solution (for further discussion of this point see Christensen, Chapter 8, this volume).

US firms have occupied nearly every important Internet-related software niche. These firms rapidly expanded their businesses into other countries, either by establishing offices or using their stock to purchase the much smaller international competitors. Whether American or foreign, most Web sites operate on US software and hardware. Regardless of the outcome of international competition concerning portals or e-commerce, or the different privacy issues and government policies, it will be US software toolmakers and service providers that will become the dominant vendors. Judging from the current situation, there will be fewer significant European and Asian firms. One possible exception to this scenario would be if mobile phones become a dominant Internet access device – an uncertain proposition (Kenney, 2003).

4.4 E-Commerce

Of all of the fields that received funding during the Internet frenzy, business-to-business and business-to-consumer e-commerce attracted the most attention from the media. There was a proliferation of startups predicated on extraordinarily risky business models. In the excitement of the moment many predicted that these platforms would entirely replace physical stores (bricks and mortar). Put differently, the on-line operations were expected to disintermediate the traditional sales, retail and wholesale. Accomplishing this proved difficult. The first idea was to create e-malls, that is, retail sites like physical-world shopping malls, where retailers could 'locate' their shops. The proposition was that these business-to-consumer (B-to-C) sites would attract consumers because of the convenience of having a centralized on-line 'shopping centre'. These 'standalone' malls failed.

In July 1994, only a few months after the establishment of Netscape and Yahoo!, Amazon was established, and in July 1995, its on-line bookstore opened. Amazon's founder, Jeff Bezos, was not attracted to books, because he was interested in the book business per se; rather, he was searching for a retail sector that would be easy to penetrate. Books were chosen because they are an easy-to-ship, undifferentiated product. Moreover, there was an existing set of distributors that could be used for order fulfilment. From its inception, Amazon aimed to expand from books to other items, with the eventual goal of becoming a multiproduct retailer – in other words, Wal-Mart was the real target. Even though Amazon consistently lost money, and did not have the advantage of being the first on-line bookstore, it was able to grow rapidly and swamp its bookstore competitors because of the venture capital backing it received in June 1996. As of late 2002, Amazon was marginally profitable.

Amazon was a pioneer. Its fabulously successful listing on the NASDAQ ignited a frenzy of investment in other on-line retail startups. Very soon there were specialized sites selling groceries, pet supplies, air travel, vitamins, pharmaceutical prescriptions, stocks, CDs, electronics, PCs, home improvement supplies, and nearly every other commonly consumed item. In this investment frenzy, often four or five on-line firms were established in each product category. At times these firms would have different business models, but for the most part, they were simply clones. Of course, part of the problem was that the venture capitalists that funded this plethora of firms selling almost any product never recognized the fact that Amazon was not meant to end up as an on-line bookstore. It was meant to be an on-line Wal-Mart. When the IPO boom ended in early 2000, many of these e-retailers had not yet gone public and were not profitable. With no exit opportunity, their backers rejected entreaties for more funds, sparking a wave of distress mergers and bankruptcies. Many of those that had gone public in 1998 and 1999 had gone bankrupt by 2002.

The on-line retailers soon discovered the importance of complementary assets such as product line expertise. For example, they learned what off-line retailers had always known: predicting demand is one of the most difficult skills in retailing. For example, in 1999 Amazon purchased the wrong toys and after Christmas it had to write off $35 million in unsold inventory. In response to these problems, in August 2000 Amazon.com entered a joint venture with Toysrus.com in which Toys'R'Us would be responsible for buying and managing the inventory, while Amazon would operate the Web site development, order fulfilment, and customer service for a new joint site (Farmer and Junnarkar, 2000). In effect, Amazon acknowledged the fact that it did not have the expertise to predict toy demand effectively, while Toys'R'Us conceded that it was not as successful in interfacing with Internet buyers and handling fulfilment.

Only six months to one year after the establishment of the first B-to-C firms, venture capitalists began funding entrepreneurs to establish Web sites aimed at becoming on-line marketplaces where businesses could buy and sell, i.e., B-to-B sites. The B-to-B market quickly outstripped B-to-C in sales, though most of these sales were through the Web sites of firms such as Dell, Cisco and Intel. However, by mid-1998, independent on-line marketplaces had been established for nearly every business imaginable. A 1999 report by a Robertson Coleman analyst listed 253 separate on-line B-to-B sites (Upin, 1999). By 2002, many of these had closed.

The history of a couple of the most important B-to-B firms provides an insight into the precipitous rise and collapse of this entire genre of Internet firms. One of the first independent B-to-B firms, VerticalNet, was established in October 1995, and by November 2000 it was operating more than 60 separate industry Web sites through which specific industrial commodities could be traded (VerticalNet, 2001). In October 1999, VerticalNet's stock reached $239 per share, but by October 2002 it had dropped to $.86 per share and was being delisted from the NASDAQ. Another firm, the Internet Capital Group (ICG), was established in 1996 with the express purpose of investing in fledgling B-to-B startups. Its investment record is directly correlated with the Internet Bubble. In 1996, ICG invested $14 million in startups, however by 1999 this had increased to $572 million. In 2000, it had planned to invest in excess of $1 billion, but this amount was dramatically reduced due to the collapse of ICG's stock price. By November 2002, ICG's stock had dropped to $.25 per share, and it was also scheduled for delisting. These two firms were clearly among the most visible of a cohort of what would prove to be a large number of delisted and bankrupt firms.

5. THE COLLAPSE OF THE BUBBLE

In March 2000, the NASDAQ Bubble that was driven by the technology stocks began to collapse. The first to drop were the profitless e-commerce firms (Pets.com, Eve.com, Boo.com ad infinitum). They were followed by the network equipment startups (e.g., Ciena, Sycamore, Extreme Networks), and then later in 2000 by the telecommunications firms (e.g., Qwest, Winstar, Global Crossing). As their stock prices fell, venture capitalists and corporate insiders began unloading their large holdings at any price. At the same time, stock market analysts at the large investment banks recommended stocks that they were privately disparaging. By 2003, the stock market collapse would be the greatest since the Great Depression of the 1930s.

At the end of 2002, though usage of the Internet continues to increase – albeit at a far slower pace than previously – the shakeout in the industry continues, though at a slower rate. Webmergers (2002), which estimates that there are between 8,000 and 10,000 dot.com firms, has counted 862 failures of dot.com firms (this does not include mergers). It also found that the rate of failure slowed in 2002. Of course, investors, especially those that purchased stock after the initial public stock offerings, have lost hundreds of billions of dollars. With the exception of eBay, even firms that will survive, such as Amazon and Yahoo!, have experienced massive losses in value.

The startups were the most severely affected, but many established firms have also had severe difficulties. The magnitude of this downturn is such that many of these firms have lost 75 percent or more of their peak valuation. Telecommunications providers ranging from AT&T to Worldcom and Sprint faced severe difficulties, with Worldcom and Qwest collapsing into bankruptcy connected with fraud. High technology equipment providers – especially telecommunications equipment providers, such as Nortel and Lucent – were flirting with bankruptcy. For others such as Cisco and Sun Microsystems, lay-

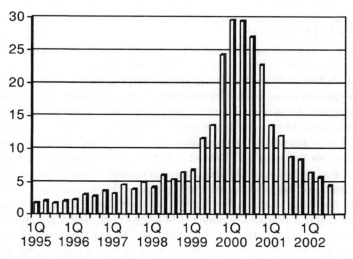

Source: Adapted from NVCA 2002.

Figure 2.1 Venture capital investments per quarter from 1995 to 2002

offs and dramatic decrease in their stock valuations were the norm. The ultimate fate of many of these firms rests with the length of the current high-technology depression.

The venture capital industry both fuelled and benefited from the Internet Bubble. Figure 2.1 shows that venture capital investment increased from approximately $2 billion per quarter in 1995 to a peak of nearly $30 billion in the second quarter of 2000. In 2002, investment had been reduced to under $5 billion in the third quarter, and it was generally expected to continue to decrease. This collapse has also been reflected in the returns on venture capital portfolios. For example, in the first quarter of 2002, the annualized rate of return for venture capital partnerships was −24.4 percent (NVCA, 2002). During the second quarter of 2002, for the first time in history, US venture capitalists have actually returned to their investors more money to investors than they received in new investments. Finally, the venture capitalists have an enormous 'overhang' of monies that are unlikely ever to be invested profitably.

There may be reasons to debate whether there ever was a 'New Economy'. Separating what has changed and what remains the same is not easy. However, it would be a mistake to treat the Bubble and the Collapse of the Bubble separately. The Bubble of the late 1990s expressed the strength and power of the US NSI. However, it is equally true that the Collapse provided an instructive lesson in the dangerous tendencies in the US NSI.

6. FINAL THOUGHTS

At this early date, writing about the commercialization of the Internet as history is fraught with uncertainty. Kindleberger (1978) noted that manias were frequently accompanied by swindles, frauds and other financial crimes, and the Internet Bubble confirms this conclusion. However, in contrast to many previous bubbles that were based on real estate, watered stock or tulip bulbs, real infrastructure was built and viable firms were created. In ten short years since the release of the Internet protocols, the Internet has become a part of everyday life. Without a doubt, the mania contributed to the rapid diffusion and commercialization of the Internet.

The enormous capital investments in everything from infrastructure through to the creation of e-commerce sites funded experimentation with new business models and activities of all sorts. The US NSI based on venture capital funding of startups turbocharged the formation of new firms, but also fed wild speculation. Despite, or possibly because of this excess, the US developed the strongest and broadest Internet industry in the world. These defining firms were supported by venture capital, and two important survivors, Yahoo! and Google, can be traced directly to US universities.

The Internet investment craze in the second half of the 1990s was extremely wasteful. Foolish business propositions of all sorts received funding. And yet, even after the evisceration of large amounts of this speculative capital, US firms remain dominant in nearly every area related to the Internet. From a systemic perspective, it is likely that in a decade hence we will reflect upon the Internet investment bubble and conclude that the willingness of investors to experiment resulted in US firms capturing a leadership role, and that the survivors gained the resources, experience and market share that only a few firms in other nations were able to achieve.

Finally, the question of whether the US is in a 'New Economy' is difficult to answer, because it is too early to separate the Bubble-induced euphoria from real changes. If what is meant by a New Economy, is that the US economy would escape from capitalist business cycles, then it seems clear that there is no New Economy. However, if a New Economy refers to the implementation of a new communication system that allows the creation of new business models that may evolve so far as to change the organizational face of capitalism, then the question is still open. Unfortunately, the next decade is still before us, and only the immodest would confidently predict the future after such a tumultuous decade.

ACKNOWLEDGEMENTS

This chapter is a significantly revised version of a paper appearing in *The Global Internet Economy* edited by Bruce Kogut. The author would like to thank Suzy Iacono of the National Science Foundation and University of California Office of the President's Industry-University Cooperative Research Program for providing funding that supported aspects of the research reported here. He also thanks Jill Archer and Jens Frøslev Christensen for comments, suggestions and improvements.

NOTES

1. For one of the most cogent and prescient critiques of this technological millenarianism, see Brown and Duguid (2000).
2. It is worth noting that in the US, many different entities including state, county and city governments can affect e-commerce. These jurisdictions have different taxation schemes and laws pertaining to retail sales, particularly with respect to tobacco, firearms, alcohol and pornography. Despite these differences, it is accurate to call the US a unified market.
3. A salient expression of this was the individuals who rushed to occupy various URLs with no intention of using them. They then offered to sell the URLs. To translate this into the Land Rush metaphor, they 'staked a claim' to an address in cyberspace. One response to this was legislation forbidding 'cybersquatting,' a reference to the registration by entrepreneurs of addresses that were trademarks and/or established firms' names.

4.   Venture capitalists had funded AOL in the 1980s as an on-line service; at the time its operations were unrelated to the Internet.
5.   For a discussion of Internet service firms, see Christensen, Chapter 8, this volume.
6.   This so-called under-pricing of securities allowed investment bankers to reward their customers with allocations of 'hot' IPOs, a practice that in late 2002 was being investigated as a possible corrupt practice.
7.   The three-year compounded average annual return was a more modest 47.9 percent!
8.   Microsoft and AOL are also leading destinations. AOL is successful because it has its captive audience of subscribers. Microsoft attracts visitors for many reasons; for instance, it is the default option on the Internet Explorer browser, and users need software assistance, etc.

REFERENCES

Abbate, Janet (1999), *Inventing the Internet*, Cambridge, US: MIT Press.

Arthur, W. Brian (1994), *Increasing Returns and Path Dependence in the Economy*, Ann Arbor: University of Michigan Press.

Berners-Lee, Tim with Mark Fischetti (1999), *Weaving the Web: The Original Design and Ultimate Destiny of the World Wide Web by Its Inventor*, San Francisco: HarperSanFrancisco.

Brown, John Seely and Paul Duguid (2000), *The Social Life of Information*, Boston: Harvard Business School Press.

Chandler, Alfred (1990), *Scale and Scope: The Dynamics of Industrial Capitalism*, Cambridge: Harvard University Press.

Christensen, Clayton (1997), *The Innovators Dilemma*, Boston: Harvard Business School Press.

Christensen, J.F., M.L. Schmidt and M.R. Larsen (2003), 'Turbulence and Competitive Dynamics of the Internet Services Industry', *Industry and Innovation*, 10 (2): 117-43.

Cohen, Stephen S., J. Bradford DeLong and John Zysman (2000), 'An E-conomy?' *Milken Institute Review*, 2 (1), 16-22.

Cusumano, Paul and David Yoffie (1998), *Competing on Internet Time: Lessons From Netscape and its Battle with Microsoft*, New York: Free Press.

David, Paul (1986), 'Understanding the economics of QWERTY: The necessity of history', in W. Parker (ed.), *Economic history and the modern economist*, New York: Basil Blackwell, pp. 30-49.

Davies, Andrew (1994), *Telecommunications and Politics: The Decentralised Alternative*, London: Pinter Publishers Ltd.

Dosi, Giovanni (1984), *Technical Change and Industrial Transformation*, London: Macmillan.

Farmer, Melanie and Sandeep Junnarkar (2000), 'Amazon-Toysrus.com Deal Signals Strategy Shift', CNET News.com (10 August).

Ferguson, Charles (1999), *High Stakes, No Prisoners: A Winner's Tale of Greed and Glory in the Internet Wars*, New York: Times Books.

Fields, Gary (forthcoming), *Territories of Profit: Communications, Capitalist Development and Innovation at G.F. Swift and Dell Computer*, Stanford: Stanford University Press.

Fransman, Martin (2001), 'Evolution of the Telecommunications Industry into the Internet Age', *Communications and Strategy*, 43 (3).

Garud, Raghu and Peter Karnoe (2001), 'Path Creation as a Process of Mindful Deviation', in R. Garud and P. Karnoe (eds), *Path Dependence and Creation*, New York: Lawrence Erlbaum, pp. 1-40.

Global Aviation Associates, Ltd. (2002), 'The Economics of Travel Distribution in an Internet Driven Environment', http://www.ga2online.com/recentwork.htm (March 2001).

Howe, Walt (2000), 'A Brief History of the Internet', (18 April). http://www0.delphi.com/navnet/faq/history.html

Hunt, Courtney Shelton and Howard Aldrich (1998), 'The Second Ecology: The Creation and Evolution of Organizational Communities as Exemplified by the Commercialization of the World Wide Web', in B. Staw and L. Cummings (eds), *Research in Organizational Behavior*, Vol. 20. Greenwich, US: JAI Press, pp. 267-302.

Jimeniz, Ed and Shane Greenstein (1998), 'The Emerging Internet Retailing Market as a Nested Diffusion Process', *International Journal of Innovation Management*, September, 2 (3).

Kenney, Martin (1986), *Biotechnology: The University-Industrial Complex*, New Haven: Yale University Press.

Kenney, Martin (2003), 'The Growth and Development of the Internet in the United States', in Bruce Kogut (ed.), *The Global Internet Economy*, Boston: MIT Press.

Kenney, Martin and James Curry (1999), 'E-Commerce: Implications for Firm Strategy and Industry Configuration', *Industry and Innovation*, 6 (2), 131-51.

Kenney, Martin and James Curry (2000), 'Beyond Transaction Costs: E-commerce and the Power of the Internet Dataspace', in T. Leinbach and S. Brunn (eds), *Worlds of E-Commerce: Economic, Geographical and Social Dimensions*, New York: John Wiley & Sons, pp. 45-66.

Kenney, Martin and James Curry (2001), 'The Internet and the Personal Computer Value Chain', in BRIE-IGCC E-conomy Project (eds), *Tracking a Transformation: E-Commerce and the Terms of Competition in Industries*, Washington: Brookings Institution Press, pp. 151-77.

Kenney, Martin and Urs von Burg (1999), 'Technology and Path Dependence: The Divergence between Silicon Valley and Route 128', *Industrial and Corporate Change*, 8 (1), 67-103.

Kindleberger, Charles P. (1978), *Manias, Panics, and Crashes: A History of Financial Crises*, New York: Basic Books.

Kogut, Bruce and Udo Zander (1992), 'Knowledge of the Firm, Combinative Capabilities, and the Replication of Technology', *Organization Science*, 3, 383-97.

Leiner, Barry M., Vinton G. Cerf, David D. Clark, Robert E. Kahn, Leonard Kleinrock, Daniel C. Lynch, Jon Postel, Lawrence G. Roberts and Stephen Wolff (2000), 'A Brief History of the Internet', http://www.isoc.org/inter net/history/ brief.html# Initial_Concepts.

Lipartito, Kenneth (1997), '"Cut-throat" Competition, Corporate Strategy, and the Growth of Network Industries', *Research on Technological Innovation, Management and Policy*, 6, 3-53.

Lissom, Steve (2002). www.insidervc.com. (September 22).

Macaluso, Nora (2001), 'Nearly 60 Percent of US Homes Are Online', www.EcommerceTimes.com (13 August).

Markoff, John (1993), 'A Free and Simple Computer Link', *The New York Times* (8 December).

Mayer, David and Martin Kenney (2002), 'Economic Action Does Not Take Place in a Vacuum: Understanding Cisco's Acquisition and Development Strategy', Berkeley Roundtable on the International Economy Working Paper No. 148.

Moore, Richard K (1996), 'Telecom Regimes', http://www.cni.org/Hforums/ roundtable/1996-02/0056.html.

Mowery, David and Nathan Rosenberg (1993), 'The US National Innovation System', in R. Nelson (ed.), *National Innovation Systems: A Comparative Analysis*, New York: Oxford University Press, pp. 29-75.

Mowery, David and Timothy S. Simcoe (2002), 'Is the Internet a US Invention? – An Economic and Technological History of Computer Networking', forthcoming in *Research Policy*.

NVCA (National Venture Capital Association) (2000a), 'Venture Capital Funds Raise A Record $46.55 Billion in 1999' (27 March).

NVCA (2000b), *2000 National Venture Capital Association Yearbook*, Washington: NVCA.

NVCA (2001), *2001 National Venture Capital Association Yearbook*, Washington: NVCA.

NVCA (2002), 'Private Equity Performance Continues to Reflect Industry Realities' (7 August), www.nvca.org/Vepress08_07_02.pdf.

Nonaka, Ikujiro and Hirotaka Takeuchi (1995), *The Knowledge-Creating Company*, New York: Oxford University Press.

Perkins, Anthony (2000), 'Investors: Brace Yourselves for the Next Bubble Bath', *Red Herring* (13 November), 21-2.

Reich, Robert (1991), *The Work of Nations*, New York: Knopf.

Rogers, Juan (1998), 'Science and the Politics of Internetworking: NSFNET in Internet History', *The Information Society*, 14 (3) July-September.

Rosenberg, Nathan and Manuel Trajtenberg (2002), 'A General Purpose Technology at Work: The Corliss Steam Engine in the Late 19th Century US', NBER Working Paper No. 8485 (September).

Sturgeon, Timothy J. (2002), 'Modular Production Networks: A New American Model of Industrial Organization', *Industrial and Corporate Change*, 11 (3), 451-96.

Taylor, Humphrey (2001), 'Internet Penetration Has Leveled Out Over The Last 12 Months', (7 November) http://www.harrisinteractive.com/harris_poll/ index.asp?PID= 266

Teece, David J. (1986), 'Profiting from technological innovation: Implications for integration, collaboration, licensing, and public policy', *Research Policy*, 15, 285-305.

Upin, Eric (1999), 'The B-to-Bs Are Coming', Presentation to 2 November Venture Capitalist Luncheon, Menlo Park, CA.

Usher, Abbott Payson (1954), *A History of Mechanical Inventions*, revised edition, Cambridge, US: Harvard University Press.

Utterback, James and Fernando Suarez (1993), 'Innovation, competition and industry structure', *Research Policy*, 22 (1), 1-21.

Venture Economics (2002), 'The Internet Boom', *Venture Capital Journal* (April).

VerticalNet (2001), www.verticalnet.com.

von Hippel, Eric (1988), *The Sources of Innovation*, New York: Oxford University Press.

Webmergers (2002), 'First Half Report: Dot Com Failures down 73% from 2001 Levels in First Half', http://www.webmergers.com/editorial/article. php?id=60.

Zook, Matthew (2002), 'Grounded Capital: Venture Financing and the Geography of the Internet Industry 1994-2000', *Journal of Economic Geography*, 2 (2), 151-77.

3. 'Changing Gear': Productivity, ICT and Service Industries in Europe and the United States

Bart van Ark, Robert Inklaar and Robert H. McGuckin[1]

1. INTRODUCTION

A wide variety of recent studies – at firm, industry and macro levels of detail – have assessed the impact of information and communication technologies (ICT) on productivity growth during the 1990s. In addition, there have been many case studies of the way in which ICT influences performance. For the United States, there is widespread agreement that production of ICT goods has strongly contributed to acceleration in productivity growth during the 1990s.[2] Although there are a few dissenters, a consensus is emerging on the proposition that the diffusion of ICT is also a prime contributor to productivity growth elsewhere in the economy. In particular, service sectors are among the main beneficiaries of increased investment in ICT, leading to faster growth in labour productivity and in many cases also in total factor productivity growth.[3]

In the case of Europe, there is some evidence that ICT investment has contributed to faster output growth, although in most cases to a lesser extent than in the United States.[4] However, it has been widely acknowledged that European countries generally have not exploited the productivity enhancing potentials to the extent of the United States.[5] In fact, productivity growth in Europe has declined since the mid-1990s, but relatively little is known about how widespread this productivity slowdown has been across industries.[6]

This chapter examines international differences in the labour productivity performance across ICT-producing industries, intensive ICT-using industries and less intensive users (hereafter, for the sake of simplicity, called 'non-ICT' industries), with an additional breakdown into manufacturing and service industries. The database includes output and employment information for 52

Table 3.1 Productivity growth and GDP shares of ICT-producing, ICT-using and non-ICT industries in the EU

| | Productivity growth | | | | GDP share | |
| | 1990-1995 | | 1995-2000 | | 2000 | |
	EU^b	US	EU^b	US	EU^b	US
Total Economy	1.9	1.1	1.4	2.5	100.0	100.0
ICT-Producing Industries	6.7	8.1	8.7	10.1	5.9	7.3
ICT-Producing Manufacturing	11.1	15.1	13.8	23.7	1.6	2.6
ICT-Producing Services	4.4	3.1	6.5	1.8	4.3	4.7
ICT-Using Industries[a]	1.7	1.5	1.6	4.7	27.0	30.6
ICT-Using Manufacturing	3.1	-0.3	2.1	1.2	5.9	4.3
ICT-Using Services	1.1	1.9	1.4	5.4	21.1	26.3
Non-ICT Industries	1.6	0.2	0.7	0.5	67.1	62.1
Non-ICT Manufacturing	3.8	3.0	1.5	1.4	11.9	9.3
Non-ICT Services	0.6	-0.4	0.2	0.4	44.7	43.0
Non-ICT Other	2.7	0.7	1.9	0.6	10.5	9.8

Notes: Productivity is defined as value added per person employed.
a) excluding ICT-producing.
b) EU includes Austria, Denmark, Finland, France, Germany, Ireland, Italy, Netherlands, Spain, Sweden and the United Kingdom. which represents over 90% of EU GDP.

Source: Tables 2 and 3.

individual industries (ISIC rev 3) for 16 OECD countries, of which 13 are European countries (Austria, Denmark, Finland, France, Germany, Ireland, Italy, Netherlands, Norway, Sweden, Spain, Switzerland and the United Kingdom) as well as Canada, Japan and the United States, for the period from 1990 to 2000. Section 2 discusses the measures of ICT intensity by industry, which we use to group our industries into ICT-using and non-ICT industries and the differences in productivity growth between groups. In addition, we apply in section 3 some simple regressions to assess the importance and statistical significance of the widely different trends among industries. In section 4 we look at the dynamics of productivity growth for individual industries – and in particular services industries – classified as ICT-using or non-using.

Table 3.1 summarizes our results in terms of labour productivity growth rates and GDP shares for major industry groups for the European Union and the United States. The first impression from the table is a widespread acceleration in US productivity growth in particular for ICT-producing manufacturing and ICT-using services. Secondly, in contrast to the US, overall productivity growth in the European Union slowed, except for the ICT-producing sector of the economy where it accelerated. In the ICT-using sector in Europe productivity growth did not improve, whereas growth rates declined in non-ICT industries.

The latter suggests that differences with the US go beyond differences in the diffusion of new technologies. There are surely many factors involved, among them overall performance of product and labour markets, differences in initial capital-labour ratios and the widespread moderation of initially high wages in Europe since the mid-1990s. Nonetheless, technology diffusion is a big part of the story. Diffusion of ICT has taken place in Europe, but at a slower pace than in the United States, particularly during the second half of the 1990s.

Looking beyond the aggregate numbers there are three factors that stand out. First, European countries show rapid increases in labour productivity growth in ICT-producing manufacturing and service industries alike. The contribution of these industries to aggregate productivity growth was slightly lower than in the US due to the smaller size of these industries.

Second, since 1995 most European countries have shown a significant difference between productivity growth in ICT-using services and non-ICT services, although this difference in performance is much larger for the US than for Europe. Of particular importance, the US-EU differential in productivity growth is largely associated with much faster productivity growth in three ICT-using service industries, namely in retail and wholesale trade and in securities. Because of their large share in output and employment, these service industries feature prominently in accounting for the aggregate productivity growth differential. Moreover, compared to the US, each of these industries can be linked to restricted opportunities for expansion and implementation of ICT in Europe.

Third, it appears that ICT diffusion in Europe is following patterns across industries that are similar to those experienced in the US. Not only is there a reasonable correlation between the industry distributions of productivity growth in the US during the earlier half of the 1990s and the European industry productivity pattern from 1995-2000, but the industry distributions of ICT capital across countries are similar as well.

2. DOES ICT MAKE A DIFFERENCE FOR PRODUCTIVITY?

2.1 Measures of ICT Use and Industry Grouping by ICT-Categories

To distinguish between industries that use ICT more or less intensively, we must choose, for practical purposes, between three possible measures of ICT use by industry. These are the share of ICT investment in total investment, the share of ICT capital in total capital, and the share of the flow of capital services from ICT in total capital services. The latter measure has our preference, as the service flow per unit of ICT capital can be quite different from the flow from a unit of non-ICT capital. Service flows are calculated by estimating a user cost for each type of capital, and this can be relatively high for ICT capital because of high rates of depreciation. Thus, a simple measure of ICT's share of total assets may understate the flow of services from it.[7]

Unfortunately, detailed measures of capital services by industry that also distinguish between ICT and non ICT-assets are only available for the United States. We therefore largely base our grouping on US estimates for 1995 from Stiroh (2001). The rationale behind our choice of this indicator (in addition to our preference for capital services measures as discussed above) is the assumption that the US distribution of ICT intensity across industries defines the opportunity set for productive use of ICT. Then we use this distribution to study to what extent other countries have used the opportunities ICT provides in these industries. The use of the US distribution of ICT provides an independent standard that helps us identify where to expect differential productivity performance in Europe. For example, the US has shown acceleration of productivity growth in industries like finance, banking and business services which are heavy users of ICT. In addition, case studies of ICT use in industries as diverse as retail trade and trucking support the contention that ICT makes an important contribution to enhanced productivity growth.

A distinction between heavy users of ICT and less intensive ICT-users (non-ICT) is necessarily arbitrary as there are few, if any, industries that do not use ICT at all, so it requires an arbitrary cut-off point. For example, Stiroh's cut-off point is the median of the 57 industries he studied. Despite this, the use of a single set of estimates of ICT intensity can have advantages when such measures contain substantial noise, making international comparisons difficult.[8] Moreover this type of industry grouping has worked well in several earlier US studies to identify the industries with the highest impact from increased ICT use (McGuckin and Stiroh, 2001, 2002; Stiroh, 2001).

2.2 Data

The database for this study largely draws on the new STAN database for national accounts from the OECD.[9] STAN includes industry series of GDP in current basic prices, and constant price series expressed as index numbers. Employment refers to all persons employed, including self-employed persons. As hours per employee at industry level were only available for a limited number of countries, our computations relate only to output per person employed.[10]

For some ICT-producing industries, like insulated wire (ISIC 313) and instruments (ISIC 331), the STAN database does not report the detail separating them from the broader industry to which they belong, which we do in this study. In addition, we break down repairs, retail and wholesale trade (ISIC 50-52) and distinguish between ICT-intensive business services (ISIC 741-743) and non-ICT business services (ISIC 749). Although the procedures differed from country to country, in most cases output and employment shares for these more detailed industries were obtained from the OECD Structural Statistics for Industry and Services and the OECD Services Statistics on Value Added and Employment and applied to the more aggregated series from STAN.[11]

To obtain constant price series in national currencies we linked index series for real value added to 1995 GDP levels in current prices. These constant price series were distributed by industry within each of the industry groups distinguished above and then aggregated on the basis of chain-weighted Törnqvist indexes. As a result, our aggregated series do not exactly match the original GDP series for each country.

Prior to these procedures, however, we faced a serious methodological problem concerning the deflation of output in ICT-producing industries – a problem already identified in earlier studies (e.g., Schreyer, 2000, 2002; Daveri, 2001). Since many countries develop price indices for ICT goods by matching prices of comparable models between two periods in time, the rapid changes in quality of ICT equipment are not adequately reflected in measured output. Only a limited number of countries, including the United States, Australia, Canada and France, use hedonic output price indexes in their national accounts that capture the quality changes. Therefore measured prices in these countries typically decline much more rapidly. Some countries in Europe, for example Denmark and Sweden, do not create their own hedonic price indexes, but make use of the US price index for ICT equipment with a correction for the US dollar exchange rate.

To improve comparability fo the deflators for ICT output across countries, we adopted a procedure based on Schreyer (2000). The US value added deflators for ICT-producing manufacturing industries were applied to the other countries, after an adjustment for the ratio of the aggregate GDP deflator (excluding the deflators for ICT-producing manufacturing) for each country relative to the US GDP deflator. For most countries, this procedure leads to considerably higher growth of real output in ICT-producing manufacturing industries compared to the estimates reported in the national statistics (see Table 3.4 below).

In making comparisons between Europe and other countries, we calculated a European Union average based on 11 EU member states in our sample (covering more than 90 percent of EU GDP).[12] The 1995-based value added in each industry was converted to euros using the exchange rate between each national currency and the value of the euro as fixed on 1 January 1999. This method assumes, somewhat problematically, that there are no price differences between countries in the EU area.[13]

2.3 GDP Shares by Industry Group

Table 3.2 shows the relative importance of seven industry groups in the year 2000 for each country in our sample and for the European Union average. It shows the proportion of GDP accounted for by ICT-producing industries in manufacturing, ICT-producing industries in services, ICT-using industries in manufacturing (excluding the ICT-producing manufacturing industries), ICT-using industries in services (excluding the ICT-producing service industries), non-ICT industries in manufacturing, non-ICT industries in services and other non-ICT industries (including agriculture, mining, construction and public utilities).

ICT-producing industries make up at most 8 percent of GDP, with Finland being a notable exception (just over 10 percent of GDP) because of its large communication equipment industry. Most countries in Europe have lower GDP shares in ICT-producing manufacturing and ICT-producing services than the United States. ICT-using industries (other than ICT-producing industries) also account for bigger shares in the United States than in Europe, but there is a clear difference between manufacturing and services.

In ICT-using manufacturing, almost every European country has higher GDP shares than the US, with Germany and Switzerland having notably larger

Table 3.2 GDP shares of ICT-producing, ICT-using and non-ICT industries, 2000 (current prices in percentage of total)

	ICT-Producing		ICT-Using[a]		Non-ICT		
	Manufac-turing	Services	Manufac-turing	Services	Manufac-turing	Services	Other[d]
Austria	1.7	2.8	5.7	22.7	13.5	40.7	12.7
Denmark	1.1	3.6	5.9	20.6	10.1	47.7	11.0
Finland	5.9	4.7	6.1	15.3	13.9	43.1	11.1
France[b]	1.4	4.1	5.0	20.3	11.8	47.8	9.7
Germany	1.6	4.0	7.4	21.1	13.1	44.3	8.4
Ireland	7.0	5.3	6.2	25.2	18.9	24.8	12.5
Italy	1.0	3.7	6.8	22.8	12.8	42.8	10.3
Netherlands	1.4	4.4	4.7	24.1	10.3	42.7	12.5
Spain[b]	0.7	3.6	4.5	18.9	13.1	44.7	14.6
Sweden	2.1	5.7	5.6	18.1	12.2	48.2	8.1
UK	1.8	5.3	5.8	21.5	9.8	44.7	11.1
EU	1.6	4.3	5.9	21.1	11.9	44.7	10.5
Canada[b]	1.2	5.2	4.7	26.4	15.4	30.5	16.7
Japan[c]	2.9	3.3	7.0	20.4	11.2	41.3	13.8
Norway	0.6	2.9	3.6	17.2	6.0	36.4	33.2
Switzerland	2.2	4.0	7.2	30.0	12.5	34.9	9.3
US	2.6	4.7	4.3	26.3	9.3	43.0	9.8

Notes:
a) excluding ICT-producing; b) 1999; c) 1998; d) agriculture, mining, construction and public utilities.

Table 3.3 Labour productivity growth (value added per person employed) by industry group, 1990-95 and 1995-2000

1990-95	Austria	Denmark	Finland	France	Germany	Ireland	Italy	Netherlands	Spain	Sweden	UK	EU	Canada	Japan	Norway	Switzerland	US
Total Economy	2.3	1.6	3.3	1.0	2.1	3.0	1.8	0.7	1.6	2.8	2.8	1.9	1.1	0.8	3.3	-0.1	1.1
ICT-Producing Industries	5.8	7.6	6.9	4.7	7.1	11.2	2.5	3.8	4.3	4.8	8.8	6.7	2.6	8.8	3.2	1.5	8.1
ICT-Producing Mnf.	7.6	6.5	8.9	10.0	6.8	17.1	4.6	5.7	8.3	-0.7	15.8	11.1	11.8	12.4	8.4	1.4	15.1
ICT-Producing Services	4.8	7.9	4.8	2.6	5.9	2.2	1.6	2.3	3.1	6.8	5.6	4.4	0.4	4.2	2.1	1.5	3.1
ICT-Using Industries[b]	2.2	1.1	1.9	1.1	1.6	1.4	2.2	0.6	-0.2	3.4	2.3	1.7	1.8	0.7	4.3	-1.5	1.5
ICT-Using Mnf.	1.9	2.7	4.7	3.3	2.6	6.1	3.4	1.8	1.7	5.6	2.1	3.1	2.1	-1.1	1.3	0.0	-0.3
ICT-Using Services	2.1	0.6	0.7	0.5	1.1	0.2	1.6	0.4	-0.7	2.5	2.5	1.1	1.9	1.4	5.2	-2.0	1.9
Non-ICT Industries	2.1	1.4	3.4	0.7	2.0	2.6	1.5	0.5	2.0	2.4	2.5	1.6	0.5	0.1	3.0	0.7	0.2
Non-ICT Mnf.	4.6	2.9	6.2	3.4	4.4	7.8	2.7	3.7	3.5	6.3	4.0	3.8	2.1	0.4	2.2	4.4	3.0
Non-ICT Services	0.1	0.5	2.0	-0.3	0.9	-0.9	0.6	-0.2	0.9	1.5	1.5	0.6	-0.2	-0.2	0.7	-0.2	-0.4
Non-ICT Other	4.5	4.1	4.2	1.6	2.7	2.9	3.0	0.9	2.9	2.8	6.1	2.7	1.4	0.2	9.3	-0.2	0.7
Pro memoria:																	
with national deflators																	
Total Economy	2.2	1.6	3.3	1.1	2.1	2.4	1.8	0.6	1.5	2.8	2.7	1.9	1.0	0.7	3.2	0.0	1.1
ICT-Producing Mnf.	3.8	6.7	12.4	9.5	4.3	4.0	3.5	4.3	0.5	-0.1	9.8	7.8	6.8	6.8	2.3	4.8	15.1

Notes:
a) 1991-1995; b) excluding ICT-producing industries.

63

Table 3.3 (continued)

1995-2000	Austria	Denmark	Finland	France[a]	Germany	Ireland	Italy	Netherlands	Spain[a]	Sweden	UK	EU	Canada[a]	Japan[b]	Norway	Switzerland	US
Total Economy	2.3	1.9	2.5	1.2	1.3	5.3	0.8	0.9	0.4	2.1	1.8	**1.4**	1.4	0.9	1.7	1.1	**2.5**
ICT-Producing Industries	3.4	5.9	10.9	8.7	12.7	23.5	6.3	3.2	5.9	2.7	8.3	**8.7**	5.3	12.1	8.4	-1.9	**10.1**
ICT-Producing Mnf.	9.6	5.7	13.2	15.0	13.7	42.3	6.0	-1.9	13.1	1.1	16.1	**13.8**	16.9	19.5	4.9	-4.3	**23.7**
ICT-Producing Services	-0.4	5.9	8.1	6.2	11.9	-0.2	6.2	4.5	4.1	3.3	5.2	**6.5**	2.8	4.0	9.2	-0.7	**1.8**
ICT-Using Industries[c]	3.0	2.0	2.5	1.0	1.3	2.9	1.0	2.0	0.1	2.9	2.3	**1.6**	2.5	0.1	3.7	1.3	**4.7**
ICT-Using Mnf.	6.0	0.1	1.5	1.9	2.4	8.7	1.5	2.7	1.1	1.7	1.7	**2.1**	1.1	0.5	-1.3	3.3	**1.2**
ICT-Using Services	2.1	2.5	3.0	0.7	0.9	1.4	0.6	1.9	-0.1	3.3	2.6	**1.4**	2.8	0.0	4.8	0.8	**5.4**
Non-ICT Industries	1.8	1.5	1.4	0.7	0.5	2.7	0.4	0.2	0.1	1.6	0.8	**0.7**	0.5	0.1	0.7	1.1	**0.5**
Non-ICT Mnf.	4.6	3.8	3.0	2.7	0.5	10.4	0.6	2.0	-0.3	3.3	0.5	**1.5**	1.3	-0.3	1.7	4.4	**1.4**
Non-ICT Services	-0.4	1.2	0.6	0.1	-0.1	-1.2	-0.4	0.1	-0.1	1.4	0.9	**0.2**	-0.4	0.6	0.4	0.8	**0.4**
Non-ICT Other	4.0	1.2	2.3	1.1	2.3	1.2	2.5	0.0	1.3	0.5	1.5	**1.9**	1.1	-1.5	1.4	-1.3	**0.6**
Pro memoria: *with national deflators*																	
Total Economy	2.2	1.8	2.9	1.2	1.3	3.3	0.8	1.0	0.3	2.5	1.6	**1.4**	1.3	0.7	1.7	1.2	**2.5**
ICT-Producing Mnf.	4.6	3.9	19.9	13.9	6.8	8.6	1.4	3.3	1.6	21.1	5.5	**10.1**	6.6	9.3	3.2	0.7	**23.7**

Notes:
a) 1995-99; b) 1995-98; c) excluding ICT-producing industries.

shares.[14] This partly reflects the proportionally declined importance of the manufacturing sector in the US economy, but also the comparative advantage of many European countries in ICT-using (and non-ICT) industries in manufacturing outside the ICT-producing sector. In contrast, ICT-using services in the US clearly account for a higher share of GDP than in Europe, with the exception of Switzerland, where the banking sector dominates. In section 4, we look in more detail at some of the main ICT-using service industries contributing to the American productivity growth advantage over Europe.

2.4 Productivity Growth by Industry Group

Table 3.3 shows the productivity growth rates for the seven industry groupings distinguished above for individual countries and for the EU as a whole for the periods 1990-1995 and 1995-2000. During the first half of the decade, aggregate productivity growth in Europe was considerably faster than in the United States, but since 1995 US productivity growth has been 1.1 percentage points faster. But there are some important differences in growth dynamics between industry groups. First, productivity growth in the ICT-producing industries in manufacturing (i.e., office and computer equipment and telecommunication equipment) is much faster than in the rest of the economy for virtually all countries. Hence, once comparable price indexes reflecting the rapid technological change in ICT-producing manufacturing are adopted for all countries – and not just for the US – ICT-producing industries exhibit rapid productivity growth in this (small) part of the economy nearly everywhere.[15]

The clearest and most systematic differences between Europe and the US, however, arise in services, particularly in ICT-producing and ICT-using services. In ICT-producing services productivity growth in many European countries is faster than in the United States.[16] As we will see in section 4, this is mainly due to the faster productivity growth in telecommunication services in Europe. In contrast, in ICT-using services (excluding the ICT-producing services), US performance has been substantially better than that of other countries since 1995. Productivity in ICT-using services grew at 5.4 percent in the US compared to 1.4 percent for Europe in the 1995-2000 period. This difference is mainly due to better US productivity performance in the securities and trade sectors.

2.5 Industry Group Contributions to Aggregate Productivity Growth

The impact of each industry group on labour productivity at the aggregate level depends not only on the average productivity growth rate of each industry, but also on the relative size of that industry. Hence labour productivity for

Table 3.4 Contribution of industry groups to labour productivity growth, 1990-95 and 1995-2000

1990-95	Austria	Denmark	Finland	France[a]	Germany	Ireland	Italy	Netherlands	Spain	Sweden	UK	EU	Canada	Japan	Norway	Switzerland	US
Total Economy	2.3	1.6	3.4	1.0	2.1	3.0	1.8	0.7	1.6	2.8	2.9	**1.9**	1.1	0.8	3.3	-0.1	**1.1**
ICT-Producing Industries	0.3	0.3	0.3	0.2	0.3	0.9	0.1	0.2	0.1	0.3	0.5	**0.3**	0.1	0.5	0.1	0.1	**0.5**
ICT-Producing Mnf.	0.1	0.1	0.2	0.1	0.1	0.8	0.1	0.1	0.1	0.0	0.3	**0.2**	0.1	0.4	0.1	0.0	**0.4**
ICT-Producing Services	0.2	0.3	0.2	0.1	0.2	0.1	0.0	0.1	0.1	0.3	0.2	**0.2**	0.0	0.1	0.1	0.0	**0.1**
ICT-Using Industries[b]	0.6	0.3	0.4	0.3	0.4	0.4	0.6	0.2	-0.1	0.8	0.7	**0.4**	0.6	0.2	1.0	-0.5	**0.4**
ICT-Using Mnf.	0.1	0.2	0.3	0.2	0.2	0.4	0.2	0.1	0.1	0.3	0.1	**0.2**	0.1	-0.1	0.1	0.0	**0.0**
ICT-Using Services	0.5	0.1	0.1	0.1	0.2	0.0	0.4	0.1	-0.1	0.4	0.5	**0.2**	0.5	0.3	0.9	-0.5	**0.4**
Non-ICT Industries	1.2	1.0	2.4	0.5	1.4	1.5	1.0	0.5	1.4	1.9	1.9	**1.1**	0.5	0.0	2.8	0.4	**0.2**
Non-ICT Mnf.	0.6	0.3	0.8	0.4	0.7	1.3	0.4	0.4	0.5	0.8	0.5	**0.5**	0.3	0.0	0.2	0.5	**0.3**
Non-ICT Services	0.0	0.2	0.9	-0.1	0.4	-0.3	0.2	-0.1	0.4	0.8	0.6	**0.2**	0.0	-0.1	0.3	0.0	**-0.2**
Non-ICT Other	0.6	0.5	0.6	0.2	0.3	0.5	0.4	0.1	0.5	0.3	0.8	**0.3**	0.2	0.0	2.3	0.0	**0.1**
Shift effect	0.2	0.0	0.3	0.0	0.0	0.2	0.1	-0.2	0.2	-0.1	-0.2	**0.0**	-0.1	0.1	-0.6	-0.1	**-0.1**

Notes: contributions of industry groups refer to the 'intra-effect' only, that is the weighted average productivity growth of the group (see text). The 'shift-effect', which refers to the effect of reallocations between groups on aggregate productivity growth, is reported separately.
a) 1991-1995; b) excluding ICT-producing industries.

66

Table 3.4 *(continued)*

1995-2000	Austria	Denmark	Finland	France [a]	Germany	Ireland	Italy	Netherlands	Spain [a]	Sweden	UK	EU	Canada [a]	Japan [b]	Norway	Switzerland	US
Total Economy	2.3	1.9	2.6	1.2	1.4	5.5	0.8	0.9	0.4	2.1	1.8	**1.4**	1.4	0.9	1.7	1.1	**2.5**
ICT-Producing Industries	0.2	0.3	0.9	0.5	0.7	2.7	0.3	0.2	0.2	0.2	0.6	**0.5**	0.3	0.7	0.3	-0.1	**0.7**
ICT-Producing Mnf.	0.2	0.1	0.6	0.2	0.2	2.8	0.1	0.0	0.1	0.0	0.3	**0.2**	0.2	0.6	0.0	-0.1	**0.7**
ICT-Producing Services	0.0	0.2	0.3	0.2	0.5	0.0	0.2	0.2	0.1	0.2	0.2	**0.3**	0.1	0.1	0.3	0.0	**0.1**
ICT-Using Industries [c]	0.8	0.5	0.6	0.2	0.4	0.9	0.2	0.6	0.0	0.7	0.7	**0.4**	0.8	0.0	0.8	0.5	**1.4**
ICT-Using Mnf.	0.3	0.0	0.1	0.1	0.2	0.6	0.1	0.1	0.0	0.1	0.1	**0.1**	0.0	0.0	-0.1	0.2	**0.0**
ICT-Using Services	0.5	0.5	0.5	0.2	0.2	0.3	0.1	0.4	0.0	0.6	0.6	**0.3**	0.7	0.0	0.9	0.2	**1.4**
Non-ICT Industries	1.0	1.1	1.0	0.5	0.2	1.6	0.2	0.2	0.1	1.2	0.6	**0.5**	0.2	0.0	0.7	0.7	**0.4**
Non-ICT Mnf.	0.6	0.4	0.4	0.3	0.1	1.8	0.1	0.2	0.0	0.4	0.0	**0.2**	0.2	0.0	0.1	0.6	**0.1**
Non-ICT Services	-0.1	0.6	0.3	0.0	0.0	-0.3	-0.2	0.0	-0.1	0.7	0.4	**0.1**	-0.1	0.2	0.2	0.3	**0.2**
Non-ICT Other	0.6	0.1	0.3	0.1	0.2	0.2	0.3	0.0	0.2	0.1	0.2	**0.2**	0.2	-0.2	0.4	-0.1	**0.1**
Shift effect	0.3	0.0	0.2	0.0	0.1	0.2	0.1	0.0	0.0	0.1	0.0	**0.0**	0.1	0.1	-0.1	0.0	**0.0**

Notes: contributions of industry groups refer to the 'intra-effect' only, that is the weighted average productivity growth of the group (see text). The 'shift-effect', which refers to the effect of reallocations between groups on aggregate productivity growth, is reported separately.
a) 1995-99; b) 1995-98; c) excluding ICT-producing industries.

67

the total economy (P) can be perceived as the sum of the productivity contributions of each industry group (i) weighted with the labour share ($L_i/L=S_i$):[17]

$$P \;=\; \frac{Y}{L} \;=\; \sum_{i=1}^{n}(\frac{Y_i}{L_i})(\frac{L_i}{L}) \;=\sum_{i=1}^{n}(P_i S_i) \tag{3.1}$$

In a time perspective, the change in productivity between year t (P_t) and year $t-1$ (P_{t-1}) can be written as follows:

$$\frac{P_t - P_{t-1}}{P_t} = \frac{\Delta P}{P_t} = \frac{\sum_{i=1}^{n}(\Delta P_i \cdot \overline{S}_i)}{P_t} + \frac{\sum_{i=1}^{n}(\overline{P}_i \cdot \Delta S_i)}{P_t} \tag{3.2}$$

where $\overline{S}_i$ and $\overline{P}_i$ are the average employment share and the average productivity level in year t and $t-1$ respectively. Thus, aggregate productivity growth is decomposed into the productivity growth within each industry group (the first term on the right-hand side, called 'intra-effect') and the effects of the reallocation of labour between industry groups (the second term, called the 'shift-effect'). The intra-effect is positive as long as labour productivity growth in industry group i is positive. The contribution of the shift effect can be either positive or negative, depending on whether the labour productivity level in the expanding industry groups is higher or lower than the average labour productivity level in the industry groups where the labour share is declining.[18]

Table 3.4 shows the contributions by ICT-producing industries, ICT-using industries and the rest of the economy to labour productivity growth for 1990-1995 and 1995-2000. The combined shift effect is shown separately and is generally quite small, which suggests that gross effects from shifts between industry groups largely cancel out at the aggregate level. The contributions of each individual industry group in Table 3.4 therefore refer to the intra effects only. The table shows that, despite their relatively small share in GDP, ICT-producing manufacturing industries contributed substantially to labour productivity growth, and for most countries this contribution increased during the second half of the 1990s. However, the contribution of ICT-producing manufacturing is substantially bigger in the US than in Europe. For some European countries (in particular Germany, the Netherlands and Norway) the contribution of ICT-producing services even exceeded that of ICT-producing manufacturing.

While the contribution of ICT-using manufacturing (excluding the producers) has generally been somewhat higher in Europe (and in particular in Germany) than in the US, ICT-using services (again excluding the producers) accounts for by far the largest contributions to productivity growth in the US. In contrast, the productivity contribution of the non-ICT group has been smaller in the US than in most other countries. Although the non-ICT contribution to labour productivity growth has seriously diminished in almost all countries since 1995, its fall has been much greater outside the US. Indeed, the deceleration of productivity contributions from the non-ICT sector has accounted for much of the aggregate slowdown that European countries experienced during the second half of the 1990s (van Ark, 2001; McGuckin and van Ark, 2001).

3. ARE THE DIFFERENCES IN PRODUCTIVITY GROWTH BETWEEN INDUSTRY GROUPS SIGNIFICANT?

Even though the decomposition in section 2 suggests substantive differences in growth rates across industry groupings, it is useful to determine the statistical strength of the differences between ICT-producing, ICT-using and other industries while taking account of variations in industry productivity growth associated with each group. For this purpose we carried out a number of country-specific regressions using a simple difference model for which we progressively increased the number of industry groupings. First we estimated the simplest model, which distinguishes only between ICT-using (including ICT-producing industries) and non-ICT industries:

$$\Delta P_{i,t} = \alpha + \gamma C + \varepsilon_{i,t} \qquad\qquad (3.3)$$

where $\Delta P_{i,t}$ is the annual productivity growth rate, i denotes the industry group and t is years between 1990 and 2000. With 52 industries, this leads to a maximum of 520 observations per country. C is a dummy that is one if the industry is an ICT-intensive industry (which here means either an ICT-producing or an ICT-using industry). The estimated coefficients in Table 3.5 have the following interpretations: α is the average productivity growth rate for non-ICT industries and $\alpha + \gamma$ is the mean growth rate of ICT-intensive industries. Hence γ shows the difference between the growth rate of ICT-using industries and non-ICT industries. We ran the regressions for two sub-periods, 1990-1995 and 1995-2000.[19] The left-hand side of Table 3.5 focuses on the first half of the 1990s. It shows that in nearly all countries (except Austria and Spain) productivity growth was faster in ICT-using industries than in non-ICT industries. However, during the early 1990s, the difference between ICT-using and non-ICT industries was statistically significant for only four of the 16 countries (the US at the 1 percent level, Japan and Norway at the 5 percent level and Canada at the 10 percent level). The right-hand side of Table 3.5 shows that during the second half of the 1990s, the difference in growth between ICT and non-ICT industries became significant for more than half of the countries, namely Canada, Finland, France, Germany, Ireland, the Nether-lands, Norway, the UK, the US and the EU as a whole. It should be noted that the degree (or lack) of significance not only depends on the average growth difference between the two industry groups, but also on the variation within each group.

Using a slight modification of equation (3.3) we allow for differential effects between ICT-producing and ICT-using industries (excluding ICT-pro-ducing):

$$\Delta P_{i,t} = \alpha + \gamma_1 P + \gamma_2 U + \varepsilon_{i,t} \tag{3.4}$$

where the dummy variable P is one if the industry is an ICT-producing indus-try and U is one if it is an ICT-using industry. Table 3.6 shows that the ICT-producing industry group accounts for much of the difference in productivity growth rates relative to the non-ICT industry. Between 1990-95, most coun-tries (except France, Ireland, Italy, Norway, Spain and Sweden) showed signif-icantly higher growth rates in ICT-producing compared to the non-ICT indus-tries. On the other hand, only Norway and the United States showed signifi-cantly faster growth in other ICT-using (excluding ICT-producing) industries. For the second half of the 1990s the difference between productivity growth in ICT-producing and non-ICT is still strong and significant at the 1 percent sig-nificance level for most countries (including the EU as a whole). Moreover, the coefficient on the differences is higher than for the period 1990-1995 in eight countries as well as for the EU as a whole. Still, apart from the United States, only Canada, Norway, the UK and the EU as a whole showed signifi-cantly higher growth for ICT-using industries as well.[20]

Table 3.7 provides estimates of a model that focuses on the distinction between manufacturing and services. The model in equation (3.4) was modi-fied to:

$$\Delta P_{i,t} = \alpha_1 + \gamma_3 Q + \gamma_4 R + \gamma_5 S + \varepsilon_{i,t} \tag{3.5}$$

where α_1 represents the average productivity growth rate for non-ICT-using services industries, dummy Q is one if the industry is an ICT-using industry in manufacturing, dummy R is one if the industry is ICT-using and in services, and dummy S is one when the industry is a non-ICT and a non-services indus-try. So the differences in productivity growth estimated in equation (3.5) are

Table 3.5   Impact of non-ICT and ICT-using industry groupings on productivity growth

	Productivity Growth (1990-95)		Difference over non-ICT	Productivity Growth (1995-2000)		Difference over non-ICT
	Non-ICT (α)	ICT-Using ($\alpha+\gamma$)	ICT-Using (γ)	Non-ICT (α)	ICT-Using ($\alpha+\gamma$)	ICT-Using (γ)
Austria	2.238 (1.074)**	1.878 (0.442)***	-0.360 (1.161)	1.491 (0.700)**	2.821 (0.546)***	1.330 (0.888)
Canada[b]	0.036 (0.420)	1.962 (0.954)**	1.926 (1.042)*	0.401 (0.365)	2.881 (0.402)***	2.481 (0.543)***
Denmark	1.264 (0.981)	2.209 (0.844)***	0.945 (1.294)	1.710 (1.002)*	2.051 (0.850)**	0.341 (1.314)
Finland	2.249 (0.641)***	2.673 (1.380)*	0.424 (1.522)	1.138 (0.386)***	3.340 (0.725)***	2.202 (0.821)***
France[b]	0.631 (0.442)	1.714 (0.609)***	1.082 (0.753)	0.538 (0.431)	1.953 (0.646)***	1.415 (0.777)*
Germany[a]	1.629 (0.602)***	1.946 (0.686)***	0.317 (0.913)	0.144 (0.329)	1.743 (0.684)**	1.599 (0.759)**
Ireland	0.799 (0.542)	1.690 (1.303)	0.891 (1.411)	0.358 (1.042)	4.842 (1.749)***	4.485 (2.036)**
Italy	1.528 (0.464)***	1.985 (0.583)***	0.457 (0.745)	0.506 (0.311)	1.221 (0.446)***	0.714 (0.544)
Japan[c]	-0.600 (0.523)	1.218 (0.679)*	1.819 (0.857)**	-0.910 (0.714)	0.920 (1.257)	1.830 (1.445)
Netherlands	0.585 (0.343)*	0.921 (0.418)**	0.336 (0.541)	0.640 (0.356)*	1.741 (0.510)***	1.101 (0.622)*
Norway	2.308 (0.495)***	4.191 (0.731)***	1.883 (0.883)**	0.832 (0.371)**	4.125 (0.759)***	3.293 (0.845)***
Spain[b]	1.523 (0.341)***	1.044 (0.441)**	-0.479 (0.558)	0.097 (0.235)	0.841 (0.441)*	0.744 (0.500)
Sweden	1.863 (0.347)***	3.377 (0.939)***	1.514 (1.001)	1.913 (0.584)***	2.567 (0.498)***	0.654 (0.768)
Switzerland	-1.287 (0.691)*	-0.933 (0.886)	0.354 (1.124)	-0.093 (0.461)	0.100 (0.570)	0.194 (0.733)
UK	2.382 (0.536)***	3.258 (0.462)***	0.876 (0.708)	1.015 (0.443)**	2.923 (0.662)***	1.908 (0.797)**
EU	1.462 (0.286)***	2.184 (0.347)***	0.722 (0.450)	0.703 (0.183)***	2.160 (0.351)***	1.456 (0.396)***
US	0.041 (0.324)	2.361 (0.527)***	2.320 (0.619)***	0.529 (0.242)**	5.105 (0.622)***	4.576 (0.667)***

Notes:
The dependent variable is yearly productivity growth (see Equation 3.3).
Standard errors, consistent for heteroscedasticity and autocorrelation, are in brackets.
All estimations are done using weighted least squares, where employment is used as weights.
* significant at 10% level; ** significant at 5% level; *** significant at 1% level.
a) 1991-95; b) 1995-99; c) 1995-98.

Table 3.6 Impact of non-ICT, ICT-producing and ICT-using industry groupings on productivity growth

	Productivity Growth (1990-95)			Difference over non-ICT		Productivity Growth (1995-2000)			Difference over non-ICT	
	Non-ICT (α)	ICT-Producing ($\alpha+\gamma_1$)	ICT-Using[d] ($\alpha+\gamma_2$)	ICT-Producing (γ_1)	ICT-Using[d] (γ_2)	Non-ICT (α)	ICT-Producing ($\alpha+\gamma_1$)	ICT-Using[d] ($\alpha+\gamma_2$)	ICT-Producing (γ_1)	ICT-Using[d] (γ_2)
Austria	2.238 (1.076)**	5.098 (1.018)***	1.467 (0.451)***	2.860 (1.481)*	-0.771 (1.167)	1.491 (0.701)**	3.440 (2.498)	2.740 (0.523)***	1.948 (2.594)	1.248 (0.875)
Canada[b]	0.036 (0.421)	3.850 (1.078)***	1.737 (1.059)	3.814 (1.157)***	1.701 (1.140)	0.401 (0.366)	6.775 (1.840)***	2.366 (0.402)***	6.374 (1.876)***	1.965 (0.544)***
Denmark	1.264 (0.983)	7.013 (1.738)***	1.485 (0.930)	5.748 (1.997)***	0.221 (1.353)	1.710 (1.004)*	6.136 (1.760)***	1.451 (0.918)	4.427 (2.027)**	-0.258 (1.360)
Finland	2.249 (0.642)***	5.870 (1.684)***	2.079 (1.602)	3.620 (1.802)**	-0.171 (1.726)	1.138 (0.387)***	8.847 (2.253)***	2.001 (0.564)***	7.709 (2.286)***	0.863 (0.684)
France[b]	0.631 (0.443)	4.332 (2.587)*	1.326 (0.584)**	3.701 (2.624)	0.694 (0.734)	0.538 (0.432)	7.629 (2.273)***	1.099 (0.613)*	7.091 (2.313)***	0.562 (0.750)
Germany[a]	1.629 (0.604)***	6.860 (1.963)***	1.224 (0.697)*	5.231 (2.054)**	-0.405 (0.922)	0.144 (0.329)	11.712 (2.760)***	0.459 (0.548)	11.569 (2.779)***	0.315 (0.640)
Ireland	0.799 (0.543)	8.945 (5.252)*	0.528 (1.178)	8.147 (5.280)	-0.271 (1.297)	0.358 (1.044)	14.922 (5.946)**	2.472 (1.623)	14.564 (6.037)**	2.114 (1.930)
Italy	1.528 (0.465)***	2.110 (1.892)	1.970 (0.614)***	0.582 (1.948)	0.442 (0.770)	0.506 (0.312)	5.965 (1.686)***	0.653 (0.422)	5.459 (1.714)***	0.147 (0.524)
Japan[c]	-0.600 (0.525)	8.328 (2.796)***	0.341 (0.647)	8.928 (2.845)***	0.941 (0.833)	-0.910 (0.717)	12.257 (6.254)*	-0.499 (1.019)	13.168 (6.295)**	0.411 (1.246)
Netherlands	0.585 (0.344)*	3.636 (1.326)***	0.571 (0.423)	3.051 (1.370)**	-0.014 (0.545)	0.640 (0.357)*	2.533 (2.272)	1.627 (0.483)***	1.893 (2.300)	0.987 (0.600)
Norway	2.308 (0.496)***	3.247 (3.314)	4.344 (0.651)***	0.939 (3.351)	2.036 (0.819)**	0.832 (0.371)**	8.338 (2.385)***	3.436 (0.773)***	7.506 (2.414)***	2.604 (0.858)***
Spain[b]	1.523 (0.342)***	3.605 (1.226)***	0.543 (0.459)	2.082 (1.272)	-0.980 (0.572)*	0.097 (0.236)	2.015 (1.908)	0.582 (0.325)*	1.918 (1.923)	0.485 (0.402)

Table 3.6 (continued)

	Productivity Growth (1990-95)			Difference over non-ICT		Productivity Growth (1995-2000)			Difference over non-ICT	
	Non-ICT (α)	ICT-Producing ($\alpha+\gamma_1$)	ICT-Using^d ($\alpha+\gamma_2$)	ICT-Producing (γ_1)	ICT-Using^d (γ_2)	Non-ICT (α)	ICT-Producing ($\alpha+\gamma_1$)	ICT-Using^d ($\alpha+\gamma_2$)	ICT-Producing (γ_1)	ICT-Using^d (γ_2)
Sweden	1.863 (0.348)***	3.343 (2.731)	3.383 (0.990)***	1.480 (2.753)	1.520 (1.050)	1.913 (0.585)***	2.549 (1.415)*	2.572 (0.522)***	0.636 (1.531)	0.658 (0.784)
Switzerland	-1.287 (0.693)*	1.726 (1.453)	-1.284 (0.988)	3.014 (1.610)*	0.003 (1.206)	-0.093 (0.462)	-1.443 (1.437)	0.330 (0.627)	-1.350 (1.509)	0.423 (0.779)
UK	2.382 (0.537)***	7.778 (1.493)***	2.610 (0.470)***	5.396 (1.587)***	0.228 (0.714)	1.015 (0.444)**	6.019 (1.920)***	2.410 (0.708)***	5.004 (1.971)**	1.395 (0.836)*
EU	1.462 (0.287)***	6.187 (1.310)***	1.632 (0.317)***	4.725 (1.341)***	0.170 (0.427)	0.703 (0.184)***	7.482 (1.836)***	1.413 (0.225)***	6.779 (1.845)***	0.710 (0.291)**
US	0.041 (0.324)	6.382 (1.976)***	1.784 (0.542)***	6.341 (2.002)***	1.743 (0.631)***	0.529 (0.242)**	6.655 (2.538)***	4.858 (0.626)***	6.126 (2.549)**	4.329 (0.671)***

Notes:

The dependent variable is yearly productivity growth (see Equation 3.4). Standard errors, consistent for heteroscedasticity and autocorrelation, are in brackets.

All estimations are done using weighted least squares, where employment is used as weights.

* significant at 10% level; ** significant at 5% level; *** significant at 1% level.

a) 1991-95; b) 1995-99; c) 1995-98; d) excluding ICT-producing.

Table 3.7   *Impact of non-ICT services, ICT-using manufacturing,*
                ICT-using services and other non-ICT on productivity growth

	Productivity Growth (1990-95)				Difference over non-ICT Services		
	Non-ICT Services (α_1)	ICT-using Manufct. $(\alpha_1+\gamma_3)$	ICT-using Services $(\alpha_1+\gamma_4)$	Other non-ICT $(\alpha_1+\gamma_5)$	ICT-using Manufct. (γ_3)	ICT-using Services (γ_4)	Other non-ICT (γ_5)
Austria	-0.025 (0.379)	2.280 (0.707)***	1.726 (0.542)***	4.537 (1.987)**	2.305 (0.802)***	1.751 (0.662)***	4.562 (2.023)**
Canada[b]	-0.327 (0.542)	3.850 (1.066)***	1.693 (1.081)	0.731 (0.654)	4.176 (1.196)***	2.019 (1.209)*	1.057 (0.849)
Denmark	0.515 (1.323)	2.855 (1.794)	1.971 (0.957)**	2.982 (1.150)**	2.340 (2.229)	1.456 (1.633)	2.467 (1.753)
Finland	0.980 (0.373)***	4.201 (2.195)*	1.981 (1.755)	4.311 (1.462)***	3.222 (2.227)	1.001 (1.794)	3.331 (1.509)**
France[b]	-0.230 (0.467)	3.872 (1.247)***	1.060 (0.695)	2.284 (0.905)**	4.102 (1.331)***	1.290 (0.837)	2.514 (1.019)**
Germany[a]	0.363 (0.594)	3.499 (1.380)**	1.232 (0.728)*	3.547 (1.302)***	3.136 (1.502)**	0.869 (0.940)	3.183 (1.431)**
Ireland	-1.029 (0.601)*	6.459 (3.319)*	-0.063 (1.175)	2.769 (0.712)***	7.488 (3.373)**	0.966 (1.320)	3.797 (0.932)***
Italy	0.547 (0.508)	3.707 (1.050)***	1.229 (0.657)*	2.932 (0.795)***	3.161 (1.167)***	0.682 (0.831)	2.385 (0.943)**
Japan[c]	-0.601 (0.478)	1.211 (1.606)	1.222 (0.665)*	-0.599 (0.965)	1.812 (1.676)	1.823 (0.819)**	0.002 (1.077)
Netherlands	0.070 (0.395)	2.508 (0.965)**	0.507 (0.447)	1.782 (0.672)***	2.438 (1.043)**	0.438 (0.596)	1.712 (0.779)**
Norway	1.416 (0.437)***	1.973 (0.924)**	4.908 (0.888)***	4.714 (1.052)***	0.557 (1.022)	3.492 (0.990)***	3.298 (1.139)***
Spain[b]	1.006 (0.303)***	1.608 (1.122)	0.814 (0.428)*	2.837 (0.898)***	0.602 (1.162)	-0.192 (0.524)	1.831 (0.948)*
Sweden	1.056 (0.306)***	3.580 (2.354)	3.294 (0.917)***	4.004 (0.892)***	2.525 (2.374)	2.238 (0.966)**	2.949 (0.943)***
Switzerland	-2.489 (1.019)**	0.063 (0.982)	-1.262 (1.141)	0.526 (0.813)	2.552 (1.415)*	1.228 (1.529)	3.016 (1.303)**
UK	1.822 (0.720)**	3.756 (1.180)***	3.122 (0.496)***	3.664 (0.630)***	1.934 (1.382)	1.301 (0.874)	1.843 (0.957)*
EU	0.515 (0.287)*	4.081 (0.804)***	1.490 (0.334)***	3.057 (0.559)***	3.566 (0.854)***	0.975 (0.440)**	2.542 (0.628)***
US	-0.452 (0.292)	2.944 (1.301)**	2.214 (0.578)***	1.535 (0.917)*	3.396 (1.334)**	2.666 (0.648)***	1.987 (0.962)**

Notes:
The dependent variable is yearly productivity growth (Equation 3.5). Standard errors, consistent for heteroscedasticity and autocorrelation, are in brackets. All estimations are done using weighted least squares, where employment is used as weights.
* significant at 10% level; ** significant at 5% level; *** significant at 1% level.
a) 1991-95; b) 1995-99; c) 1995-98.

Table 3.7 (continued)

	Productivity Growth (1995-2000)				Difference over non-ICT Services		
	Non-ICT Services (α_1)	ICT-using Manufct. ($\alpha_1+\gamma_3$)	ICT-using Services ($\alpha_1+\gamma_4$)	Other non-ICT ($\alpha_1+\gamma_5$)	ICT-using Manufct. (γ_3)	ICT-using Services (γ_4)	Other non-ICT (γ_5)
Austria	-0.361 (0.818)	6.209 (1.212)***	1.725 (0.591)***	3.676 (1.030)***	6.570 (1.463)***	2.086 (1.009)**	4.036 (1.315)***
Canada[b]	-0.178 (0.390)	3.866 (1.731)**	2.750 (0.399)***	1.490 (0.671)**	4.044 (1.775)**	2.928 (0.558)***	1.669 (0.776)**
Denmark	1.604 (1.345)	0.551 (1.661)	2.561 (1.006)**	1.972 (1.039)*	-1.053 (2.137)	0.956 (1.680)	0.368 (1.699)
Finland	0.326 (0.282)	3.482 (1.253)***	3.271 (0.892)***	2.619 (0.898)***	3.156 (1.284)**	2.945 (0.935)***	2.293 (0.942)**
France[b]	0.111 (0.461)	3.652 (1.566)**	1.489 (0.700)**	1.495 (0.996)	3.541 (1.632)**	1.378 (0.838)	1.383 (1.097)
Germany[a]	-0.452 (0.355)	3.708 (1.294)***	1.012 (0.766)	1.207 (0.644)*	4.160 (1.342)***	1.464 (0.845)*	1.660 (0.736)**
Ireland	-0.373 (1.412)	14.056 (4.688)***	1.692 (1.651)	1.295 (1.550)	14.429 (4.896)***	2.065 (2.172)	1.668 (2.097)
Italy	-0.172 (0.277)	1.797 (0.794)**	0.991 (0.531)*	1.585 (0.622)**	1.969 (0.841)**	1.163 (0.599)*	1.757 (0.681)**
Japan[c]	0.007 (0.907)	4.377 (2.729)	-0.535 (1.229)	-1.986 (1.144)*	4.370 (2.875)	-0.542 (1.528)	-1.993 (1.460)
	0.356 (0.386)	1.250 (1.640)	1.847 (0.513)***	1.395 (0.789)*	0.894 (1.685)	1.491 (0.642)**	1.039 (0.878)
Norway	0.935 (0.385)**	-0.388 (1.167)	5.586 (0.801)***	0.538 (0.929)	-1.323 (1.229)	4.651 (0.889)***	-0.397 (1.005)
Spain[b]	0.023 (0.208)	0.650 (0.988)	0.917 (0.479)*	0.289 (0.665)	0.626 (1.009)	0.894 (0.522)*	0.266 (0.697)
Sweden	1.904 (0.774)**	1.816 (1.000)*	2.858 (0.567)***	1.939 (0.554)***	-0.087 (1.265)	0.954 (0.959)	0.035 (0.952)
	-0.194 (0.501)	1.984 (1.154)*	-0.456 (0.633)	0.079 (0.922)	2.178 (1.258)*	-0.261 (0.807)	0.274 (1.049)
UK	1.131 (0.574)*	2.394 (1.389)*	3.058 (0.751)***	0.713 (0.576)	1.262 (1.503)	1.927 (0.946)**	-0.418 (0.813)
EU	0.230 (0.176)	3.211 (0.913)***	1.826 (0.351)***	1.615 (0.392)***	2.981 (0.930)***	1.596 (0.393)***	1.385 (0.430)***
US	0.216 (0.243)	4.891 (1.791)***	5.153 (0.645)***	1.510 (0.621)**	4.675 (1.807)**	4.937 (0.689)***	1.294 (0.667)*

Notes:
The dependent variable is yearly productivity growth (Equation 3.5). Standard errors, consistent for heteroscedasticity and autocorrelation, are in brackets. All estimations are done using weighted least squares, where employment is used as weights.
* significant at 10% level; ** significant at 5% level; *** significant at 1% level.
a) 1991-95; b) 1995-99; c) 1995-98.

Table 3.8   Impact of non-ICT services, ICT-using manufacturing, ICT-using services and other non-ICT on productivity acceleration

	Productivity Acceleration (1995-2000 over 1990-95)				Difference over Productivity Acceleration in non-ICT Services		
	Non-ICT Services (β)	ICT-using Manufct. $(\beta+\delta_1)$	ICT-using Services $(\beta+\delta_2)$	Other non-ICT $(\beta+\delta_3)$	ICT-using Manufct. (δ_1)	ICT-using Services (δ_2)	Other non-ICT (δ_3)
Austria	-0.336 (0.902)	3.929 (1.403)***	-0.001 (0.802)	-0.861 (2.238)	4.265 (1.668)**	0.335 (1.207)	-0.526 (2.413)
Canada[b]	0.148 (0.668)	0.015 (2.031)	1.057 (1.152)	0.759 (0.936)	-0.133 (2.138)	0.909 (1.331)	0.611 (1.150)
Denmark	1.089 (1.887)	-2.303 (2.445)	0.589 (1.389)	-1.009 (1.550)	-3.392 (3.088)	-0.500 (2.343)	-2.098 (2.442)
Finland	-0.654 (0.467)	-0.719 (2.528)	1.291 (1.969)	-1.692 (1.716)	-0.065 (2.571)	1.944 (2.023)	-1.038 (1.779)
France[b]	0.341 (0.656)	-0.220 (2.000)	0.430 (0.986)	-0.790 (1.345)	-0.561 (2.105)	0.088 (1.184)	-1.131 (1.496)
Germany[a]	-0.815 (0.692)	0.209 (1.892)	-0.220 (1.058)	-2.339 (1.453)	1.024 (2.015)	0.595 (1.264)	-1.524 (1.609)
Ireland	0.656 (1.535)	7.586 (5.744)	1.754 (2.026)	-1.483 (1.705)	6.930 (5.945)	1.099 (2.542)	-2.138 (2.294)
Italy	-0.719 (0.578)	-1.911 (1.317)	-0.238 (0.845)	-1.347 (1.009)	-1.191 (1.438)	0.482 (1.024)	-0.628 (1.163)
Japan[c]	0.608 (1.022)	3.166 (3.158)	-1.757 (1.394)	-1.387 (1.493)	2.558 (3.319)	-2.366 (1.728)	-1.995 (1.810)
Netherlands	0.286 (0.552)	-1.259 (1.903)	1.340 (0.680)*	-0.387 (1.036)	-1.545 (1.982)	1.054 (0.876)	-0.673 (1.174)
Norway	-0.481 (0.582)	-2.360 (1.489)	0.678 (1.196)	-4.176 (1.403)***	-1.879 (1.598)	1.158 (1.330)	-3.695 (1.519)**
Spain[b]	-0.983 (0.368)***	-0.958 (1.493)	0.103 (0.642)	-2.549 (1.116)**	0.024 (1.538)	1.086 (0.740)	-1.566 (1.175)
Sweden	0.848 (0.832)	-1.767 (2.558)	-0.435 (1.078)	-2.064 (1.050)*	-2.615 (2.690)	-1.283 (1.362)	-2.912 (1.340)**
Switzerland	2.295 (1.135)**	1.927 (1.515)	0.806 (1.305)	-0.448 (1.229)	-0.369 (1.893)	-1.489 (1.729)	-2.743 (1.673)
UK	-0.691 (0.921)	-1.363 (1.822)	-0.065 (0.900)	-2.952 (0.854)***	-0.673 (2.041)	0.626 (1.287)	-2.261 (1.256)*
EU	-0.285 (0.337)	-0.870 (1.216)	0.336 (0.484)	-1.442 (0.683)**	-0.585 (1.262)	0.621 (0.590)	-1.157 (0.761)
US	0.669 (0.380)*	1.947 (2.214)	2.939 (0.866)***	-0.024 (1.107)	1.279 (2.246)	2.271 (0.946)**	-0.693 (1.171)

Notes:
The dependent variable is yearly productivity growth (see Equation 3.6).
Standard errors, consistent for heteroscedasticity and autocorrelation, are in brackets.
All estimations are done using weighted least squares, where employment is used as weights.
* significant at 10% level; ** significant at 5% level; *** significant at 1% level.
a) 1991-95; b) 1995-99; c) 1995-98.

Table 3.9 Labour productivity growth and productivity differential for EU and US, 1990-95 and 1995-2000

ISIC Rev3		1990-95			1995-2000			Acceleration		
		EU	US	US-EU	EU	US	US-EU	EU	US	US-EU
	Total Economy	**1.9**	**1.1**	**-0.8**	**1.4**	**2.5**	**1.1**	**-0.5**	**1.4**	**1.9**
	ICT-Producing Industries	**6.7**	**8.1**	**1.4**	**8.7**	**10.1**	**1.4**	**2.0**	**2.0**	**0.0**
	Manufacturing	**11.1**	**15.1**	**4.0**	**13.8**	**23.7**	**10.0**	**2.6**	**8.6**	**6.0**
30	Computers	33.2	28.6	-4.6	49.3	52.3	3.0	16.1	23.7	7.6
321	Semiconductors	37.7	36.8	-1.0	56.4	52.1	-4.3	18.7	15.3	-3.4
322	Communication eq.	5.0	6.6	1.7	3.5	-0.4	-3.9	-1.5	-7.0	-5.6
313	Fibre optics	6.9	5.6	-1.3	2.9	5.7	2.8	-4.0	0.1	4.1
331	Instruments	-2.6	-4.5	-1.9	-7.2	-5.9	1.3	-4.7	-1.4	3.3
323	Radio and TV eq.	-2.6	-4.6	-2.1	-13.9	-12.5	1.4	-11.3	-7.9	3.4
	Services	**4.4**	**3.1**	**-1.3**	**6.5**	**1.8**	**-4.7**	**2.1**	**-1.4**	**-3.4**
64	Telecommunications	5.7	3.3	-2.5	9.9	6.5	-3.4	4.2	3.2	-0.9
72	Computer services	1.5	2.7	1.2	1.5	-4.5	-6.0	0.0	-7.2	-7.2
	ICT-Using Industries	**1.7**	**1.5**	**-0.2**	**1.6**	**4.7**	**3.2**	**-0.1**	**3.3**	**3.4**
	Manufacturing	**3.1**	**-0.3**	**-3.4**	**2.1**	**1.2**	**-1.0**	**-1.0**	**1.4**	**2.4**
31-31.3	Electrical machinery	2.2	0.5	-1.6	2.3	-0.7	-3.0	0.1	-1.3	-1.3
33-33.1	Watches & instruments	7.5	2.1	-5.3	5.1	14.2	9.1	-2.3	12.1	14.4
18	Apparel	5.2	3.4	-1.8	2.9	3.8	0.9	-2.4	0.3	2.7
36-37	Misc. manufacturing	1.1	1.3	0.3	1.5	2.4	0.9	0.4	1.0	0.6
353	Aircraft	0.5	-1.0	-1.5	6.4	1.1	-5.3	5.9	2.1	-3.8
29	Machinery	4.2	0.9	-3.3	1.0	0.3	-0.7	-3.3	-0.7	2.6
352+359	Railroad and other	5.9	-2.0	-7.9	3.1	-0.1	-3.1	-2.8	1.9	4.8
22	Printing & Publishing	1.9	-2.6	-4.6	2.5	-0.2	-2.7	0.5	2.4	1.9
351	Ships	4.1	-3.8	-7.9	0.4	-0.2	-0.6	-3.8	3.6	7.4
	Services	**1.1**	**1.9**	**0.8**	**1.4**	**5.4**	**4.0**	**0.3**	**3.5**	**3.2**
67	Securities trade	1.1	3.2	2.1	2.0	15.3	13.4	0.9	12.1	11.3
52	Retail trade	1.1	2.3	1.2	1.4	6.9	5.5	0.3	4.7	4.4
51	Wholesale trade	2.9	3.4	0.5	1.2	6.1	4.9	-1.7	2.7	4.4
65	Banks	0.4	1.3	0.9	3.0	2.8	-0.2	2.6	1.5	-1.0
73	R&D	-0.2	1.0	1.2	-0.5	3.1	3.6	-0.3	2.1	2.4
741-743	Professional services	-0.4	-0.7	-0.3	0.4	1.0	0.6	0.8	1.8	0.9
71	Renting of machinery	2.4	6.7	4.2	0.5	5.7	5.2	-2.0	-1.0	1.0
66	Insurance	0.2	3.0	2.8	0.2	-1.0	-1.1	-0.1	-4.0	-3.9
	Non-ICT Industries	**1.6**	**0.2**	**-1.4**	**0.7**	**0.5**	**-0.2**	**-0.9**	**0.2**	**1.1**
	Manufacturing	**3.8**	**3.0**	**-0.8**	**1.5**	**1.4**	**-0.1**	**-2.4**	**-1.6**	**0.7**
24	Chemicals	6.8	3.4	-3.4	4.7	4.4	-0.4	-2.0	1.0	3.0
25	Rubber & plastics	3.2	4.6	1.4	1.6	4.1	2.5	-1.6	-0.5	1.1
17	Textiles	3.5	3.0	-0.4	1.4	3.3	2.0	-2.1	0.3	2.4
27	Basic metals	6.9	3.9	-3.0	0.9	3.1	2.2	-6.0	-0.8	5.2
26	Stone. clay & glass	2.5	2.8	0.3	1.4	2.6	1.3	-1.1	-0.2	1.0
23	Petroleum & coal	9.6	5.0	-4.5	0.2	1.5	1.3	-9.3	-3.5	5.8
34	Motor vehicles	3.2	4.9	1.7	0.9	1.4	0.5	-2.3	-3.5	-1.2
19	Leather	3.3	4.9	1.6	0.7	1.3	0.5	-2.5	-3.6	-1.1
28	Fabricated metals	2.2	3.2	1.0	0.9	0.6	-0.3	-1.3	-2.6	-1.3
20	Wood	2.5	-2.8	-5.3	2.7	0.3	-2.4	0.1	3.1	2.9
21	Paper	3.5	0.0	-3.5	2.3	0.2	-2.1	-1.2	0.2	1.4
15-16	Food & beverages	2.9	3.5	0.6	0.0	-4.5	-4.5	-2.9	-8.0	-5.1
	Services	**0.6**	**-0.4**	**-0.9**	**0.2**	**0.4**	**0.2**	**-0.4**	**0.8**	**1.2**
70	Real estate	-0.7	1.6	2.3	-0.8	1.7	2.5	-0.1	0.1	0.2
60-63	Transportation	3.2	2.1	-1.1	1.7	1.6	0.0	-1.5	-0.4	1.0
55	Hotels & restaurants	-1.8	-1.1	0.7	-1.2	0.4	1.6	0.6	1.5	0.9
95	Private households		2.2			0.7			-1.5	
75	Government	1.4	0.0	-1.4	1.1	0.2	-0.8	-0.3	0.3	0.6
74.9	Other business services	-1.1	-1.0	0.1	-0.3	1.4	1.7	0.8	2.4	1.6
85	Health	0.8	-2.2	-2.9	0.4	-0.3	-0.7	-0.3	1.9	2.3
80	Education	0.9	-0.2	-1.1	-0.1	-1.2	-1.1	-0.9	-1.0	0.0
50	Repairs	-0.1	-1.4	-1.2	1.0	-2.5	-3.4	1.1	-1.1	-2.2
90-93	Personal & social serv.	-0.4	0.3	0.7	-0.5	-0.9	-0.5	-0.1	-1.3	-1.2
	Other non-ICT industries	**2.7**	**0.7**	**-2.0**	**1.9**	**0.6**	**-1.3**	**-0.8**	**-0.1**	**0.7**
01-05	Agriculture	5.2	-1.0	-6.3	4.0	6.3	2.3	-1.3	7.3	8.5
40-41	Utilities	4.5	2.5	-2.0	4.9	2.3	-2.7	0.5	-0.2	-0.7
45	Construction	0.4	0.5	0.1	0.2	0.2	0.0	-0.2	-0.3	-0.1
10-14	Mining	7.5	5.4	-2.1	3.5	-1.8	-5.4	-3.9	-7.2	-3.3

Note:

EU includes Austria, Denmark, Finland, France, Germany, Ireland, Italy, Netherlands, Spain, Sweden and the United Kingdom.

all relative to the non-ICT-using services group. The results provide further support for the hypothesis that ICT use, in particular in services, is driving productivity growth. Between 1990 and 1995, six countries showed significantly faster growth in ICT-using services than in non-ICT-using services and, between 1995 and 2000, that number went up to ten countries. For the EU average, the difference between ICT-using and non-ICT services was already significant between 1990-1995 but became significant at the 1 percent level for the period 1995-2000. A comparison of the left and right-hand sides of Table 3.7 shows that despite an increasing spread in productivity growth between ICT-using and non-ICT services from 1995-2000, productivity growth in ICT-using services was still somewhat slower compared to 1990-1995 for five European countries. For the US there was a substantial increase in both the spread between ICT and non-ICT services and in the productivity growth of industries within the ICT-using services group itself.

Finally, we assessed the possibility that productivity growth accelerated between the second half of the 1990s compared with the first half because of increased use of ICT. Such acceleration is found in the aggregate results for the United States, as well as in industry-specific work such as McGuckin and Stiroh (2001, 2002) and Stiroh (2001). For this purpose we transformed equation (3.5) by adding specific dummies to pick up differences in growth rates between the pre- and post-1995 period:

$$\Delta P_{i,t} = \alpha_2 + \beta D + \gamma_3 Q + \gamma_4 R + \gamma_5 S + \delta_1 Q \cdot D + \delta_2 R \cdot D + \delta_3 S \cdot D + \varepsilon_{i,t} \quad (3.6)$$

where the parameter β is the acceleration in productivity growth of non-ICT service industries after 1995, $\beta + \delta_1$ is the acceleration for ICT-using industry in manufacturing, $\beta + \delta_2$ is the acceleration for ICT-using services, $\beta + \delta_3$ is the acceleration for other non-ICT industries, and δ_1, δ_2 and δ_3 are the additional accelerations of each industry group beyond the acceleration in non-ICT services. Table 3.8 confirms the earlier contribution analysis. Non-ICT services experienced decelerating growth during the second half of the 1990s compared to the first half for most European countries, but not for Canada and the United States. Still only the United States showed an acceleration of productivity in ICT-using services that was significantly different from that in non-ICT services. In fact, in Denmark, Japan, Sweden and Switzerland, ICT-using services showed deceleration relative to non-ICT services, even though none of these differences is statistically significant.

In summary, the regressions show that the difference in productivity growth between ICT-using and non-ICT industries is in part linked to ICT-production. Apart from that, a sizeable number of countries have also shown significantly faster growth in ICT-using services compared to non-ICT services since 1995. This suggests that the diffusion of ICT in Europe is proceeding, but at a slower pace than in the US. The US stands out since it is the only country that has also shown a significantly faster acceleration in ICT-using services compared to non-ICT services since 1995. In turn, this suggests that the diffusion of ICT in Europe has been 'too slow' to accommodate the rapid improvement in employment growth in Europe since the 1990s.

4. IS DIFFUSION IN EUROPE SLOWER THAN IN THE US?

Even though the grouping of industries based on ICT intensity is useful, it hides much of the variation within each of these groups. Table 3.9 shows the labour productivity growth rates by industry for 1990-1995 and 1995-2000, the accelerations between the two sub-periods, and the differential between the United States and the EU.[21] Within each of the seven industry groupings, individual industries are ranked by the US productivity growth rates from 1995-2000.

4.1 ICT-Producing Industries

In the ICT-producing sector, both the US and the EU show very strong productivity growth. Turning first to the ICT-producing manufacturing industries, our attention is drawn to the very rapid productivity growth in office and computer equipment and semiconductors. These manufacturing industries clearly benefited from the rapid technological progress in ICT which lowered prices and led to increased adoption of these technologies. It is striking that the labour productivity growth rates in these industries for both the EU and the US are relatively close, but the acceleration of productivity growth in the ICT-producing manufacturing sector as a whole has been faster in the US in the second half of the decade. Also noteworthy is the negative productivity growth in some ICT-producing manufacturing industries, like radio and TV equipment. The reason for that decline is that these industries make intensive use of semiconductors and other electronic components. While the prices of these inputs have spectacularly decreased, the output of these industries is valued at roughly unchanged prices. As a result, the (implicit) price of value added is rising rapidly and productivity is declining.

While the ICT-producing services industries showed notably slower productivity growth than the ICT-producing manufacturing industries, ICT-producing services clearly stand out compared to other services industries. This can be mainly attributed to the strong productivity growth in the telecommunications sector. While this industry had fast productivity growth in both the EU and the US, the EU had a clear advantage over the United States in particular because of the rapid take-off of the wireless market. From 1995-2000 Europe showed positive productivity growth rates in computer services, whereas negative growth rates were reported for the US.[22]

4.2 ICT-Using Industries

The ICT-using sector (excluding the ICT-producing industries) was the sector in which the US showed the most clear-cut performance advantage over the EU. Most US manufacturing and service industries in this group showed a faster acceleration in productivity growth than the EU after 1995.

In ICT-using manufacturing, productivity growth accelerated faster in the US, with the exception of the 'other electrical machinery' industry and the aircraft industry. However, these widespread gains in the US come against the backdrop of generally lower productivity growth compared to the EU. Even as late as 1995-2000, US productivity growth in most ICT-using manufacturing industries was still lower than in Europe.

The story is very different for ICT-using services (other than ICT-producing) where the EU experienced a negligible improvement in productivity growth of 0.3 percentage points compared to an increase of 3.5 percentage points in the US. Some individual industries of course show bigger differences. For example, the United States experienced the strongest productivity growth in securities trade, and wholesale and retail trade. In fact, all ICT-using services but two (renting of machinery and insurance) show acceleration in labour productivity growth in the United States, whereas in the European Union most of these industries experienced a decelerating growth performance.

The strong acceleration of productivity in trade is recognized in the literature.[23] In fact, as we will see below, the trade sector and securities together account for the largest part of the whole difference in productivity growth between Europe and the United States since 1995.

Europe's very slow productivity growth in this sector is a key factor in explaining the economy-wide differences in productivity acceleration in the late 1990s. The banking sector was the only ICT-using service industry (excluding ICT-producing) for which the EU showed acceleration in productivity growth after 1995, which was also higher than in the United States. The higher productivity growth in banking for the EU reflects the experience of most EU member states, except Austria, Ireland and the Netherlands (see Appendix). Part of Europe's higher growth rate in banking is due to restructuring of the sector, which has led to a continuous fall in employment with little offset in measured output. In contrast, employment in US banking has increased since 1995. In banking, measurement issues are of major concern. Strikingly, the Netherlands is among the few countries that (like the United States) recently shifted from measuring real output in the banking sector based on deflated interest receipts and service charges to genuine volume measures of banking output. Hence some of the differences across countries may reflect measurement procedures.

4.3 Non-ICT Industries

In the 'non-ICT' sector (representing the less intensive users of ICT) there are substantial differences in productivity growth across industries, with mostly better productivity performance in manufacturing industries (such as chemicals and textiles) than in service industries, particularly in the 1990-95 period. The difference in productivity growth between the manufacturing and service non-ICT sectors narrowed considerably in the 1995-2000 period in both the US and the EU. There was also a narrowing of the differences in productivity growth rates between the EU and the US as US productivity growth slowed less in non-ICT manufacturing and modestly accelerated in non-ICT services. Nonetheless, compared to the ICT-using sector both the EU and the US showed slower productivity growth throughout the non-ICT sector.

Given their sheer size, service industries are mainly responsible for the overall slower growth of productivity in the non-ICT sector compared to the ICT-using sector. Unfortunately, measurement issues cloud interpretation of the differences. While measurement of service sector output is a problem in the ICT-using sector, these problems may be even bigger for some of the non-ICT service sectors. One of the major issues is that the real output of service sectors is still largely based on information on inputs (such as employment input and labour income). While in both Europe and the United States improvements in the measurement of non-market services output are discussed, for example, in health and education, details on the actual implementation of improved measurement methods in the national accounts are often missing.[24] Since it is likely that the problems in developing suitable output measures are similar across countries, we can only assume that progress towards solutions is not all that different.

Table 3.9 shows that the average productivity growth for a considerable part of non-ICT services in the US was lower than in the EU, particularly in health, repairs, education, and personal and social services. The latter may simply reflect faster growth of nominal wages in Europe (i.e., it is a measurement problem), but there may also be explanations of a more economic nature. For example, employment in education, health, personal and social services and government has increased much more slowly in Europe than in the United States since 1995, although the difference between the EU and the US has diminished as European employment growth has at least turned positive since 1995. There is also some scattered – and partly anecdotal – evidence of greater efficiency in terms of output per person in European health and education services.[25] At the same time, the acceleration in productivity growth in some non-ICT services in the United States (in particular health – though still negative – and non-ICT business services) has been greater than in the EU since 1995. But clearly all these measures are unlikely to take adequate account of quality improvements so these arguments should not be pushed too far.

What is clear, however, is that the largest part of the observed difference in productivity performance between Europe and the US arises from the much better performance of ICT-using services relative to non-ICT services in the US. While ICT-using services performed better than the non-ICT services in both the US and the EU in 1995-2000, the differential was greater in the US (1.5 percentage points in the EU versus 5.0 percentage points in the US). Moreover, US productivity accelerated in both sectors, though by substantially more in the ICT-using sector (3.5 percent in ICT-services versus 0.8 percent in non-ICT services). At the same time, European productivity growth more or less stalled in ICT-using services, and decelerated in non-ICT services (from 0.6 percent to 0.2 percent).

4.4 Industry Contribution to the US–EU Productivity Growth Differential

While the differences in performance between ICT and non-ICT services is a primary factor in accounting for the aggregate productivity growth differential between the US and the EU since 1995, it is largely driven by a limited number of industries. In order to examine the importance of particular industries accounting for the rise in the productivity gap between Europe and the United States between 1995 and 2000, we return to our decomposition analysis – introduced by equations (3.1) and (3.2) in section 2. Using this decomposition, aggregate productivity growth in both countries was allocated to the 50 industries used in the industry-by-industry analysis.

By taking the difference between the EU and the US in terms of industry contributions to aggregate productivity growth, we can allocate the aggregate difference in productivity growth between the US and the EU (which was 1.1 percentage points from 1995-2000) to the individual industries. The results of this exercise are displayed in Figures 3.1a to 3.1c. Figure 3.1a shows the contribution to the US–EU productivity differential from ICT-using services (including ICT-producing services). Figure 3.1b provides the same information for non-ICT services. The analysis is extended to ICT-using manufacturing in Figure 3.1c.

Figure 3.1a shows that securities, retail and wholesale trade contributed more than 0.90 percentage points less to aggregate productivity growth in Europe than in the United States. This number is close to the overall productivity differential of 1.1 percentage points between the US and the EU from 1995-2000. Figure 3.1b shows that most non-ICT services in Europe show faster productivity growth than in the US, offsetting part of the slower growth in Europe's ICT-using services. Figure 3.1c shows that office and computer machinery and semiconductors add substantially to the US–EU productivity differential, but the contributions of other manufacturing industries to the differences in productivity growth between the EU and the US are small.

In Figures 3.1a to 3.1c, we not only show the total difference in contribution, but also (between brackets) the part that is due to higher or lower productivity growth. The second figure in brackets is the sum of three remaining effects, i.e., differences in each industry's share in total employment, differences in the changes in employment shares and differences in productivity levels by industry relative to the aggregate productivity level.[26] As Figure 3.1a shows, the majority of the difference in contribution in ICT-using services can be explained by differences in productivity growth. This is especially true in the two trade industries and to a lesser extent for the other industries. Figure 3.1b shows that in non-ICT services, the contributions of individual industries generally have a small effect on the aggregate US–EU productivity differential. The largest positive impact on the US–EU gap is real estate, which contributes 0.09 percentage points to the productivity growth differential. In this case, a much lower productivity growth rate in the EU (−0.8 percent versus 1.7 percent in the US) has a reduced impact because of the smaller size of the industry in the EU. The majority of industries in the non-ICT services grouping in fact narrow the gap between the EU and the US. As mentioned above, although the productivity differentials have become smaller relative to the 1990-1995 period, most non-ICT services have still shown faster productivity growth in the EU than in the US between 1995-2000.

Figure 3.1c shows that ICT-using manufacturing industries (including ICT-producing) also account for part of the aggregate productivity differential. Here the role of the semiconductor industry is especially noteworthy. Its contribution to the US–EU growth differential is actually the largest of all industries. This is mostly because the US industry has a much larger employment share than in the EU (0.4 versus 0.2 percent of employment).[27] The computer industry also makes a considerable contribution to the difference between the US and EU, but the remainder of the industries makes only limited contributions. This is because differences in productivity growth rates in ICT-using manufacturing between the US and the EU are not as large as those found in ICT-using services. In addition, the size differences between the EU and the US in ICT-using manufacturing are much smaller than those in ICT services.

4.5 Testing the 'Lagging Diffusion' Hypothesis for Europe

So far we have presented some evidence from industry labour productivity data supporting the idea that diffusion rates for ICT have been slower in

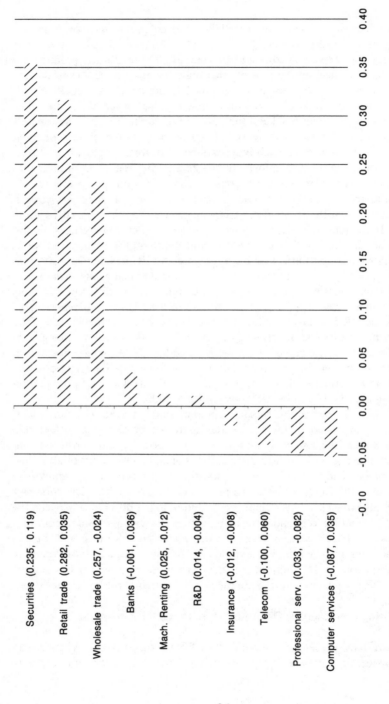

Securities (0.235, 0.119)

Retail trade (0.282, 0.035)

Wholesale trade (0.257, -0.024)

Banks (-0.001, 0.036)

Mach. Renting (0.025, -0.012)

R&D (0.014, -0.004)

Insurance (-0.012, -0.008)

Telecom (-0.100, 0.060)

Professional serv. (0.033, -0.082)

Computer services (-0.087, 0.035)

-0.10   -0.05   0.00   0.05   0.10   0.15   0.20   0.25   0.30   0.35   0.40

Figure 3.1a Contribution of ICT-using services to US–EU productivity differential, 1995-2000

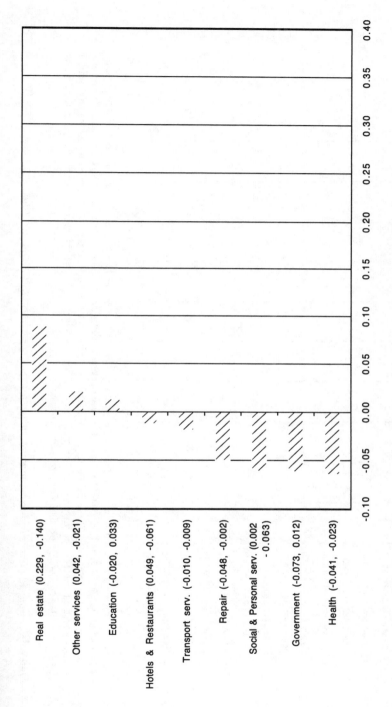

Real estate (0.229, -0.140)

Other services (0.042, -0.021)

Education (-0.020, 0.033)

Hotels & Restaurants (0.049, -0.061)

Transport serv. (-0.010, -0.009)

Repair (-0.048, -0.002)

Social & Personal serv. (0.002 - 0.063)

Government (-0.073, 0.012)

Health (-0.041, -0.023)

-0.10   -0.05   0.00   0.05   0.10   0.15   0.20   0.25   0.30   0.35   0.40

Figure 3.1b Contribution of non-ICT services to US–EU productivity differential, 1995-2000

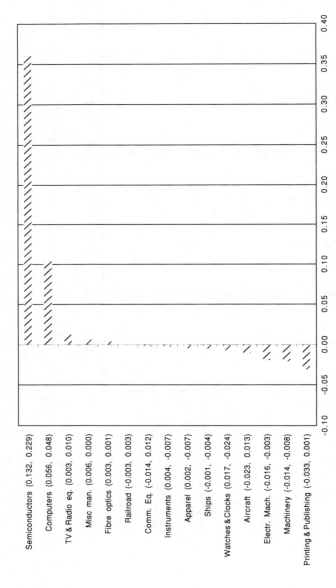

Note: Each bar measures the contribution of an industry to the aggregate differential in labour productivity growth between the US and the EU, which was 1.1 percent higher in the US from 1995-2000. The first term between brackets shows the part of the US–EU differential that is attributable to higher or lower productivity growth of that industry. The second figure between brackets is the sum of three remaining effects, i.e., differences in each industry's share in total employment, differences in the changes in employment shares and differences in productivity levels by industry relative to the aggregate productivity level. See van Ark et al. (2002), appendix E for a more detailed discussion.

Figure 3.1c Contribution of ICT-using manufacturing to US–EU productivity differential, 1995-2000

Europe than in the US, although the direct evidence on ICT diffusion is relatively sparse. But the evidence that labour productivity growth, and changes in growth rates, are linked to ICT-using and ICT-producing industries extends to Europe. Moreover, the differences in productivity performance between the EU and the US are strongly associated with major ICT-using industries, particularly trade and securities. We conclude this line of reasoning by looking at the patterns of productivity growth across the entire distribution of industries.

Table 3.10 provides correlations of productivity growth between the EU and the US for all industries, for all industries with the two major ICT-producing industries (office and computer equipment, and semiconductors) omitted, and for service industries only. The first column shows Spearman rank correlation coefficients for productivity growth rates and the second and third columns provide Pearson correlations on productivity growth rates and productivity contributions respectively. The calculations are carried out on productivity growth in the EU and the US between 1995 and 2000, on acceleration in productivity growth in 1995-2000 relative to 1990-1995, and on EU productivity growth from 1995-2000 relative to US growth from 1990-1995. The latter type of correlation comes closest to the 'lagging diffusion' hypothesis as it tests whether the EU growth pattern during the second period resembles the US growth pattern during the first period.

Reading across the top panel of Table 3.10, which shows the correlations when all industries are included, the relationships are positive and, when the productivity growth measure (in column 2) is used, in fact they are quite strong. However, as is shown in the second panel, the originally high correlation coefficients in column (2) drop significantly once the office and computer equipment (ISIC 30) and semiconductors (ISIC 32.1) are dropped from the sample. While the Spearman coefficient (column 1) in the second panel drops somewhat, the Pearson correlations on productivity contributions in column (3) (which take into account the relative size of industries) hold up fairly well. In particular, the correlation between EU and US productivity growth rates in the 1995-2000 period, and the comparison of the EU productivity growth rates in 1995-2000 with those in the US in the earlier period, 1990-1995, remain strongly significant.[28]

In the third panel of Table 3.10 we concentrate on the service industries only, and find again that the results support the argument that Europe's diffusion process is ongoing but lagging behind that of the US. In particular, the correlations are uniformly positive and follow a reasonable pattern for comparisons of EU growth from 1995-2000 with US growth from 1990-1995. While the correlation coefficients are somewhat smaller than in the other two panels, they are still significantly positive.

Table 3.10 Correlation between EU and US productivity growth by industry

	Spearman Rank Correlations (1)	Pearson correlations On productivity growth (2)	Pearson correlations On contributions to aggregate productivity growth (3)
All industries			
EU and US (1995-2000)	0.47**	0.95**	0.61**
EU and US Acceleration 1995-2000/1990-95	0.47**	0.70**	0.24*
EU (1995-2000) and US (1990-95)	0.31**	0.92**	0.58**
All industries (except 30 and 32.1)			
EU and US (1995-2000)	0.40**	0.60**	0.51**
EU and US Acceleration 1995-2000/1990-95	0.40**	0.38**	0.15
EU (1995-2000) over US (1990-95)	0.23	0.40**	0.48**
Service industries			
EU and US (1995-2000)	0.36**	0.35**	0.35**
EU and US Acceleration 1995-2000/1990-95	0.26	0.27*	0.22
EU (1995-2000) over US (1990-95)	0.50**	0.33**	0.38**

Notes:
Asterisks denote significance: * 10%; ** 5%.
30 and 32.1 represent Office and Computing Equipment and Semiconductors respectively.

5. CONCLUDING COMMENTS AND FURTHER RESEARCH

The main conclusion from this chapter is that the diffusion of ICT in Europe is underway. It is following patterns similar to those experienced in the US, but the pace is considerably slower overall.

ICT production, particularly the computers and semiconductor industries, showed strong productivity growth and acceleration in virtually all countries. The contribution of these industries to aggregate productivity growth was higher in the US due to their larger size. But in many European countries, ICT-producing service industries (in particular telecommunication services) performed better than in the US.

The key differences between Europe and the US are in the services sector, in particular in intensive ICT-using services. Productivity growth in the US accelerated strongly during the second half of the decade, whereas it more or less stalled in the EU. While there was great diversity among industries and countries, a couple of patterns stand out. The US, in contrast to Europe, showed strong productivity improvements in retail and wholesale trade and securities. Moreover, even though these sectors were larger in the US, it was productivity, not size differences, which explained most of the differences in the aggregate productivity growth rates between the US and the EU since 1995. In addition, there were almost universal productivity gains in banking but very mixed performances in insurance and securities services, with the larger countries, including the US, doing poorly in the insurance industry.

Clear patterns were less obvious among the non-ICT industries. Productivity performances were very mixed across industries, but on the whole, Europe showed higher productivity growth in both 1990-95 and 1995-2000. The gap narrowed, however, as the US was one of the few countries to show some improvement in productivity growth for the aggregate of non-ICT services.

These results raise several questions that deserve further research. First, how important are measurement issues as contrasted with economic explanations in interpreting our findings? We cannot be sure how many of the differences we observe are the result of inadequate measurement of services output and differences across countries in measurement methodology. It is clear that the measurement issues need to remain a key item on the future agenda for productivity research. The importance of service industries in accounting for the US–EU gap in aggregate productivity growth underscores the central role that measurement issues are to take in the research agenda.

Second, why was ICT diffusion faster in the US? It is clear that ICT equipment is sold in worldwide markets and that European productivity growth in manufacturing matches that in the US. This means the technology is available to potential users almost everywhere. Moreover, stronger productivity performance in European ICT-producing services, in particular telecom services, suggests plenty of support for ICT users.

Finally, despite the importance of ICT, it should be noted that ICT is not the only factor explaining differences in productivity growth between Europe and the US. A broad literature has addressed a wide range of causes for Europe's slowdown in productivity growth during the 1990s. In turn, these same factors may be behind the slower diffusion of ICT in Europe compared to the US.[29] Indeed business organization and the opportunities to exploit technologies depend on the constraints and restrictions that firms face. For example, McGuckin and van Ark (2001) argue that in many European industries, regulations and structural impediments in product and labour markets limit the opportunities to invest in ICT. Examples of product market restrictions include limits on shop opening hours, and transport regulations that make it difficult for manufacturers and wholesalers to supply customers frequently. Restrictive labour rules and procedures limit flexibility in organizing the workplace and the hiring and firing of workers. Furthermore, barriers to entry and restrictions on the free flow of capital are still an issue in many countries. We note that such queries would not just focus on European rigidities. The relatively poor performance of telecom services in the US may be associated with cable and broad-spectrum regulations and the lack of universal standards that limit entry and competition in telecommunications services.

More research on these issues may also help with the related question posed in the chapter: How was the US able to simultaneously expand employment in industries such as retail trade and increase labour productivity? In Europe it appears that the slower pace of ICT diffusion meant that employment gains went together with declining productivity. This slower pace involves a risk that Europe may enter a low-productivity growth path, which will make it difficult to raise output and living standards in the long run.

NOTES

1. This is an abbreviated version of a working paper (with the same title) from the Groningen Growth and Development Centre and The Conference Board that can be obtained from http://www.eco.rug.nl/ggdc. The authors thank Colin Webb (OECD) for his advice on the use of the OECD STAN database. We are grateful to Kevin Stiroh (NY Fed) for advice on the US. ICT capital data, and to Brian Moyer (BEA), Robert Yuskavage (BEA) and Christopher Kask (BLS) for advice on US deflators for ICT-producing industries. We also received useful comments on earlier drafts of the paper at various occasions, including the DRUID Summer Conference 2002 on Industrial Dynamics of the New and Old Economy (6-8 June 2002, Copenhagen).
2. See, for example, Jorgenson (2001).

3. See, for example, Baily and Lawrence (2001), Jorgenson, Ho and Stiroh (2002) and Triplett and Bosworth (2002). Among the main dissenters are Gordon (2000, 2002) and McKinsey Global Institute (2001).
4. See, for example, Daveri (2001, 2002), ECB (2001) and Colecchia and Schreyer (2001).
5. See, for example, OECD (2001, 2002).
6. See van Ark (2001) and McGuckin and van Ark (2001). A limited number of country-specific studies in Europe have recognized the smaller contribution of ICT to productivity growth in ICT-using industries, mainly in services, including Oulton (2001) for the UK, Jalava and Pohjola (2001) and Niiniinen (1999) for Finland, van der Wiel (2001) for the Netherlands, Cette, Mairesse and Kocuglu (2001) for France, and De Arcangelis, Jona-Lasinio and Manzocchi (2001) for Italy.
7. In addition, user cost measures by industry will also take into account possible high returns on ICT capital in particular industries. For example, in the oil extraction industry, a small investment in ICT has fundamentally changed the methods by which this industry explores new oil reserves (Olewiler, 2002 and Carlsson, Chapter 1, this volume). But when using the capital services approach, capital returns can be high even with small amounts of investment in ICT.
8. One way to crosscheck the sensibility of the US industry grouping for international comparisons is to look at industry measures of ICT and IT intensities that we have for some other countries. Van Ark et al. (2002) provide the average proportion of total IT investment (i.e., excluding investment in communication equipment) in total investment for France, Germany, the Netherlands, the UK and the US over the 1993-97 period, as well as the share of ICT capital in the total capital stock for France and the UK. While the data are spotty, they show wide variation across industries in IT and ICT intensities across industries as was also observed in the US data. However, rank correlations of these industry intensities between each pair of countries are positive and mostly above 0.50. This suggests that the intensive ICT-using industries are similar across countries, so that using the US experience with ICT diffusion as a measure of the opportunity set is reasonable.
9. See http://www.oecd.org/EN/document/0,,EN-document-0-nodirectorate-no-1-3245-0,00. html. A detailed description of the data and adjustments is given in van Ark et al. (2002), Appendix B.
10. Even though the decline in working hours in Europe means that labour productivity grew faster when measured in hours than when measured on a person employed-basis, differences across industries are not strongly affected by these different measures of labour productivity.
11. In the case of the United States, we also relied heavily on detailed series from the Bureau of Economic Analysis on the value of shipments at the 4-digit level for manufacturing industries and gross output at the 3-digit level for non-manufacturing industries (http://www. bea.gov/bea/dn2/gpo.htm). In addition, we used Input/Output tables from the Bureau of Labour Statistics (http://www.bls.gov/emp) to obtain shares of intermediate inputs in gross output, which are needed for the double deflation (i.e., separate deflation of series on gross output and intermediate inputs) at the value added level (see below).
12. Belgium, Luxembourg, Greece and Portugal are not included in the database, because the industry detail in the national accounts was insufficient for the analysis applied in this chapter.
13. This procedure follows the actual practice of the OECD concerning data for years before 1999 (see OECD, 2001b). For Sweden, Denmark and the UK, which do not have the euro as their currency, we used their average exchange rate for the euro for 1999. Obviously cross-country purchasing power parities would be the preferable measure, but these are only available for a limited number of countries and not on a disaggregated level as used in this chapter (van Ark et al., 2003).
14. Here the exceptions are the Netherlands and Norway, where the non-ICT sector dominated because of large mineral extraction industries (natural gas and oil). In Norway in particular, the oil extraction industry accounted for more than 10 percent of GDP.
15. In Ireland, productivity growth in ICT-producing manufacturing is faster than in the US because of the large impact of the computer and semiconductor industries. The bottom line of Table 3.2 shows the estimates for all countries based on the original price indexes for ICT-

producing manufacturing. This shows that the procedure adopted here makes substantial differences at the level of ICT-producing manufacturing. However, at the aggregate level the differences between the original and adjusted estimates are much smaller.

16. We also find that productivity growth in ICT-using manufacturing is higher than in the US for many countries.
17. Based on Fabricant (1942).
18. The shift effect may be further decomposed into a static and dynamic shift effect. The latter effect is the product of changes in shares and changes in labour productivity levels and is quite small when using annual data, as is the case here.
19. All parameters are estimated with weighted least-squares (WLS), where the weight of each industry is its employment in the relevant year (this multiplies the dependent and the independent variable by the square root of employment).
20. The significant result for the EU as a whole is caused by the fact that industries within the ICT-using group showed less volatility in productivity growth than individual EU member countries.
21. See the Appendix for numbers for individual countries.
22. But recently concerns have surfaced concerning the still too fragmented market structure of the European telecom market. See, for example, Isern and Rios (2002).
23. See, for example, McKinsey Global Institute (2001).
24. In the United States, the US Bureau of Labour Statistics (which is responsible for the development of price indices) and the Bureau of Economic Analysis (which produces the National Income and Product Accounts) have introduced various improvements in measurement methods (Dean, 1999; Gullickson and Harper, 1999; Landefeld and Fraumeni, 2001). In a series of reports, Eurostat recently evaluated measurement practices in various service activities, such as financial services and public services (Eurostat, 1998a, 1998b, 2000, 2001).
25. But in health services, some countries (Austria, Germany and the Netherlands) have shown an even faster decline in labour productivity than the United States since 1995.
26. See van Ark et al. (2002), Appendix E for a detailed explanation. We distinguish between the four effects by running counterfactual shift-share analyses. The employment shares of the US are imposed on the EU and vice versa. By comparing the 'intra-effect' using the same employment shares, we isolate the effect of differences in productivity growth. The remaining difference in the intra-effect is then due to the other three effects. In the end, we take the average of each of the effects under US and EU employment shares.
27. Productivity growth in the semiconductor industry also contributes positively to the US–EU differential. While Table 3.9 shows higher productivity growth in the EU, the shift-share analysis decomposes the absolute change in productivity (value added per person in currency units) in each industry. Despite the higher European growth rates, the US semiconductor industry has shown a larger absolute increase in productivity.
28. The acceleration test performs badly across the board, which is no surprise given the slowdown of productivity growth in many European industries and the acceleration in many US industries since 1995 (see Table 3.9).
29. A useful summary is in Scarpetta et al. (2000).

REFERENCES

Ark, B. van (2001), 'The Renewal of the Old Economy: Europe in an Internationally Comparative Perspective', *OECD STI Working Paper*, 2001/5   (http://www.olis.oecd.org/olis/2001doc.nsf/LinkTo/DSTI-DOC (2001)5)

Ark, B. van (2002), 'Measuring the New Economy: An International Comparative Perspective', *Review of Income and Wealth*, 48 (1), 1-14, March.

Ark, B. van, R. Inklaar and R.H. McGuckin (2002), 'Changing Gear': Productivity, ICT and Services: Europe and the United States', *Research Memorandum*, GD-60, Groningen Growth and Development Centre (http:// www.eco.rug.nl/GGDC/).

Ark, B. van, R. Inklaar and E. Stuivenwold (2003), 'Purchasing Power Parities for Industry Comparisons of Productivity Levels', Groningen Growth and Development Centre, mimeographed.

Baily, M.N. and Lawrence, R.Z. (2001), 'Do we have a New E-conomy?', *NBER Working Paper*, no. 8243, April.

Cette, G., J. Mairesse and Y. Kocuglu (2001), 'Diffusion des technologies de l'information et de la communication et croissance économique, le cas de la France sur une longue période (1980-2000)', *Croissance*, No. 6, 14, November.

Colecchia, A. and Schreyer, P. (2001), 'ICT Investment and Economic Growth in the 1990s: Is the United States a Unique Case? A Comparative Study of Nine OECD Countries', *OECD STI Working Paper*, 2001/7, October (http:// www.olis.oecd.org/olis/2001doc.nsf/LinkTo/DSTI-DOC(2001)7).

Daveri, F. (2001), 'Information Technology and Growth in Europe', University of Parma and IGIER, May (http://digilander.iol.it/crenos/cnr67701/Daveri. pdf).

Daveri F. (2002), 'The New Economy in Europe (1992-2001)', *IGIER Working Paper*, 213, April.

De Arcangelis, G, C. Jona-Lasinio and F. Manzocchi (2001), 'Sectoral Determinants and Dynamics of ICT Investment in Italy', mimeo, University of Bari, ISTAT and University of Perugia.

Dean, E.R. (1999), 'The Accuracy of BLS Productivity Measures', *Monthly Labour Review*, February, 24-34.

ECB (2001), 'New technologies and productivity in the euro area', *ECB Monthly Bulletin*, July, 37-48

Eurostat (1998a), Report of the Task Force Volume Measure for Non-Market Services, September, Luxembourg.

Eurostat (1998b), Report of the Task Force Prices and Volumes for Health, September, Luxembourg.

Eurostat (2000), Report of the Task Force Price and Volume Measures for Financial Intermediation, May, Luxembourg.

Eurostat (2001), *Handbook on price and volume measures in national accounts*, Eurostat.

Fabricant, S. (1942), *Employment in Manufacturing, 1899-1939*, National Bureau of Economic Research: New York.

Gordon, R.J. (2000), 'Does the 'New Economy' Measure up to the Great Inventions of the Past?', *Journal of Economic Perspectives*, 14 (4), 49-77.

Gordon, R.J. (2002), 'Technology and Economic Performance in the American Economy', *NBER Working Paper*, no. 8771, February.

Griliches, Z., ed. (1992), *Output Measurement in the Service Sectors, Studies in Income and Wealth*, Volume 56, National Bureau of Economic Research, Chicago University Press.

Gullickson, W. and Harper, M.J. (1999), 'Possible measurement bias in aggregate productivity growth', *Monthly Labour Review*, February, 47-67.

Hulten, C.R. (2000), 'Measuring Innovation in the New Economy', paper prepared for the National Bureau of Economic Research Summer Institute joint workshop of the Productivity Program and the Conference on Research in Income and Wealth, 31 July and 1 August (http://www.bsos. umd.edu/econ/neweconf.pdf).

Isern, J. and Rios, M. (2002) 'Facing Disconnection: Hard Choices for Europe's Telecos', *The McKinsey Quarterly*, 2002, no. 1.

Jalava, J. and Pohjola M. (2001), 'Economic Growth in the New Economy: Evidence from Advanced Economies', mimeo UNU/WIDER.

Jorgenson, D.W. (2001), 'Information Technology and the US Economy', *American Economic Review*, 91 (1), 1-32.

Jorgenson, D.W. and K.J. Stiroh (2000), 'Raising the Speed Limit: US Economic Growth in the Information Age', *Brooking Papers on Economic Activity*, pp. 125-211.

Jorgenson, D.W., M.S. Ho and K.J. Stiroh (2002), 'Growth of US Industries and Investments in Information Technology and Higher Education', paper presented at Conference on Research in Income and Wealth, *Measuring Capital in the New Economy*, 26-27 April, 2002 (http://post.economics. harvard.edu/faculty/jorgenson/papers/jhscriw.pdf).

Kask, C. and E. Sieber (2002), 'Productivity growth in 'high-tech' manufacturing industries' *Monthly Labour Review*, March, 16-31.

Landefeld, J.S. and B.M. Fraumeni, (2001), 'Measuring the New Economy', *Survey of Current Business*, March, 23-40.

McGuckin, R. and B. van Ark (2001), 'Making the Most of the Information Age: Productivity and Structural Reform in the New Economy', *Perspectives on a Global Economy*, Report 1301-01-RR, October.

McGuckin, R. and B. van Ark (2002), *Performance 2001, Productivity, Employment, and Income in the World's Economies*, New York: The Conference Board.

McGuckin, R.H. and K.J. Stiroh (2001), 'Do Computers Make Output Harder to Measure?', *Journal of Technology Transfer*, 26, 295-321.

McGuckin, R.H. and K.J. Stiroh (2002), 'Computers and Productivity: Are Aggregation Effects Important?', *Economic Inquiry*, 40 (1), 42-59, January.

McKinsey Global Institute (2001), *US Productivity Growth 1995-2000, Understanding the contribution of Information Technology relative to other factors*, October.

Niiniinen, P. (2001), 'Computers and Economic Growth in Finland', in M. Pohjola (ed.), *Information Technology, Productivity and Economic Growth*, WIDER/United Nations University, Oxford University Press.

OECD (2001a), *OECD Productivity Manual: A Guide to the Measurement of Industry-Level and Aggregate Productivity Growth*, Paris: OECD.

OECD (2001b), 'Introduction of the Euro in OECD Statistics', mimeo, downloadable from www.oecd.org/doc/M00017000/M00017083.doc

OECD (2002), *Measuring the Information Economy*, Paris: OECD.

Olewiler, N. (2002), 'Natural Capital, Sustainability and Productivity: An Exploration of the Linkages', in A. Sharpe, F. St-Hilaire and K. Banting (eds), *The Review of Economic Performance and Social Progress: Towards a Social Understanding of Productivity*, CSLS/IRPP, pp. 117-42.

Oliner, S.D. and D.E. Sichel (2000), 'The Resurgence of Growth in the Late 1990s: Is Information Technology the Story', *Journal of Economic Perspectives*, 14 (4), 3-22.

O'Mahony, M. and W. de Boer (2002), 'Britain's relative productivity performance: Updates to 1999', Final report to DTI/Treasury/ONS, March.

Oulton, N. (2001), 'ICT and Productivity Growth in the United Kingdom', *Working Paper*, no. 140, Bank of England, July.

Scarpetta, S., A. Bassanini, D. Pilat and P. Schreyer (2000), 'Economic Growth in the OECD Area: Recent Trends at the Aggregate and Sectoral Level,' *Economics Department Working Papers*, No. 248, OECD, Paris.

Schreyer, P. (2000), 'The contribution of information and communication technology to output growth: a study of the G7 countries', *STI Working Papers 2000/2*, OECD, Paris.

Schreyer, P. (2002), 'Computer price indices and international growth and productivity comparisons', *Review of Income and Wealth*, 48 (1), 5-31, March.

Stiroh, K.J. (2002), 'Information Technology and the US Productivity Revival: What Do the Industry Data Say?', *American Economic Review*, 92 (5), December, 1559-76.

Triplett, J.E. and B.P. Bosworth (2001), 'Productivity in the Services Sector', in R. M. Stern (ed.) *Services in the International Economy*, Michigan: University of Michigan Press.

Triplett, J.E. and B.P. Bosworth (2002), '"Baumol's Disease" has been Cured: IT and Multifactor Productivity in US Services Industries', Brooking Institution, mimeo.

Wiel, H.P. van der (2001), 'Does ICT boost Dutch productivity growth?', *CPB Document*, No. 016, December.

Yuskavage, R.E. (1996), 'Improved Estimates of Gross Product by Industry, 1959-94', *Survey of Current Business*, August, pp. 133-55.

Table 3A.1 Labour productivity growth (value added per person engaged) by individual industry, 1990-95

1990-95		Austria	Denmark	Finland	France[b]	Germany[a]	Ireland	Italy	Netherlands	Spain[b]	Sweden	UK	EU	Canada[b]	Japan[c]	Norway	Switzerland	US
Total Economy		2.3	1.6	3.3	1.0	2.1	3.0	1.8	0.7	1.6	2.8	2.8	1.9	1.1	0.8	3.3	-0.1	1.1
Total ICT-producing manuf.		**7.6**	**6.5**	**8.9**	**10.0**	**6.8**	**17.1**	**4.6**	**5.7**	**8.3**	**-0.7**	**15.8**	**11.1**	**11.8**	**12.4**	**8.4**	**1.4**	**15.1**
Office and Comp. Eq.	30	24.2	24.3	11.0	26.2	26.8	29.1	28.7	34.2	28.4	25.2	33.8	33.2	16.6	26.9	33.7	27.8	28.6
Fibre optics	31.3	4.5	11.8	9.2	5.0	6.5	13.6	6.3	10.5	11.1	18.3	-0.3	6.9	4.9	13.3	7.1	2.6	5.6
Semiconductors	32.1	24.7	28.9	22.8	32.3	41.9	32.0	33.4	31.0	26.5	19.0	36.1	37.7	29.7	23.5	33.5	31.5	36.8
Communication eq.	32.2	5.1	2.4	9.8	3.2	11.3	0.5	-4.1	4.4	-3.2	-3.6	13.0	5.0	6.2	2.0	10.5	4.9	6.6
Radio and TV eq.	32.3	1.6	-0.8	-1.3	-5.0	-10.9	-12.6	4.9	1.2	-3.1	-13.7	7.4	-2.6	13.5	-2.2	1.1	1.7	-4.6
Instruments	33.1	-3.1	1.3	-0.4	-4.0	-2.7	-10.9	-5.6	-1.8	-3.7	-17.2	-1.7	-2.6	-3.0	-6.9	-0.5	-2.2	-4.5
Total ICT-producing services		**4.8**	**7.9**	**4.8**	**2.6**	**5.9**	**2.2**	**1.6**	**2.3**	**3.1**	**6.8**	**5.6**	**4.4**	**0.4**	**4.2**	**2.1**	**1.5**	**3.1**
Telecommunications	64	5.8	5.1	6.6	2.5	7.7	4.8	4.4	4.0	4.0	8.0	6.2	5.7	2.1	4.7	2.3	3.2	3.3
Computer services	72	1.3	12.3	0.0	2.8	0.5	-3.5	-3.4	-1.6	0.9	3.3	5.3	1.5	1.6	3.7	1.5	-3.3	2.7
Total ICT-using manuf.		**1.9**	**2.7**	**4.7**	**3.3**	**2.6**	**6.1**	**3.4**	**1.8**	**1.7**	**5.6**	**2.1**	**3.1**	**2.1**	**-1.1**	**1.3**	**0.0**	**-0.3**
Apparel	18	2.8	3.2	2.0	3.2	3.6	-6.6	8.0	1.3	4.1	5.8	3.6	5.2	4.1	-5.9	1.8	-10.5	3.4
Printing & Publishing	22	-0.7	-0.7	3.7	1.5	2.7	6.4	0.2	1.9	-1.1	8.2	0.2	1.9	-0.8	-2.5	1.3	-3.1	-2.6
Machinery	29	1.9	2.6	4.4	5.3	4.6	7.5	3.2	3.0	2.9	3.1	2.6	4.2	2.7	-1.8	0.8	1.6	0.9
Electrical machinery	31-31.3	4.5	11.8	9.2	5.0	6.5	13.6	6.3	10.5	11.1	18.3	-0.3	6.9	4.9	13.3	7.1	2.6	5.6
Watches & instruments	33-33.1	5.4	9.7	7.9	6.3	4.2	2.2	2.9	4.4	4.7	14.0	23.1	7.5	4.2	1.5	-2.8	1.4	2.1
Ships	351	7.8	10.6	8.9	0.7	-1.2	-5.5	2.6	0.0	3.1	-4.2	10.7	4.1	5.8	14.6	0.2	-13.5	-3.8
Aircraft	353			4.0	6.5	-8.1		-5.8	-1.5	-3.0	-2.5	1.3	0.5	-0.1	4.7	8.3		-1.0
Railroad and other	352+359	7.8	0.6	-7.4	8.0	0.7	-6.8	8.7	1.6	7.9	-2.2	2.7	5.9	10.1	5.8	6.5		-2.0
Misc. manufacturing	36-37	-0.3	0.8	3.1	0.9	-0.7	6.0	3.9	0.2	0.1	5.6	-0.9	1.1	4.7	-2.6	-2.1	4.1	1.3
Total ICT-using services		**2.1**	**0.6**	**0.7**	**0.5**	**1.1**	**0.2**	**1.6**	**0.4**	**-0.7**	**2.5**	**2.5**	**1.1**	**1.9**	**1.4**	**5.2**	**-2.0**	**1.9**
Wholesale trade	51	0.7	2.6	-1.9	2.9	3.1	-0.6	4.1	-0.4	0.7	3.8	4.9	2.9	3.7	2.0[f]	5.3	-6.0	3.4
Retail trade	52	0.7	2.6	4.3	1.3	0.2	-0.6	0.7	0.1	1.6	3.8	2.6	1.1	1.1	0.0	5.3	2.9	2.3
Banks	65	5.3	-1.1	-0.3	-2.1	1.4	4.8	0.6	4.3	-2.9	3.1[d]	2.2	0.4	2.3	0.0[d]	5.1	-0.9	1.3
Insurance	66	-0.4	-6.5	-3.5	0.3	3.0	4.8	3.3	0.8	-11.9		1.4	0.2	2.5		8.8	4.1	3.0
Securities trade	67	-3.1	1.9	7.0	3.4	-2.2	4.8	1.6	-0.7	1.0		0.9	1.1			9.8	-10.2	3.2
Renting of machinery	71	5.9		0.4	-0.3	0.7	-3.5	0.0	-3.8	1.1	-6.3	5.5	2.4		3.7	8.6	-5.0	6.7
R&D	73	13.6	-2.5	0.1	-0.1	0.5	-3.5	-1.4	-3.8	-1.7	-0.6	2.3	-0.2	1.1	3.7	5.3	-4.8	1.0
Professional services	74.1-74.3	1.6	-2.0	3.7	-0.9	-2.2	-3.5	-0.5	0.5	0.5	-0.6	2.1	-0.4	-0.3	3.7	5.3	-5.4	-0.7

Table 3A.1 (continued)

1990-95		Austria	Denmark	Finland	France [b]	Germany	Ireland	Italy	Netherlands	Spain [b]	Sweden	UK	EU	Canada [d]	Japan [c]	Norway	Switzerland	US
Total Non-ICT manuf.		**4.6**	**2.9**	**6.2**	**3.4**	**4.4**	**7.8**	**2.7**	**3.7**	**3.5**	**6.3**	**4.0**	**3.8**	**2.1**	**0.4**	**2.2**	**4.4**	**3.0**
Food & beverages	15-16	3.7	3.1	5.9	2.2	3.6	3.9	2.1	6.1	1.2	6.5	3.1	2.9	1.4	-1.7	3.3	4.1	3.5
Textiles	17	0.5	2.8	8.6	5.4	4.3	2.1	1.3	1.4	4.1	4.8	2.5	3.5	3.0	0.6	1.7	5.8	3.0
Leather	19	1.4	1.7	3.6	1.5	8.3	-4.5	3.8	2.1	2.1	4.7	0.1	3.3	2.8	-2.7	8.3	-0.2	4.9
Wood	20	1.2	4.5	5.5	2.9	5.7	0.5	3.0	1.3	2.2	1.1	0.8	2.5	-2.0	-2.7	-2.9	1.1	-2.8
Paper	21	8.3	5.8	7.6	1.2	0.6	1.5	3.5	3.2	3.1	3.8	3.8	3.5	-0.8	-2.6	3.7	1.1	0.0
Petroleum & coal	23	51.5	-18.9	5.9	15.7	-1.6	17.1	5.7	4.0	5.2	11.9	8.6	9.6	4.0	-3.0	-15.9	-22.3	5.0
Chemicals	24	3.4	5.2	4.4	5.9	8.3	10.5	3.5	5.3	3.9	6.7	7.6	6.8	3.6	2.4	1.9	11.5	3.4
Rubber & plastics	25	4.9	-3.7	3.2	4.3	3.2	5.9	2.2	1.5	3.1	6.3	2.4	3.2	3.6	0.8	0.7	-0.6	4.6
Stone, clay & glass	26	-0.7	1.7	3.9	0.1	6.7	6.9	1.4	-0.4	2.8	2.0	4.3	2.5	0.0	0.1	4.6	-1.1	2.8
Basic metals	27	3.9	4.9	7.9	3.9	10.6	-5.0	4.3	2.7	7.5	9.1	4.5	6.9	3.8	1.7	-3.8	3.5	3.9
Fabricated metals	28	4.4	3.4	4.9	1.3	1.8	0.5	4.3	2.0	2.1	6.1	0.9	2.2	2.0	2.2	12.2	-0.6	3.2
Motor vehicles	34	7.9	-3.3	0.7	2.8	2.4	-3.6	0.1	5.8	8.1	8.8	3.1	3.2	5.0	-1.3	8.9	-10.1	4.9
Total Non-ICT serv.		**0.1**	**0.5**	**2.0**	**-0.3**	**0.9**	**-0.9**	**0.6**	**-0.2**	**0.9**	**1.5**	**1.5**	**0.6**	**-0.2**	**-0.2**	**0.7**	**-0.2**	**-0.4**
Repairs	50	0.7	-20.2	4.0	-1.9	-3.1	-0.6	5.4	-0.7	-0.4	3.8	1.4	-0.1			5.3	-1.4	-1.4
Hotels & restaurants	55	-1.0	2.1	3.1	-4.6	-5.2	-1.5	-1.4	-3.8	0.6	1.5	-0.6	-1.8	0.1		0.9	-5.8	-1.1
Transport	60-63	-0.3	2.3	4.0	0.8	4.9	4.8	5.5	0.8	3.2	-0.3	3.6	3.2	1.4	-2.1	4.0	-3.3	2.1
Real estate	70	-0.4	1.6	6.9	1.4	-3.3	-3.5	0.0	-1.8	5.1	6.3	-5.0	-0.7		1.1	-3.3	6.2	1.6
Other business serv.	74.9	1.6	1.5	-0.2	-1.7	-2.2		-2.2	2.0		-0.6	2.7	-1.1		10.1	5.3		-1.0
Government	75	1.2	1.8	-0.2	1.2	2.2	0.7	2.5	0.9	1.2	0.9 [e]	-0.1	1.4	1.3	0.4	2.0	2.7	0.0
Education	80	-1.4	1.7	0.4	0.4	0.4	-3.7	0.0	1.2	0.7		2.6	0.9	-1.4	1.2	0.4	-7.5	-0.2
Health	85	0.7	1.4	0.0	0.5	1.6	-1.3	-1.4	-0.7	1.6		2.9	0.8	-0.6	1.4	0.0	-1.0	-2.2
Personal & social serv.	90-93	-0.2	1.3	0.0	-3.0	-1.1	-2.4	-0.7	-0.4	-1.3		3.7	-0.4	-1.5	-1.6	0.5	-0.6	0.3
Private households	95	1.3	-0.7	0.7	0.1	-0.1	-0.5	-1.4	-0.4								0.8	2.2
Extra-terr. org.	99																	
Total Non-ICT other industries		**4.5**	**4.1**	**4.2**	**1.6**	**2.7**	**2.9**	**3.0**	**0.9**	**2.9**	**2.8**	**6.1**	**2.7**	**1.4**	**0.2**	**9.3**	**-0.2**	**0.7**
Agriculture	01-05	6.8	7.2	5.1	4.4	10.1	3.9	7.1	3.3	1.8	2.0	2.1	5.2	0.6	0.4	7.5	-0.8	-1.0
Mining	10-14	-1.2	8.1	5.4	-36.7	10.4	8.4	5.8	1.5	9.3	4.4	23.6	7.5	3.8	-0.9	8.2	-2.1	5.4
Utilities	40-41	2.0	5.5	7.2	2.2	4.0	5.6	2.8	3.1	1.6	2.5	9.8	4.5	1.1	0.7	1.7	6.1	2.5
Construction	45	2.0	-0.4	0.8	0.9	-1.1	-1.6	-0.6	-1.5	1.9	2.6	3.3	0.4	-1.4	-1.9	4.9	-2.3	0.5

Notes: a) 1991-1995; b) 1995-99; c) 1995-98; d) Refers to total finance (65-67); e) Refers to total non-market services (75-99); f) Refers to Trade (50-52) as a whole.

Table 3A.2 Labour productivity growth (value added per person engaged) by individual industry, 1995-2000

1995-2000		Austria	Denmark	Finland	France[b]	Germany[a]	Ireland	Italy	Netherlands	Spain[b]	Sweden	UK	EU	Canada[b]	Japan[c]	Norway	Switzerland[c]	US
Total Economy		**2.3**	**1.9**	**2.5**	**1.2**	**1.3**	**5.3**	**0.8**	**0.9**	**0.4**	**2.1**	**1.8**	**1.4**	**1.4**	**0.9**	**1.7**	**1.1**	**2.5**
Total ICT-producing manuf.		**9.6**	**5.7**	**13.2**	**15.0**	**13.7**	**42.3**	**6.0**	**-1.9**	**13.1**	**1.1**	**16.1**	**13.8**	**16.9**	**19.5**	**4.9**	**-4.3**	**23.7**
Office and Comp. Eq.	30	87.4	54.4	-0.1	45.7	54.8	49.1	41.0	45.2	50.7	57.2	45.7	49.3	46.2	54.7	50.9	57.4	52.3
Fiber optics	31.3	7.5	3.6	4.8	3.5	7.0	-3.0	-0.4	-4.0	-3.3	5.4	1.6	2.9	12.8	3.4	-13.5	10.7	5.7
Semiconductors	32.1	47.0	56.2	52.6	53.9	66.3	82.0	53.5	53.6	48.0	40.9	55.2	56.4	56.0	47.7	56.1	48.7	52.1
Communication eq.	32.2	3.3	0.6	10.5	0.4	10.9	-12.3	-6.1	-2.0	-10.2	-4.8	3.3	3.5	0.7	-3.1	6.1	-6.9	-0.4
Radio and TV eq.	32.3	-12.1	-9.7	-7.7	-12.8	-18.6	-12.4	-11.9	-12.3	-16.0	-13.4	-13.2	-13.9	-10.5	-15.7	-20.3	-17.2	-12.5
Instruments	33.1	-4.5	-5.4	-6.3	-8.6	-3.2	-1.1	-9.6	-10.5	-6.7	-5.5	-11.8	-7.2	-4.9	-7.7	-6.7	-9.0	-5.9
Total ICT-producing services		**-0.4**	**5.9**	**8.1**	**6.2**	**11.9**	**-0.2**	**6.2**	**4.5**	**4.1**	**3.3**	**5.2**	**6.5**	**2.8**	**4.0**	**9.2**	**-0.7**	**1.8**
Telecommunications	64	3.6	6.6	13.5	9.8	16.3	-0.6	8.6	7.7	6.2	5.6	9.1	9.9	6.9	6.8	13.8	1.1	6.5
Computer services	72	-9.8	5.4	-1.3	0.4	4.9	-2.1	3.9	1.1	0.3	-0.6	0.3	1.5	1.1	0.7	-1.9	-3.6	-4.5
Total ICT-using manuf.		**6.0**	**0.1**	**1.5**	**1.9**	**2.4**	**8.7**	**1.5**	**2.7**	**1.1**	**1.7**	**1.7**	**2.1**	**1.1**	**0.5**	**-1.3**	**3.3**	**1.2**
Apparel	18	5.4	11.2	-0.1	4.4	6.1	2.2	2.2	3.9	0.7	-1.1	3.7	2.9	0.9	-0.8	0.4	6.6	3.8
Printing & Publishing	22	7.4	-1.3	2.6	0.7	2.5	8.0	1.9	4.3	0.9	3.8	1.2	2.5	-1.4	1.6	-3.8	3.6	-0.2
Machinery	29	5.3	1.2	0.7	2.5	0.9	-3.1	0.4	2.2	1.3	0.6	-1.4	1.0	-5.4	-1.2	-0.5	2.3	0.3
Electrical machinery	31-31.3	7.5	3.6	4.8	3.5	7.0	-3.0	-0.4	-4.0	-3.3	5.4	1.6	2.9	12.8	3.4	-13.5	10.7	5.7
Watches & instruments	33-33.1	7.6	5.0	1.1	3.1	5.8	13.3	3.6	4.3	3.8	3.8	2.0	5.1	5.6	7.1	5.7	5.8	14.2
Ships	351	-1.1	-15.7	-2.7	15.3	-0.8	2.4	2.8	-0.5	-1.0	-2.7	-8.1	0.4	7.7	0.1	0.8	-12.3	-0.2
Aircraft	353			1.6	-9.7	9.9		1.9	11.0	6.1	-4.9	18.8	6.4	6.3	-2.3	11.8		1.1
Railroad and other	352+359	-1.1	0.5	3.6	-0.4	6.6	14.7	1.3	25.9	7.4	4.2	-6.0	3.1	-13.4	-11.0	-1.4	2.5	-0.1
Misc. manufacturing	36-37	3.7	0.2	2.5	2.9	0.9	-1.3	3.0	0.3	0.8	4.6	-0.9	1.5	4.9	2.9	-2.6		2.4
Total ICT-using services		**2.1**	**2.5**	**3.0**	**0.7**	**0.9**	**1.4**	**0.6**	**1.9**	**-0.1**	**3.3**	**2.6**	**1.4**	**2.8**	**0.0**	**4.8**	**0.8**	**5.4**
Wholesale trade	51	2.2	0.3	2.1	1.6	-0.3	6.2	-0.2	4.2	0.3	3.6	0.4	1.2	2.9	0.2[d]	6.3	0.0	6.9
Retail trade	52	2.7	0.8	1.6	0.9	-0.2	6.2	0.6	0.8	1.4	3.0	3.5	1.4	2.9	-2.7	7.0	5.0	2.8
Banks	65	4.4	5.2	11.9	-1.3	8.3	-1.9	4.9	-0.1	0.1	5.4[d]	1.3	3.0	3.7	1.7[d]	4.8	0.8	-1.0
Insurance	66	4.1	8.9	0.4	-0.8	-9.4	-1.9	-3.2	-2.3	-11.0		3.6	0.2	4.8		12.9	4.3	15.3
Securities trade	67	-5.9	-13.3	16.5	1.1	1.0	-1.9	-2.7	2.4	5.1		6.5	2.0					
Renting of machinery	71	0.8	-1.9	2.0	-1.0	2.5	-2.1	-0.6	3.1	0.5	7.4	0.8	0.5		0.7	5.4	0.2	5.7
R&D	73	-2.2	4.1	-0.8	-1.2	6.3	-2.1	3.9	-3.2	-3.0	-0.4	-5.8	-0.5	0.4	0.7	-1.8	-7.1	3.1
Professional services	74.1-74.3	-2.2	5.8	-0.2	2.3	-3.4	-2.1	-1.4	0.7	-0.2	-0.4	4.6	0.4	0.0	0.7	0.6	-2.3	1.0

Table 3A.2 (continued)

1995-2000		Austria	Denmark	Finland	France[b]	Germany[a]	Ireland	Italy	Netherlands	Spain[b]	Sweden	UK	EU	Canada[d]	Japan[c]	Norway	Switzerland	US
Total Non-ICT manuf.		**4.6**	**3.8**	**3.0**	**2.7**	**0.5**	**10.4**	**0.6**	**2.0**	**-0.3**	**3.3**	**0.5**	**1.5**	**1.3**	**-0.3**	**1.7**	**4.4**	**1.4**
Food & beverages	15-16	2.4	0.8	3.0	-1.8	0.3	2.4	0.7	1.4	-0.2	1.8	-1.0	0.0	-0.4	0.4	-1.9	-0.7	-4.5
Textiles	17	5.4	7.0	2.1	0.8	1.6	-3.9	1.5	6.4	-0.6	3.9	0.3	1.4	0.9	-4.7	0.2	2.5	3.3
Leather	19	5.8	11.4	2.4	0.6	2.8	-2.3	-0.9	4.8	0.5	2.5	12.0	0.7	0.9	-1.0	-0.9	1.1	1.3
Wood	20	5.4	0.0	5.5	1.9	2.3	6.5	3.5	1.8	0.9	6.3	-1.7	2.7	-0.5	-6.7	4.3	1.7	0.3
Paper	21	5.1	3.0	4.3	5.8	5.4	1.1	0.1	3.2	-3.1	4.6	-2.3	2.3	-1.4	1.4	5.7	2.3	0.2
Petroleum & coal	23	16.9	19.0	-0.3	2.7	11.9	25.7	-13.1	-3.2	0.2	3.6	0.2	0.2	4.4	4.0	9.0	16.6	1.5
Chemicals	24	5.6	11.2	4.7	4.8	2.6	17.0	1.6	3.9	0.6	5.3	3.7	4.7	1.8	2.3	4.3	9.6	4.4
Rubber & plastics	25	7.2	8.8	0.0	3.1	1.3	-3.3	0.1	3.2	0.8	2.2	-0.2	1.6	3.3	-0.8	-3.3	0.0	4.1
Stone, clay & glass	26	4.4	-0.2	2.1	4.2	0.9	3.9	1.0	2.7	0.7	-0.8	-0.2	1.4	6.1	-0.1	-2.7	2.1	2.6
Basic metals	27	8.8	1.6	4.3	0.6	2.7	-3.8	-1.7	2.7	-3.4	3.2	-1.6	0.9	1.4	-0.6	3.9	1.8	3.1
Fabricated metals	28	2.1	0.6	0.7	1.2	1.0	-4.8	0.6	0.6	-0.8	0.7	1.9	0.9	0.8	-2.2	8.8	1.8	0.6
Motor vehicles	34	0.3	5.4	5.5	12.0	-5.2	6.2	3.4	2.9	1.2	4.5	-1.8	0.9	3.7	-4.4	-1.0	0.9	1.4
Total Non-ICT services		**-0.4**	**1.2**	**0.6**	**0.1**	**-0.1**	**-1.2**	**-0.4**	**0.1**	**-0.1**	**1.4**	**0.9**	**0.2**	**-0.4**	**0.6**	**0.4**	**0.8**	**0.4**
Repairs	50	2.2	20.7	1.4	-3.2	0.2	6.2	0.5	1.6	-1.1	2.2	3.1	1.0			5.1	1.4	-2.5
Hotels & restaurants	55	0.5	-1.3	-0.6	-0.4	-5.2	4.2	0.1	0.8	-0.6	2.5	-2.1	-1.2	0.6	-0.7	2.4	0.9	0.4
Transport	60-63	2.5	3.3	2.2	3.0	3.1	-0.6	-1.8	1.8	0.8	1.7	2.1	1.7	1.5	1.7	0.7	2.5	1.6
Real estate	70	-1.6	0.1	0.7	-0.5	-2.7	-2.1	-0.6	-0.4	-6.4	3.0	1.1	-0.8		-0.3	-0.3	1.5	1.7
Other business services	74.9	-2.4	2.7	-2.0	-1.3	-3.4		-1.5	0.7		-0.4	5.9	-0.3		13.8	2.3		1.4
Government	75	0.1	0.0	1.1	1.2	1.2	-0.8	0.8	1.2	1.1	1.9[e]	0.3	1.1	1.3	1.8	1.0	0.3	0.2
Education	80	-0.1	-0.1	-0.3	0.8	0.0	-5.8	-0.6	0.3	0.4		-1.0	-0.1	-1.6	1.9	1.5	-3.7	-1.2
Health	85	-3.5	0.2	-0.1	0.3	-0.2	-1.8	0.6	-1.2	-0.2		2.6	0.4	-0.8	0.2	-0.5	0.0	-0.3
Personal & social serv.	90-93	-1.0	0.8	0.6	-2.5	-0.4	-1.1	0.4	0.1	-0.3		-0.8	-0.5	-0.6	-1.1	2.1	-1.3	-0.9
Private households	95	-3.1	1.3	-0.9	-2.7	-0.3	17.0	-0.5	3.2								-1.7	0.7
Extra-terr. org.	99																	
Total Non-ICT **other Industries**		**4.0**	**1.2**	**2.3**	**1.1**	**2.3**	**1.2**	**2.5**	**0.0**	**1.3**	**0.5**	**1.5**	**1.9**	**1.1**	**-1.5**	**1.4**	**-1.3**	**0.6**
Agriculture	01-05	3.9	5.0	4.5	4.8	5.2	2.9	4.8	2.2	3.4	1.8	1.9	4.0	4.1	0.1	2.4	4.0	6.3
Mining	10-14	4.3	8.8	-3.3	-5.9	-3.6	-0.7	-0.4	1.6	0.3	0.8	0.8	3.5	-0.5	5.0	2.9	4.0	-1.8
Utilities	40-41	5.0	-0.5	4.7	4.6	5.8	7.4	3.8	2.5	6.0	-0.4	6.4	4.9	1.6	4.1	6.0	1.0	2.3
Construction	45	2.4	-1.4	0.0	-2.7	1.0	-1.4	0.5	-0.3	-1.1	0.0	0.8	-0.5	0.9	-4.2	-3.9	-0.7	0.2

Notes: a) 1991-95; b) 1995-99; c) 1995-98; d) Refers to total finance (65-67); e) Refers to total non-market services (75-99); f) Refers to Trade (50-52) as a whole.

PART II

4. What are Advances in Knowledge Doing to the Large Industrial Firm in the 'New Economy'?*

Keith Pavitt

1. WHITHER THE LARGE MANUFACTURING FIRM?

Contemporary theories of the firm (e.g. resource-based, dynamic competencies) typically take as the object of their enquiry the large, integrated and diversifying manufacturing firm, as described by Chandler (1977) and Penrose (1995). In this chapter, I shall argue that its nature and development have been strongly conditioned by the two characteristics of the production of technological knowledge since the industrial revolution. The first – clearly identified by Adam Smith (Pavitt, 1998) – is the continuous increase in specialization in both the production of artefacts, and in the production of knowledge on which they are based. The second is the appearance of periodic waves of major innovations based on rapid improvements in specific technologies. It is in the context of these two trends that the effects on industrial practice and on organization of the latest of the periodic radical changes in Information and Communications Technology (ICT) can best be judged.

The large integrated manufacturing firm emerged through the exploitation of economies of scale and speed in production, and the reduced transport costs, both made possible by the availability of the new power sources (e.g. coal, electricity, oil) and better materials (e.g. iron and steel). Increasing size led to increasing functional specialization with the firm, and the need for co-ordinated planning between material purchase, production and marketing. Later, advances in specialized mechanical, chemical and electrical knowledge opened up major new opportunities for product innovation, not only in machinery and parts, but also in consumer goods, transportation, materials and communications. The development of these new products required the integration of partly tacit knowledge across disciplines (e.g. purely mechanical products became electro-mechanical), and between the R&D and other functions within the firm. As a consequence, the dominant sources of technical change in the 20th century have been large manufacturing firms with in-house R&D labs, combined with a myriad of small firms providing specialized capital goods.

However, established manufacturing firms have begun to have a rough ride over the past twenty years in dealing with emerging technological opportunities. I shall explore the reasons why, and suggest some further causes of concern for the future. In section 2, I shall argue that Penrose's exploration of the implications of knowledge-based product diversification needs to be linked to those of increasing specialization in the production of knowledge. In section 3, I shall further argue that Chandler's explanations of the emergence of mass production need to be linked to continuing processes of technological convergence and vertical disintegration. I therefore conclude in section 4 that, in addition to being subject to greater disruption, the large industrial firm will increasingly outsource elements of product design and manufacture. In section 5, I speculate that the core activities of the industrial firm will in future shift towards systems design and integration, and to advanced uses of ICT; manufacturing will increasingly be located in developing countries.

2. PENROSE: PRODUCT DIVERSIFICATION AND KNOWLEDGE SPECIALIZATION

2.1 Product Diversification

Penrose (1959) identified a sound corporate base of technological knowledge as a major source of product diversification and growth. As an example, she showed that the capabilities of General Motors in the technologies underlying automobiles – mass production and power systems – were major vectors of the company's diversification into markets for aircraft and diesel engines, refrigerators and other household equipment. In her study of the Hercules Powder Company (1960), she also illustrated in depth the story of a typical chemical company diversifying on the basis of its mastery of organic chemistry. Similar stories can be told of electrical and electronic companies diversifying on the basis of their competencies in electromagnetism and radio waves (Reich, 1985), and now of telecommunications equipment and software companies by exploiting Moore's Law and digital compression.[1] Experience tells us that not all design and production competencies enable product diversification: the core competence of steel firms turns out to be ... making steel. Nonetheless, pervasive technologies emerge periodically from knowledge-based, step-jump improvements in the performance of key productive inputs (e.g. materials, energy, transportation, machinery, information) that have potential applications in all sectors (Freeman and Louçã, 2001). Firms developing and exploiting these opportunities have diversified and grown on the basis of an ever-widening range of applications, just as Penrose described.

The continuing importance of knowledge-based product diversification has been matched by the continuing importance of specific managerial tasks, some of which were identified by Penrose:

- Integrating learning activities across specialized corporate functions, and particularly between R&D and marketing (Burns and Stalker, 1961)
- Dealing with an inevitably imperfect M-form organization, given the impossibility of neatly decomposing technological activities with pervasive applications into specific product divisions (Tunzelmann, 1995)
- Coping with the difficulty of *ex ante* evaluation of R&D activities, given the high levels of technical and market uncertainties (Mansfield et al., 1972; Schnaars and Berenson, 1986). As a consequence, firms tend to oscillate between judgement-based systems (which fail because it is difficult to distinguish between good judgement and luck), and rule-based systems (which fail because rules inevitably simplify, and may miss critically important variables)
- Keeping technological practice ahead (but not too far ahead) of underlying scientific theory, by developing new engineering disciplines – most recently, software engineering, and by exploiting major scientific breakthroughs – most recently, in molecular biology (Rosenberg and Nelson, 1994; Constant, 2000).[2]

2.2 The Specialized and Organizational Nature of Knowledge-Based Entrepreneurship

However, this is only part of the story. Writing in the 1950s, when the dominant sources of new technology were still the large established chemical companies, Penrose – like the late Schumpeter – saw the entrepreneurial function as a relatively tidy and manageable process. However, the experience of the past twenty years and the emergence of ICT suggest otherwise.

First, entrepreneurship in practice cannot be separated from the specialized knowledge on which it is based. The occupants of both Silicon Valley and an Arab street market are entrepreneurial, but they know about, develop and sell different things. Similarly, there are differences in entrepreneurship between chemical firms and electronic firms. Both are knowledge-based and both typically have R&D departments, but they exploit different bodies of specialized knowledge, and explore new knowledge in different directions. Knowledge-based entrepreneurship is not therefore a general-purpose management skill that can be deployed in all places at all times.

Second, the major new opportunities for knowledge-based entrepreneurship emerge not from in-house 'managerial slack' but from major technological breakthroughs. As Mowery and Rosenberg (1989) amongst others have shown, these breakthroughs emerge increasingly from formal, corporate R&D activities which themselves are increasingly based on publicly funded research in the universities, and on the related training of high-level specialists. For example, entrepreneurial opportunities in the modern chemical industry emerged from fundamental breakthroughs in organic chemistry, and today's major fields of entrepreneurial opportunity – ICT and biotechnology – are based on discoveries that originally won Nobel Prizes: the transistor effect and DNA. Corporate entrepreneurship depends on access to academic resources, particularly high quality research in new disciplines (Rosenberg, 2000). It is therefore increasingly specific to field, time and place.

Third, entrepreneurship involves assimilating specialized professionals from new fields and functions, sometimes at the expense of established ones, especially in periods of step-jump improvements in technological opportunity. It involves orchestrating and changing the balance between specialized professionals, whose tribal nature had already been recognized by Adam Smith (1776). For this reason, a reading of Machiavelli[3] may be relevant, and knowledge-based firms will continue to live in turbulent times.

The dynamics of technology have therefore been disruptive to the internal organization and routines of large, established firms. Some analysts go so far as to argue that such firms are intrinsically incapable of coping with radical new technologies, and that new entrants always do better (Utterback, 1993). The empirical evidence suggests that there is no universal law preventing large firms from exploiting new technologies (Methe et al., 1996), but that – over the longer term – major new technologies often lead to major new entrants (Louçã and Mendonça, 2001). In the past, the conventional explanation of such processes of 'creative destruction' was the inability of large established firms to master radically new fields of technological knowledge (e.g. from the wooden horse-drawn carriage to the metal railway). But contemporary evidence shows that large firms have learned how to evaluate and assimilate new fields of knowledge through their corporate R&D departments (Mowery and Rosenberg, 1989; Granstrand et al., 1997).

The causes of failure are to be sought instead in the difficulties that large firms have in coping with the *organizational* implications of major technological changes. These implications are often difficult to identify at the time. With the benefit of hindsight in the examination of several cases, we can group them as follows.

• The unexpected emergence of new products and customers, with which established companies are unfamiliar. An example of the former is the personal computer in the late 1970s, and of the latter are the computer firms and military as customers for semi-conductors in the 1950s. In this context, C. Christensen (1997) has spoken of 'disruptive technologies' and Levinthal (1998) of processes of 'speciation'.

- Mismatches between the level of innovative opportunities and corporate routines for allocating resources to innovative activities. Thus, the UK-based firm GEC changed over a 25-year period from heavy engagement in high-tech electronics to becoming a routine military arsenal, through the rigorous adherence in its investments to those with short-term profitability, and a refusal to spend money on exploring emerging technological options (Aris, 1998).
- Changes (particularly reductions) in the costs of experimentation, requiring adjustments in routines for decision-making (or processes of learning) in product development. See, for example, the difficulties of IBM in coping organizationally with the personal computer, given its experience in designing, making and selling complex and costly mainframe computers.
- The emergence of major opportunities based on new specialized competencies, threatening to those with established competencies that have been successful in the past, that are powerfully entrenched at present, and that are potentially obsolete in future. Examples include 'mainframers' versus PC nerds in computing firms, and biologists versus chemists in pharmaceutical firms. See also the story of Polaroid's failure to benefit from its early lead in digital imaging (Tripsas and Gavetti, 2000). Leonard-Barton (1995) has described how 'core competencies' can become 'core rigidities'. More recently, Scarbrough and Swan (2001) have described how IT professionals have colonized the 'knowledge management' movement. 'New' is not always 'better'. Either way, novelty engenders conflict.

2.3 Coping with Increasing Knowledge Specialization: Modular Product Designs and Systems Integration

In the Foreword to the third edition of her book, written in 1995, Edith Penrose identified both the growth of knowledge and of networking as major features of the modern corporation. Increasing specialization in knowledge production means that knowledge growth and networking are closely related. As early as the 1970s, G. B. Richardson (1972) argued that individual firms were not isolated but heavily networked in co-operative agreements with their suppliers, customers and other institutions. Accessing knowledge has become an important purpose of these corporate networks (Hagedoorn, 1992).

This is because products are becoming increasingly complex, embodying both an increasing number of subsystems and components, and an increasing range of fields of specialized knowledge. Increasing product (or system) complexity is one consequence of increased specialization in knowledge production, which has resulted in both better understanding of cause-effects relations, and better and cheaper methods of experimentation (Mahdi, 2003; Perkins, 2000). This in turn has reduced the costs of technological search and experimentation, and thereby enabled greater complexity in terms of the number of components, parts or molecules that can be successfully embodied in a new product or service. Developments within ICT itself are accelerating this trend: digitalization opens options for more complex systems, and simulation techniques reduce the costs of experimentation (Pavitt and Steinmueller, 2001).

Specialization in knowledge production has also increased the range of fields of knowledge that contribute to the design of each product. Compare what originally was the largely mechanical loom, with the many fields of specialized knowledge – electrical, aerodynamic, software, materials – that are now embodied in the contemporary design; or observe the contemporary automobile that must increasingly integrate plastic and other new materials, as well as electronic and software control systems. Firms are in fact widening the range of fields in which they acquire technological competencies (Granstrand et al., 1997).

However, firms designing increasingly complex products have found it increasingly difficult to master fully the advances in all the technological fields embodied in them. Hence the growing importance of modular designs, where component interfaces are standardized, and interdependencies amongst components are decoupled. This enables the outsourcing of design and production of components and subsystems, within the constraints of overall product (or system) architecture (Sanchez and Mahony, 1996; Ulrich, 1995).

However, modularity does not reduce the function of product or systems design to one of simply defining architecture, subcontracting the design and production of components, and then assembling them. In complex systems, it is also important to have the competence for systems integration: in particular, to be able to deal with unpredicted interactions between components (e.g. resonance and vibrations in mechanical systems), and uneven rates of development in the technologies underlying different components and subsystems (e.g. electronic versus mechanical control systems). This competence in systems integration comprises a capacity to design and test systems with new architectures, as well as knowledge of the technological fields underlying the outsourced components and subsystems (Brusoni et al., 2001).

3. CHANDLER: MASS MANUFACTURE AND VERTICAL DISINTEGRATION

3.1 Product Design and Manufacture

In addition to this specialization and partial disintegration in product design, there are also signs of further progress in the partial disintegration between product design and production, following a further step-jump in technology. As we have seen, the rise of the large manufacturing company since the 19th century is closely associated with the economies of scale and speed made possible by a combination of major technical innovations in materials, machines and energy sources, with the major organizational innovation that was the vertically integrated company (Chandler, 1977). When the firm was manufacturing standard commodities with relatively simple production techniques, vertical disintegration and the emergence of a specialized machine-building sector happened relatively quickly (Rosenberg, 1963). However, when advances in the technologies of machinery and transport, chemicals, and electrical and electronic products enabled the combination of economies of scale and scope (i.e. new products), disintegration became less frequent (Chandler, 1989).

As Mowery (1983) has shown for the USA, a growing proportion of industrial R&D in the 20th century was integrated within large manufacturing firms. Until about 10 years ago, business-funded R&D in all OECD countries was almost exclusively performed within manufacturing firms. Mowery explained this lack of vertical disintegration as being due to the difficulties of writing contracts for an activity whose output is uncertain and idiosyncratic. Today, this writer would place greater emphasis on the advantages of integration in co-ordinating product and process change, which requires the combination of specialized and often tacit knowledge across functional boundaries, and where accumulated experience matters.

In any event, the strongly recommended practice in innovation management has traditionally been close collaboration and feedback between product design and production operations, often involving personal contacts and exchanges to deal with tacit elements of both product design and its successful transfer to manufacture (Tidd et al., 2001). There are many stories of product designs that turned out to be technically difficult (even impossible) to manufacture, and of the importance of largely informal processes that ensure effective feedback between the design of product and process (Iansiti and Clark, 1994).

3.2 Technological Convergence and Vertical Disintegration

However, even in industries with heavy investments in product innovation, some vertical disintegration in manufacturing process innovation has been happening since the 19th century, stimulated at each stage by technological advances. Thus, Rosenberg (1963) has shown how specialized machine tool firms emerged in the 19th century, because advances in metal cutting and metal forming techniques led to technological convergence in operations that were common to a number of manufacturing processes (e.g. boring accurate circular holes in metal was common to the making of both small arms and sewing machines). Although the skills associated with such machining operations were often craft-based and tacit, their output could be codified and standardized. The size of the market for such common operations therefore often became large enough to sustain the growth of small specialized firms designing and making the machines to perform them. Large manufacturing customers could therefore buy machines incorporating the latest improvements fed back from many users, and therefore superior to what they could do by themselves. In contemporary terms, designing and making such machines in-house no longer gave large manufacturing firms a distinctive competitive advantage.

Table 4.1 Examples of technological convergence and vertical disintegration

Underlying Technological Breakthrough	Technological Convergence	Vertical Disintegration
Metal cutting & forming	Production operations	Machine tool makers
Chemistry & metallurgy	Materials analysis & testing	Contract research
Chemical engineering	Process control	Instrument makers Plant contractors
Computing	Design Repeat operations	CAD makers Robot makers
New materials	Building prototypes	Rapid prototyping firms
ICT	Application software Production systems	KIBS* Contract manufacture

Note: * = Knowledge-Intensive Business Services.

As Table 4.1 above shows, similar processes involving technological convergence and vertical disintegration have been frequent since then. New opportunities for technological convergence have emerged from breakthroughs that have created potentially pervasive applications in production across product groups: material shaping and forming, properties of materials, continuous chemical processes, storage and manipulation of information for controlling various business functions (manufacturing operations, design).

They have led to the emergence of contract research firms specializing in materials analysis and testing (Mowery and Rosenberg, 1989), and firms making measurement and control instruments used in continuous processes, systems of computer-aided design and manufacture originally developed in the transport sectors, robots in metal manufacture, and specialized applications software and rapid prototyping in a whole range of industries. In the heavy chemical industry, vertical disintegration in production has gone further. Specialized chemical engineering firms began designing and building complete large-scale continuous production facilities for a number of products, based on technological convergence emerging from improved understanding of chemical processes (Arora and Gambardella, 1999; Landau and Rosenberg, 1992).

3.3 Contract Manufacture and its Limits

Recently, we have begun to see signs of a further step in the disintegration of product design from subsequent manufacture. Unlike most of the cases in Table 4.1 above, the technological convergence is not between similar elements of manufacturing operations in different industries, but between the total manufacture of different product designs in the same industry. Sturgeon (2002) has documented the rise of contract manufacturing in electronics: namely, firms that take over electronic product designs from other firms, and do the detailed engineering and manufacture. He reports that contract manufacturing is also growing in other industries.[4] He stresses the importance of the development of

> the modular production network, because distinct breaks in the value chain tend to form at points where information regarding product specifications can be highly formal ... within functionally specialized value chain nodes activities tend to be highly integrated and based on tacit linkages. Between these nodes, however, linkages are achieved by the transfer of codified information.

In addition to Sturgeon (2002), a number of other scholars (such as Balconi, 2002; D'Adderio, 2001; Zuboff, 1988) have analysed the nature and effects of advances in modularity and in ICT on the links between product design and manufacture. Their studies suggest that ICT has increased technological convergence in two dimensions:

- First, it has radically reduced the costs of search to identify standard components and sub-subsystems to undertake a specified function within a product architecture.
- Second, it has progressively increased the standardization of production through automation (see Sturgeon, 2002), and through the widening adoption of standard software tools: for example, integrated enterprise software systems like Product Development Manager (PDM) and Enterprise Resource Planning (ERP) (D'Adderio, 2002).

In addition, advances in ICT have reduced the risks of vertical disintegration to the product-designing firm.

- Simulation technology and modelling have increased the possibilities of 'learning before doing' (Pisano, 1997), thereby reducing the risks of 'bugs' and technical difficulties in subsequent production (D'Adderio, 2001).
- ICT has also increased the ease with which digitized information about new products can be transferred from product designer to producer. This both reduces ambiguity, and provides a common basis for debates and agreements amongst the specialized groups involved in product development and production.
- ICT now enables product designers to monitor subsequent production instantaneously.

However, in spite of these advances, ICT has yet to achieve completely the conditions for a modular production system, as specified by Sturgeon. Linkages between product design and production are not like activating the <print> instruction on a PC, after writing a paper. They are not based entirely on codified information. Products are more difficult to formalize than language, and product designers are typically dealing with products considerably more complex and technically demanding than the car trailers and desks that Ulrich (1995) uses as exemplars for modularity.

As D'Adderio (2001) has shown, the process of digitizing a product's characteristics by its designers involves simplification; digitized models must subsequently be re-actualized by the groups responsible for production. This therefore still requires personal contacts and the transfer of tacit knowledge. An equivalent division of labour in knowledge thus does not mirror the division of labour in production: product designers still have to know something about production, and producers about product design. Although vertically disintegrated, producers and designers are 'relational' and not 'arm's length', which is no different from the earlier disintegration between product designers and makers of specialized capital goods (Lundvall, 1988). Thus the complete disintegration of product design and manufacture has not yet been achieved, but recent advances in modularity and ICT have apparently shifted the balance in its favour in some industries. Amongst other things, this is reflected in the growth in markets for technology (Arora et al., 2001).

4. CONCLUSIONS: PENROSE AND CHANDLER'S INDUSTRIAL FIRM IN THE 21ST CENTURY

Many of the key characteristics of large industrial firms identified by Penrose and Chandler will probably continue into the 21st century: most notably, product diversification based on rapidly advancing fields of knowledge, and physical economies of scale and throughput in manufacturing. However, the continuing increase in specialization in the production of knowledge, coupled with increasing complexity in physical artefacts and their links with fields of knowledge, are leading to at least three significant shifts in the stability and the nature of the large industrial firm.

First, entrepreneurship turns out not to be a corporate resource that is easily identified and managed. Major new opportunities based on rapid advances in ICT technology have proved disruptive, because they have increased uncertainty and have created conflict. As the recent experiences of AOL-Time-Warner and of Vivendi show, profitable directions of knowledge-based product diversification are not obvious at the outset.[5] In addition, they have also threatened established organizational practices and markets, and required the assimilation of new, professionally specialized 'tribes'. As a consequence, some – but not all – established firms have failed. But can we expect more of the same in the future? Or have the major organizational and market impacts of ICT been identified and worked through? This is very difficult to predict. Suffice to say that the major advances in biotechnology have not yet triggered similar waves of disruption in the chemical and pharmaceutical industries.

Second, as a consequence of increasing specialization in knowledge production, firms have progressively become more dependent on external resources for useful knowledge. The exploitation of major new technological opportunities depends less on internal 'management slack' than on access to knowledge about major technological breakthroughs, often originating in universities. In addition, the increasing complexity of products, and of the fields of knowledge on which they draw, has led firms towards modular product designs, where the design and manufacture of components and subsystems is sub-contracted to specialized firms within the constraints of an overall system architecture. There is also evidence in some industries of further disintegration between product design and manufacture, through the combined effects of modular designs and advances in ICT-related management tools. This is leading to a division of labour between firms specializing in manufacture and those in systems design and integration.

To sum up, the large industrial firm in the future will have evolved from the one described by Penrose and Chandler. It could suffer greater disruption in its markets, organization and technological competencies. And it almost certainly will see greater modularity and disintegration in product design and related manufacture. The economic pressures for such disintegration are considerable. For example, Carpenter et al. (2002) have recently shown how higher priority for shareholder value has increased the outsourcing of manufacture in optical networks. Brusoni and Prencipe (2001) identify a variety of economic factors behind increases in outsourcing design and production in aircraft engines and chemical plants: spiralling development costs, pressure from developing countries, reduced defence budgets, shrinking profit margins, and the advantages of specialization. And in a Special Report on car manufacturing, *The Economist* (2002b) points to market saturation, product differentiation and uncertainty of customer reactions as the factors behind the growing experimentation with modular components and subsystems, and with radically new product architectures.

But it is doubtful that we are moving towards a complete, arm's-length division of labour, with product designers defining modular product architectures and functions in anticipation of customers' needs, subcontracting firms designing components and subsystems within the constraints of the overall product architecture, and manufacturing firms making the components and subsystems. The division of labour within product development, and between product development and manufacture will probably grow, but will be incomplete. For some products, associated manufacture will remain a strategic resource. For firms that are outsourcing production, the effective exchange and integration of specialized knowledge with producers will require them to maintain and develop technological competencies beyond what they make themselves. In particular, firms specializing in product development and systems integration will need to maintain competencies in related manufacture, components and subsystems, and in evolving applications of ICT in design, logistics, production, customer support, and co-ordination and control.

5. SPECULATIONS: SYSTEMS INTEGRATION REPLACES MANUFACTURING AS THE DOMINANT ACTIVITY IN INDUSTRIAL FIRMS

We may speculate that these trends reflect a gradual shift in the opportunities for major technical changes from the processing of materials into products, towards the processing of information into services. The locus of competition through innovation in leading companies is shifting from discrete physical product and process innovations associated with manufacturing, to innovations in the design, development, integration and marketing of increasingly complex products and systems.

As foreseen by Drucker (2001),[6] this could lead to an increasing division of labour between systems integration firms and manufacturing firms. It could also reinforce the shift of manufacturing towards certain lower-wage countries that have invested in basic education and ICT infrastructure (Ernst, 2002; Ernst and Kim, 2002). However, the high-skilled 'services' in which the high-wage countries specialize would not be 'immaterial' in the conventional sense. They would comprise high-tech machines (processing information rather than materials), mastery of the knowledge underlying manufacturing, and a capacity for designing, integrating and supporting complex physical systems, including simulations and modelling products and processes, production and logistic operations, monitoring and control, and customer support: in other words, the skilled activities that manufacturing firms undertake, except manufacturing itself.

The fact that most of these activities are defined as 'services' often confuses rather than clarifies. They are instead the prolongation of the industrial system into a period of growing specialization and complexity, and of growing capacities to store, transmit and manipulate information. High wage countries may indeed find themselves specializing increasingly in 'services' – not as an alternative to manufacturing activities; rather, they may specialize in the skill-intensive components within them. The Visible Hand of manufacturing will not become invisible (Langlois, 2001), but continue to exploit economies of physical scale, speed and scope. At the same time, the Visible Brain of product design and systems integration could become a dominant form of business organization in the world's advanced countries.

NOTES

*   This chapter is based on the Welcome Lecture on 6 June, 2002, at the DRUID Summer Conference on *Industrial Dynamics of the New and Old Economy – who is embracing whom?* It also draws heavily on:

'Can the large Penrosian firm cope with the dynamics of technology?', SPRU Electronic Working Paper, No. 68. www.sussex.ac.uk/SPRU/publications/ imprint/sewps/sewps68.pdf.
'Are systems designers & integrators 'post-industrial' firms?', to be published in A. Prencipe, A. Davies and M. Hobday (eds), *Systems Integration and Firm Capabilities*, Oxford University Press.

1. For reviews of the evidence, see Pavitt and Steinmueller (2001).
2. For an illustration of how these two features have combined to revolutionize the practice of drug development in the pharmaceutical industry, see Nightingale (2000).
3. '... There is nothing more difficult to carry out, nor more doubtful of success, nor more dangerous to handle, than to initiate a new order of things. For the reformer has enemies in all those who profit by the old order, and only lukewarm defenders in all those who would profit by the new order ... arising partly from fear of adversaries ... and partly from the incredulity of mankind, who do not truly believe in anything new until they have actual experience of it.' Machiavelli, *The Prince*, p. 21.
4. He lists apparel and footwear, toys, data processing, offshore oil drilling, home furnishings and lighting, semiconductor fabrication, food processing, automotive parts, brewing, enterprise networking and pharmaceuticals. In addition, Prencipe (1997) has shown increases in the outsourcing of production of aircraft engine components.
5. Both companies assumed that major new opportunities would be created through the integration of the Internet with traditional media: firms, TV, newspapers and magazines. So far, the opportunities have proved illusory, largely because integration with Internet Service Providers turns out not to be a competitive alternative to the traditional methods of diffusing content. See *The Economist* (2002a).
6. See his contrasting visions of the futures of GM and Toyota (pp. 18-19).

REFERENCES

Aris, S. (1998), *Arnold Weinstock and the making of GEC*, London, UK: Aurum.
Arora, A. and A. Gambardella (1999), 'Chemicals', in D. Mowery (ed.), *US Industry in 2000: Studies in Competitive Performance*, Washington: National Academy Press.
Arora, A., A. Fosfuri and A. Gambardella (2001), *Markets for Technology: the Economics of Innovation and Corporate Strategy*, Cambridge, US: MIT Press.
Balconi, M. (2002), 'Tacitness, codification of technological knowledge and the organisation of industry', *Research Policy*, 31, 357-79.
Brusoni, S. and A. Prencipe (2001), 'Unpacking the black box of modularity: technologies, products and organisations', *Industrial and Corporate Change*, 10 (1), 179-205.
Brusoni, S., A. Prencipe and K. Pavitt (2001), 'Knowledge Specialization, Organizational Coupling, and the Boundaries of the Firm: Why Do Firms Know More Than They Make?', *Administrative Science Quarterly*, 46, 597-621.
Burns, T. and G. Stalker (1961), *The Management of Innovation*, London, UK: Tavistock (republished in 1994 by Oxford University Press).

Carpenter, M., W. Lazonick and M. O'Sullivan (2002), *Corporate Strategy and Innovative Capability in the 'New Economy': the Optical Networking Industry*, France: INSEAD.

Chandler, A. (1977), *The Visible Hand*, Cambridge, US: Belknap Press.

Chandler, A. (1989), *Scale and Scope*, Boston, US: Harvard University Press.

Christensen, C. (1997), *The Innovator's Dilemma*, Boston, US: Harvard University Press.

Constant, E. (2000), 'Recursive practice and the evolution of technological knowledge' in J. Ziman (ed.), *Technological Innovation as an Evolutionary Process*, Cambridge, UK: Cambridge University Press, 219-33.

D'Adderio, L. (2001), 'Crafting the virtual prototype: how firms integrate knowledge and capabilities across organisational boundaries', *Research Policy*, 30 (9), 1409-24.

D'Adderio, L. (2002), 'Bridging Formal Tools with Informal Practices: How Organisations Balance Flexibility and Control', Research Centre for Social Centre for Social Sciences (RCSS), University of Edinburgh.

Drucker, P. (2001), 'The next society: a survey of the near future', *The Economist*, 3 November.

The Economist (2002a), 'Who's afraid of AOL-Time-Warner?', 24 January.

The Economist (2002b), 'Incredible shrinking plants', 23 February.

Ernst, D. (2002), 'Digital Information Systems and Global Flagship Networks: How Mobile is Knowledge in the Global Network Economy', East-West Working Papers, Economics Series, No. 48, Hawaii: East-West Center.

Ernst, D. and L. Kim (2002), 'Global Production Networks, Knowledge Diffusion, and Local Capability Formation', *Research Policy*, 31 (8-9), 1417-29.

Freeman, C. and F. Louçã (2001), *As Time Goes By: From the Industrial Revolutions to the Information Revolution*, Oxford, UK: Oxford University Press.

Granstrand, O., P. Patel and K. Pavitt (1997), 'Multi-Technology Corporations: Why They Have 'Distributed' Rather Than 'Distinctive Core' Competencies', *California Management Review*, 39 (4), 8-25.

Hagedoorn, J. (1992), 'Trends and Patterns in Strategic Technology Partnering since the Early Seventies', *Review of Industrial Organisation*, 11, 601-16.

Iansiti, M. and K. Clark (1994), 'Integration and Dynamic Capability: Evidence from Product Development in Automobiles and Mainframe Computers', *Industrial and Corporate Change*, 4, 557-605.

Landau, R. and N. Rosenberg (1992), 'Successful Commercialization in the Chemical Process Industries', in N. Rosenberg, R. Landau and D. Mowery (eds), *Technology and the Wealth of Nations*, Stanford, US: Stanford University Press: 73-119.

Langlois, R. (2001), 'The vanishing hand: the modular revolution in American business', (mimeo) University of Connecticut, Richard.Langlois@Uconn. edu.

Leonard-Barton, D. (1995), *Wellsprings of Knowledge*, Boston, US: Harvard Business School Press.

Levinthal, D. (1998), 'The Slow Pace of Rapid Technological Change: Gradualism and Punctuation in Technological Change', *Industrial and Corporation Change*, 7, 217-47.

Louçã, F. and S. Mendonçã (2001), 'Steady change. The 200 largest US manufacturing firms throughout the twentieth century', www.business.auc.dk/ Druid/conferences/nw/ paper1/Louca_Mendonca.pdf.

Lundvall, B.-Å. (1988), 'Innovation as an Interactive Process: from User-producer Interaction to the National System of Innovation', in G. Dosi et al. (eds), *Technical Change and Economic Theory*, London, UK: Pinter, pp. 349-69.

Machiavelli, N. (1950 edition), *The Prince*, Modern Library College Editions, London, UK: Random House.

Mahdi, S. (2003), 'Search Strategy on Product Innovation Process: Theory and Evidence from the Evolution of Agrochemical Lead Discovery Process', *Industrial and Corporate Change* (forthcoming).

Mansfield, E., J. Rapaport, J. Schnee, S. Wagner and M. Hamburger (1972), *Research and Innovation in the Modern Corporation*, London, UK: Macmillan.

Methe, D., A. Swaminathan, and W. Mitchell (1996), 'The Underemphasized Role of Established Firms as Sources of Major Innovations', *Industrial and Corporate Change*, 5, 1181-203.

Mowery, D. (1983), 'The Relationship between Contractual and Intrafirm Forms of Industrial Research in American Manufacturing, 1900-1940', *Explorations in Economic History*, 351-74.

Mowery, D. and N. Rosenberg (1989), *Technology and the Pursuit of Economic Growth*, Cambridge, UK: Cambridge University Press.

Nightingale, P. (2000), 'Economies of Scale in Experimentation: Knowledge and Technology in Pharmaceutical R&D', *Industrial and Corporate Change*, 9, 315-59.

Pavitt, K. (1998), 'Technologies, Products and Organisation in the Innovating Firm: what Adam Smith tells us and Joseph Schumpeter doesn't', *Industrial and Corporate Change*, 7, 433-51.

Pavitt, K. and W. Steinmueller (2001), 'Technology in corporate strategy: change, continuity and the information revolution', in A. Pettigrew, H. Thomas and R. Whittington (eds), *Handbook of Strategy and Management*, London, UK: Sage Publications, pp. 344-72.

Penrose, E. (1959), *The Theory of the Growth of the Firm*, Oxford, UK: Oxford University Press.

Penrose, E. (1960), 'The Growth of the Firm – A Case Study: The Hercules Powder Company', *Business History Review*, XXXIV, 1-23.

Penrose, E. (1995), *The Theory of the Growth of the Firm*, Oxford, UK: Oxford University Press (first published in 1959).

Perkins, D. (2000), 'The evolution of adaptive form', in J. Ziman (ed.), *Technological Innovation as an Evolutionary Process*, Cambridge, UK: Cambridge University Press, 159-73.

Pisano, G. (1997), *The Development Factory*, Boston, US: Harvard University Press.

Prencipe, A. (1997), 'Technological Capabilities and Product Evolutionary Dynamics: a case study from the aero engine industry', *Research Policy*, 25, 1261-76.

Reich, L. (1985), *The Making of American Industrial Research: Science and Business at GE and Bell*, Cambridge, UK: Cambridge University Press.

Richardson, G. (1972), 'The Organisation of Industry', *Economic Journal*, 82, 883-96.

Rosenberg, N. (1963), 'Technological Change in the Machine Tool Industry, 1840-1910', *Journal of Economic History*, 23, 414-46.

Rosenberg, N. (2000), *Schumpeter and the Endogeneity of Technology*, London, UK: Routledge.

Rosenberg, N. and R. Nelson, (1994), 'American Universities and Technical Advance in Industry', *Research Policy*, 23, 323-48.

Sanchez, R. and J. T. Mahoney (1996), 'Modularity, flexibility, and knowledge management in product and organization design', *Strategic Management Journal*, 17 (Winter Special Issue), 63-76.

Scarbrough, H. and Swan, J. (2001), 'Explaining the Diffusion of Knowledge Management: The role of fashion', *British Journal of Management*, 12, 3-12.

Schnaars, S. and C. Berenson (1986), 'Growth market forecasting revisited: a look back at a look forward', *California Management Review*, 28, 71-88.

Smith, A. (1776), *The Wealth of Nations*, reprinted (1910), London, UK: Dent.

Sturgeon, T. (2002), 'Modular Production Networks: A New American Model of Industrial Organization', *Industrial and Corporate Change*, 11 (3), 451-96.

Tidd, J., J. Bessant and K. Pavitt (2001), *Managing Innovation: Integrating Technological, Market and Organizational Change* (2nd edition), Chichester, UK: Wiley.

Tripsas, M. and G. Gavetti (2000), 'Capabilities, Cognition and Inertia: Evidence from Digital Imaging', *Strategic Management Journal*, 21, 1147-61.

Tunzelmann, G.N. von (1995), *Technology and Industrial Progress: The Foundations of Economic Growth*, Aldershot, UK and Brookfield, US: Edward Elgar.

Ulrich, K. (1995), 'The Role of Product Architecture in the Manufacturing Firm', *Research Policy*, 24, 419-40.

Utterback, J. M. (1993), *Mastering the Dynamics of Innovation*, Boston US: Harvard Business School Press.

Zuboff, S. (1988), *In the Age of the Smart Machine: The Future of Work and Power*, Oxford, UK: Heinemann.

5. News Out of the Old: The Evolving Technological Incoherence of the World's Largest Companies

Sandro Mendonça[1]

1. INTRODUCTION

Large established companies from a variety of industrial sectors typically show a highly diversified knowledge base. A number of authors have found that this phenomenon can be measured using several technological indicators such as educational data on engineering backgrounds and patent applications (Granstrand and Sjölander, 1990; Patel and Pavitt, 1994). The interesting feature of this trend is that companies invest to acquire competence in areas that are unrelated to their production specialization in the market. However, this paradoxical empirical pattern is more easily observed than explained. Recently, some explanations have been put forward; one of which is that large innovative firms need to internalize many different branches of engineering knowledge in order to cope with uneven rates of development in the components they rely on (Brusoni et al., 2001).

This work draws on the insights of the multi-technology corporation literature (e.g. Granstrand et al., 1997) and attempts to complement previous findings with a focus on the dynamic features of technological diversification. The chapter has two main goals: to draw a map of the rate and direction of technological diversification and, on that basis, to nourish a tentative discussion of the forces behind the evolving profile of multi-technology firms. In order to do this, we use patent counts and classifications based on the SPRU database for nearly 500 of the world's largest innovating companies from 1980 to 1996, as ranked by sales revenues.

Large companies exhibit significant command of technologies unrelated to the actual making of their principal product lines, i.e., they reveal a degree of technological diversity or 'incoherence' as it is labelled thorughout this chapter. Having underlined this contemporary stylized fact, we shall be concerned with the existence of broad changes in the rate and direction of technological diversification across and within industries. We find evidence of an emergent reorganization in corporate technological portfolios. Although the extent to which companies patent outside their core technical fields has remained stable, or has even decreased slightly, the composition of the in-house technological mix appears to have changed considerably over a period of less than two decades.

The technologies attracting the diversification movement in corporate capabilities, as revealed by patents, have increasingly become information and communication technologies (ICT), new materials and drugs and bioengineering. This is not entirely surprising since these technologies are commonly regarded as 'generic technologies' or 'general-purpose technologies'. However, this tendency coincides with a remarkable regularity: for these three technology groups, the growth in patents was consistently higher for non-specialist sectors than for specialist sectors.

Taken together, these findings can be interpreted as evidence that 'new economy' technology fields gained weight against 'older' technologies, like the chemicals and mechanical fields, within the large established companies of the 'old economy'. The observed patent regularities raise other issues. In particular, they could provide a useful perspective to an ongoing debate on whether the rise of new technologies has been associated with the substitution of or, on the contrary, complementarity with older technologies. While there is considerable inter-industry diversity, the pattern of growth in ICT, materials and drugs and bioengineering patent groups seems to suggest that there is room for both stories.

What is the meaning of this set of changes? On a macroscopic perspective we suggest these developments can be understood as an expression of an ongoing technological revolution in the neo-Schumpeterian sense of Freeman and Louçã (2001). As this chapter has a more microscopic perspective, we concentrate on the discussion of the strategic rationale behind the dynamics of diversification in the corporate knowledge base. At this stage we offer two intertwined hypotheses that fit the observations.

The chapter begins by addressing the empirical and conceptual contributions of the literature on technological diversification. Section 3 describes the data set and considers the methodological conditions necessary for a prudent use of patents as indicators of technological capabilities. Section 4 then reports on the analysis of our sample, which constitutes the core of the chapter. Section 5 critically assesses the empirical results, discusses implications for technology management and suggests some unsettled questions for innovation studies. The last section, section 6, forms the conclusion.

2. THE CORPORATE TECHNOLOGY MIX

2.1 The Case of Multi-Technology Firms

The emergence of the large innovative firm, as a fundamental institution of capitalism, is a phenomenon of the 1870s and onwards. Having matured by the 1920s, big business organizations continued to develop throughout the twentieth century and some 'early movers' still continue to play an important role in global markets today, e.g., Ford, Bayer, Shell, etc. (Chandler and Daems, 1980). An enduring characteristic of these modern industrial corporations is the strategy of multi-product lines. This stable corporate facet has also been associated with a 'non-random (coherent) distribution of product portfolios inside firms, and the relative stability in the composition of firm's product portfolios over the long run' (Dosi et al., 1992:185).

Another remarkable characteristic of large companies is the wide variety of technologies that is nurtured within them. Evidence indicates that this was not always the case. As the twentieth century went by, the corporate knowledge base became more complex, so that contemporary giants operate in a broader range of technological areas (Fai and Cantwell, 1999). This seems to suggest that the multi-technology corporation can be seen as a new organizational subspecies of late twentieth century capitalism. Today a company like Ford contributes to the advancement of semiconductors, chemicals and materials, but does not sell computers or raw materials for other companies (Granstrand et al., 1997). Likewise, tyre manufacturers are not the leading sources of polymer science, but they clearly command cutting-edge expertise in the corresponding patent classes (Acha and Brusoni, 2002). We are, therefore, led to think in terms of profiles of competencies shared on average by given industries, i.e. the varying levels of commitment and revealed advantage in a range of technological fields (Patel and Pavitt, 1997).

A crucial lesson that emerges from such an insight is that the notion of the multi-technology corporation must be set apart from that of the multi-product corporation. To use the words of Pavitt (1998a: xiv), '(t)he main analytical and policy conclusion is that we should not confuse technologies with products.' Empirical research indeed allows us to say that contemporary big business institutions exhibit a much broader portfolio of technologies or competencies than of products, i.e., they know more than they do (Brusoni et al., 2001). This suggests the existence of differences between the processes of productive and cognitive division of labour (Pavitt, 1998b).

The product and technology dimensions are distinct, but nevertheless, related. A paradigmatic expression of this connection is product evolution towards technological complexity. This has been the case of the iconic artefact of the 1990s, the mobile phone. The number of sub-technologies involved in one case of Ericsson handsets rose from 17 to 29 narrow patent classes from the early to the late 1980s (Grandstrand and Sjölander, 1992). Diversification was used in Swedish, Japanese and US companies to improve the degree of sophistication of many types of products in very specific classes (Granstrand, 1999). Thus, the number of new combinations made possible by the technological diversification trend has coincided and been reinforced by the tendency towards more complex products and systems.

Another aspect emphasized by Gambardella and Torrisi (1998) is that business diversification might also impair sales or profit performance due to exogenous factors, namely the difficulties of putting in place the necessary downstream assets and capabilities that are required for commercialization. This is the case with the electronics industry, where firms are narrowing the range of products while extending the range of ICTs in their knowledge base.

It should also be kept in mind that multi-technology profiles are not exclusive to the so-called knowledge economy or 'high-tech' sectors, those industries with a high R&D to sales ratio. For instance, there is evidence that industries like food processing have been developing new technological fields together with the extension of its more traditional technologies:

> This industry has been dominated through most of its historical development in the
> industrial era by two main technological fields: machinery and chemicals (the latter
> often working through machinery, e.g., in refrigeration). Over the past two decades,
> these fields have been added in significant ways by newer technological fields,
> including advanced instrumentation (lasers, etc), electronics, biotechnology, phar-
> maceuticals, advanced materials (especially in packaging), and so on. (von Tunzel-
> mann, 1998: 232)

2.2 The Dynamics of Technological Diversification

Here we focus not on why firms diversify their product offerings, but on how their technology portfolios evolved during the 1980s and 1990s. We provocatively borrow and adapt the phrase 'corporate coherence' introduced by Dosi et al. (1992) to emphasize the often enigmatic amplitude and composition of the corporate knowledge base. One starting point is that even if the composition of their product portfolios is 'coherent', as argued by Dosi et al. (1992), that does not mean that companies diversify into 'related' technological areas. Instead, different levels of knowledge are developed and maintained across different areas of interest not strictly related to the productive operations of firms. It is in this sense that we are interested in 'technological incoherence'. We propose to trace its evolution across industries as a possible way to learn about its underlying micro-motives and strategic rationale.

The way in which technologies change their relative importance in companies' knowledge portfolios is an aspect that still gives us considerable room to expand our understanding of the multi-technology phenomena. The data constraint is traditionally severe in this regard, both because it is a recent phenomenon for which data is scarce and because it is difficult to make inter-temporal comparisons using technology indicators. The aim of this chapter is precisely to contribute to the body of empirical papers analysing change in corporate technological diversification or incoherence.

It is also worth emphasizing the boundaries between what we are and are not researching. Indeed, by referring to the notion of coherence in the context of technological competencies, we are adopting a substantive meaning that is similar to the approach advocated by Foss and Christensen's (2001) use of the term. In an applied paper, Christensen (2000) refers to coherence as an integrated process of generating and exploiting complementarities among innovative assets and learning activities. Also partially building on the resource-based approach, Teece and Pisano (1994) use the term 'dynamic capabilities' to refer to the strategic integration and adaptation of skills in a shifting environment, a key managerial ability for sustaining competitive advantage. Like them, we are concerned with the dynamic properties of technology economics and management. However, it should be made clear that we are not discussing the issue of technological coherence at the same ontological level, i.e. we do not provide an analysis of the dynamics of firm assets for technological innovation in the context of resource-based or competence perspectives. Given the limited scope of this chapter, and because the empirical material used does not allow us to carry out such in-depth inquiry, the notion of capabilities is more instrumentally defined, as explained in the methodology section.

Theoretical and empirical research has frequently made the case that path-dependence should be expected in the accumulation of competencies. Either due to the fields of knowledge traditionally involved in manufacturing or due to the increasing complexity in coping with technological and organizational variables, this view argues that localized learning strongly constrains the directions of diversification (Patel and Pavitt, 1997; von Tunzelmann, 1998). In a nutshell, the persistence of stable and industry-specific technological profiles is to be explained by the accumulation of capabilities in the conceptual framework of learning-by-doing and investments in R&D and human capital. The corollary is the predominance of creative accumulation over creative destruction, i.e. new capabilities link with older ones in a complementary and enhancing fashion (Granstrand, 1998; Pavitt, 1998).

Recent research conspires, nevertheless, to complicate this picture of smooth and incremental change. Utilizing patent data from the Reading University database, Fai and von Tunzelmann (2001a) confirm that industry-specific competencies have endured throughout the last century and that differences in overall technological profiles remain quite distinct. Surprisingly enough, they find much stronger evidence of convergence in the direction of growing technologies across industries. In a related paper (Fai and von Tunzelmann, 2001b), the same authors argued that the range of corporate technological diversification changes over time and that this is due to the advent of new opportunities created on the basis of new emerging technologies. Coupled with the convergence in corporate technological diversification, Cantwell and his colleagues (Cantwell and Santangelo, 1999; Cantwell and Noonan, 2001) report a rising degree of inter-relatedness and co-patenting between formerly disconnected fields of technology. The authors above offer the common view that opportunities emerging outside core technological capabilities mean that large firms are obliged to move outside their typical domains of expertise, i.e., those more closely related to what they manufacture.

Interpreted in the context of the diffusion of new technological paradigms these patterns suggest the multi-technology phenomenon might have a broader explanation. In another paper, in which this author has specifically examined the tendency among large companies from all industries to patent in ICT, it was found that ICT patenting in non-ICT industries clearly intensified after 1980 as compared with other technologies (Mendonça, 2002). As in Fai and von Tunzelmann's (2001a, 2001b) empirical papers, this was taken as an indication that, in spite of the stability of diversified patent portfolios, something new is happening in the corporation's knowledge base. Although technological diversification is uneven across industries, the changes in corporate capabilities shows signs of convergence. Namely, in spite of the stability and industry-specificity of technological profiles, aggregate corporate behaviour reveals a broad and increasing attraction towards ICT, biotechnology and new materials in the last two decades of the last century. An implication is that technology diversification can be related to the concept of long waves of techno-economic change and to studies characterizing ICT as a core input or a general-purpose technology (Freeman and Louçã, 2001).

Paraphrasing a famous phrase of George Orwell: some technologies are more equal than others. Technologies are not alike in term of opportunities for future development and potential for interrelation with existing technologies. Long and medium-term changes in patenting can be related to changes in the importance of specific technologies for complex physical products and, therefore, for coping with the challenges of competition in increasingly sophisticated markets. We will explore this hypothesis in the context of the results of our empirical section.

In order to pursue this line of research, this chapter will give an account of the technology families that drove technological diversification in the period under analysis. We will contrast the changes in the most dynamic technologies with the changes in the technologies that lost share in the patent portfolio of multi-technology companies in order to assess the destructive and/or complementary character of these changes. Differences between industrial sectors will be highlighted. From the examination of the sectoral and technological shifts we will gather material for discussing the rationale(s) behind the underlying micro behaviour. In the next section, we present the methodology for our enquiry.

3. DATA AND METHODOLOGY

3.1 The Database

Technological and sectoral evolution are discussed utilizing data extracted from the SPRU database. For the years 1980-85, 1985-90 and 1991-96 we have snapshots of accumulated patent counts broken down by 14 industries and 34 patent classes. This database contains more than half a million patents granted in the US for 463 of the largest US, European and Japanese companies distributed according to principal product group. Patents come already assigned to industries; therefore, we cannot perform intra-industry analysis because the patent database ignores the profiles of individual companies.

All patents are assigned one of 34 individual technological fields as well as one industry, that of the applicant company, following information provided by the US patent office. This database represents a huge effort of consolidation of 4500 subsidiaries and divisions carried out in the SPRU since the mid-1980s. Different assignee names, kept or bought by the 463 firms up to 1992, were identified using *Who Owns Whom* and attributed to their parent company.[2]

In our work with the SPRU database characteristics we have to take aboard its original technological classes. Notwithstanding this limitation, we subjected the original SPRU patent classes to our own re-categorization. Three reasons lie behind this reorganization. The first is synthesis, i.e., simplification is important because patterns emerging from 34 individual classes times 14 sectors during 3 time periods are difficult to bear in mind or even to visualize at the same time. Second, new information on unexpected patterns can be gained with a new aggregation of patent categories. Finally, the reliability of conclusions is substantially upgraded by allowing for sensitivity testing. Thus the reorganization of the patent classification allows us to gain extra operational leverage in data manipulation and to achieve a more secure and profound scrutiny of patterns. Table 5.1 presents the new technological groups while Appendix, Table 5A.1, contains the complete descriptors of individual patent classes.

Table 5.1 Technological groups

Chemicals	Fine Chem	Drugs & Bio	Materials	Mechanical	Transport	ICT	Electrical	Other
InOrChem	OrgCh	Drugs & Bio	Materials	NonElMach	VehiEngi	Telecoms	ElectrDevi	Medical
AgrCh	ChePro			SpecMach	OthTran	Semicond	ElEqup	MiscMetProd
Hydroc				MetalWEq	Aircraft	Computers	Instrumen	Metallu Pro
Bleach				AssHandApp		Image&Sou	Photog&C	Nuclear
Plastic				Mining				PowerP
ChemApp								Food&T
								TextWoodetc
								Other(weap.etc.)

Source: SPRU's technological classes re-arranged by the author.

128

The new technological categories are constructed to represent families of associated technologies. Since all classifications are imperfect conventions it is important to look at them critically. The US patent system is a classification in which patents are clustered together according to function, effect and end product, although the same patent can have several industrial uses and be related to a wider technological area. However, there are grounds to believe, as do Narin and Olivastro (1988), that it is possible to construct reasonable (re-)classifications according to criteria of technological similarity. This will only be an approximation but, in our case, the task is made easier as we build on the efforts that lead to the current SPRU database. For instance, under the ICT label we regroup technological areas that have been strongly influenced by the advent of the microchip and incorporate a strong digital element. The electrical group, on the other hand, is more difficult to put together; therefore, it is not as reliable as the former group in terms of internal consistence.

Finally, we follow Patel's (1999) table of correspondence between industries, defined by their principal product group, and 'core technical fields' (see Appendix, Table 5A.2). Although such a correspondence is never simple and straightforward, this information is precious. By measuring the proportion of patents granted outside the industries' traditional areas of technological expertise it becomes possible to assess the extent of technological diversity and changes in diversification in each industry and for the aggregate of all industries.

3.2 Interpreting Patenting Activity

The empirical section of this work attempts to capture technological capabilities through patent data. Many studies refer to capabilities or competencies as technological knowledge that is created and reproduced by organizations and among them affecting the ability of firms to innovate in certain directions rather than others (Gambardella and Malerba, 1999). However, patents are only a very imperfect and indirect measure of industrially applicable knowledge. Many authors have examined the problems of using patents as an indicator of technological activity.[3] To minimize these problems we do not treat patents as proxies for inventive output resulting from R&D investment, and thus avoid a notion of 'knowledge production function' akin to the much-abused 'linear model of innovation'. Three potential limitations must be noted in connection with this research.

Firstly, patents account for codified knowledge, whereas a main reason why firms and industries are different is due to firm-specific tacit knowledge emerging because different firms are exposed to different circumstances and learn different things differently (Nelson, 1991). A second limitation refers to the argument that patents are not a linear indicator of innovative efforts. There are different inter-firm propensities to patent among different companies with a given national patenting system, as well as differences in the patenting patterns across technologies, across industries, across countries and over time (Patel and Pavitt, 1995). Thirdly, there are epistemological difficulties in the issue of measurement of competencies; ultimately, we have access only to the behaviour of technology indicators, not to knowledge structures or the corporate mechanisms that remain underneath and constitute the real unit of analysis (Lawson, 1997). Still, in spite of all these limitations, patents constitute a precious window (however narrow) into a deeper ontological level, i.e., the potential to generate improved technical knowledge.

On the positive side, many authors agree that the US patenting system is a particularly rich source of information, identifying it as a basis for international and, to a degree, inter-temporal comparisons (Narin and Olivastro, 1988). At present, two other observations strengthen the validity of patents to assess the technological evolution of big business institutions. Firstly, 80 percent of all patents were granted to business firms in the last quarter of the twentieth century; of these, about half were granted to the world's largest innovative firms (Patel and Pavitt, 1995). Secondly, a recent survey questionnaire (Cohen, Nelson and Walsh, 2000: 13) sent to 1478 R&D labs in the US manufacturing sector suggests that patents have become more important as a protection strategy for product innovations in a growing number of industries since the early 1980s.

4. EMPIRICAL EXPLORATION

4.1 Overview of Patenting Trends

The empirical work of this chapter assesses the magnitude of change in technological profiles among the world's largest innovative firms. Let us first draw a picture of the main developments taking place in our time period.

There is a substantial increase in the absolute number of patents granted to our population of large firms over time. Companies received a total of 274,904 patents in the period 1991-96, which corresponds to a variation of 81 percent when compared with the total patent counts in 1980-85: that is, almost twice as many patents. Individual patent classes behaved quite differently. Among those classes that experienced the highest increase in patents, ICT classes figure prominently. For instance, 'semiconductors' and 'computers' were the top two classes in terms of overall growth with more than three times as many patents granted in the early !990s than in the early 1980s. At the other extreme, two classes decreased in absolute terms. The 'inorganic chemistry' and the 'hydrocarbons' classes had fewer patents in 1991-95 than in 1980-85.

Accounting for growth in individual classes can be affected by the existence of small numbers in the initial period. Regrouping classes into groups of technology can supply a sensitivity test while giving us a more robust and manageable picture of the trends. Again, ICT grows more vigorously, now clearly followed by materials technology and drugs and bioengineering, the other two groups growing beyond the average of total patenting.

This intensity of patenting can also be captured by assessing the weight of these technologies in the total stock of patents granted. The ICT technology group constitutes 29.9 percent of all patents in 1991-96, whereas in 1980-85 it was 18.8 percent. Materials grew from 3.4 percent to 3.8 percent and drugs and bioengineering from 5.2 percent to 5.5 percent of total patents. These were the only technological groups to expand their relative sizes. The rest diminished their share of the volume of patents, namely fine chemicals, mechanical technology and chemicals.

If the absolute increase in patenting can be considered as evidence of technological opportunity (Patel and Pavitt, 1994) then it is clear that this is not evenly distributed across fields. In this heterogeneous landscape, ICT, new materials and drugs and bioengineering reflect the greatest revealed technological opportunities in our time span.

4.2 Patenting outside 'Core Technical Fields'

However, what one could not necessarily expect is that the aggregate growth pattern in patents generated by technological diversification replicates the pattern described above. In other words, not only are ICT, new materials and drugs and bioengineering the most dynamic technological categories, they are also the areas where companies patent more when they patent outside their 'core technical fields'. Figure 5.1 takes all patents that companies generate outside their traditional technological areas and sorts those technological groups that recorded the highest growth between the first and last sub-periods of our time frame.

This pattern of growth occurred while the extent of technological diversification for all industries as a whole was essentially stable, or even decreasing: the proportion of patents obtained from outside core technological fields for the periods was 51.5 percent, 50.7 percent and 48.3 percent for 1980-85, 1986-90 and 1991-96 respectively. About half of the patents generated by the companies in the database come from non-specialist sectors. This confirms the multi-technology nature of the companies in our sample. Moreover, taken together with the immense attractive power revealed by the three top technologies observed above, it suggests the occurrence of a considerable change in the structure of technological diversification.

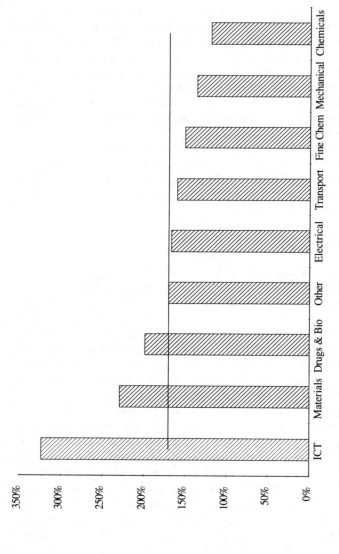

Note: Horizontal line refers to average growth; technologies are sorted by growth.

Source: Elaborations on the SPRU database.

Figure 5.1 Growth in the number of patents obtained by firms outside their core activities from 1980-85 to 1991-96

4.3 Changes in the Structure of Technological Diversification

In order to assess the evolution of technological diversification we take a look at the distribution of patents granted outside 'core technical fields' for all industries taken together and compare it across sub-periods (Table 5.2).

Note that ICT's share increases appreciably, materials grow moderately and drugs and bioengineering maintain their weight over time as overall patenting grows substantially for the world's largest companies. The ICT component of technological diversification increased 7.5 percentage points from 1980-85 up to 1991-96. Materials technology's share went up 1.6 percentage points, whereas drugs and bioengineering increased about 0.2 percent (0.88 percent in 1980-85 and 1.03 percent in 1991-96). Every other technological group decreased its relative size in total patents, except the residual category of 'other' technologies.

Now, if we consider the sequence of change in ICT share we can observe that it appears to slow down for the latest part of the period under analysis. The same is true for materials technology. In contrast, drugs and bioengineering takes on an increasing importance in technology portfolios in the sub-period 1991-96, though we cannot supply conclusive evidence of this. Another, but again weak, reinforcement of the likelihood of this emerging trend in drugs and bioengineering appears when we exclude ICT from the table for purposes of sensitivity analysis. Comparing diversification structures for different sub-periods as if ICT did not exist, the drugs and bioengineering technological group emerges as the only one increasing its relative size in the diversified patent portfolio of the average industry. While this analysis reveals that Materials technology's share grew during the 1980s, the 1990s witnessed a stabilisation of this process.

Table 5.2   The structure of technological diversification measured as the distribution of patents granted to firms outside 'core technical fields'

	1980-85	1986-90	1991-96
Chemicals	12.0	9.1	8.5
Fine Chemicals	18.0	14.5	15.6
Drugs & Bio	0.9	0.9	1.0
Materials	4.7	5.7	6.3
Mechanical	15.7	14.7	12.7
Transport	1.6	1.7	1.5
ICT	8.2	12.5	15.7
Electrical	25.5	26.0	25.2
Other	13.4	14.9	13.5
Total	100.0%	100.0%	100.0%

Source: Elaborations on the SPRU database.

4.4 ICT, Materials and Drugs and Bioengineering: the Contribution of Non-Specialist Sectors

So far our empirical exploration emphasized the uneven attractiveness of different technologies when companies patent outside their traditional competencies. The literature on technological diversification emphasizes both variety within firm as well as variety between firms. Due to the limitations of the data available we cannot go deeper than the industry level. Therefore we will be limited to applying a sectoral approach, which disregards inter-firm variability. This implies a difficulty in producing generalizations. The examination of the main features of the three most attractive patent groups offers, nevertheless, interesting insights into the process of development of technological diversification in the last two decades of the twentieth century. We will now explore the role these key technologies play in the technology portfolio of different sectors.

Those industries in which ICT patents classes do not figure as 'core technical fields' contribute consistently to about 25 percent of all ICT patents throughout the three sub-periods. This has been an impressive performance by non-specialists, since ICT patenting by specialist sectors, i.e. computers and electrical/electronic industries, exploded during this time. Indeed, the growth in the volume of ICT patents originating in non-ICT sectors was much higher than the growth in patenting in ICT sectors. The rate of variation of the ICT technology group between 1980-85 and 1991-96 was 223 percent for the non-specialist sectors, whereas for ICT specialists it was 177 percent. Meanwhile, the growth of non-ICT sectors was higher between 1980-85 and 1986-90, whereas ICT patenting grew more in ICT specialists than non-specialists between 1986-90 and 1991-96.

Additionally, while ICT industries have themselves been among those narrowing their technological scope and concentrating on their prime fields of expertise, ICTs have progressively broadened the industry base from which new patents are harvested (Mendonça, 2002). Indeed, all but the paper industry increased their patenting in ICT fields, but some industries increased more dramatically than others (see Table 5.3). These findings need to be qualified. This stylized fact is very strong but the increase in the ICT share of the non-ICT industries' portfolios was slower during the period 1986-90/1991-96.

Table 5.3   Percentage distribution in the contribution of sectors to materials patenting

	1980-85/1986-90	1986-90/1991-96	1980-85/1991-96
Non-specialists	95%	66%	123%
Specialists	61%	72%	177%

Source: Elaborations on the SPRU database.

ICT is the technological group that increased most dramatically in the average portfolio but, as could be expected and as Figure 5.2 shows, there is considerable industry variation when companies patent in ICT. ICT is important, and increasingly so, for the photography and photocopy, motor vehicles and parts, aerospace, machinery industries.[4] Another observation is that the metals and materials industries, for which ICT did not represent a large share of total patenting, are integrating that technological field in their knowledge portfolios rapidly and in a substantive way (Mendonça, 2002). An apparent implication of these findings is that cutting-edge technology capabilities, not only in utilizing, but also in generating ICT, are of key importance for an increasing number of large corporations in almost all sectors. However, it is not clear what this increasing pervasiveness in ICT activity really means. We will return to this issue in the next section.

The case of materials technology is different from ICT. Non-specialists have been the first contributors to the filling of patents in this technological category. Furthermore, the importance of the contribution of non-specialists to the total number of patents grew considerably over the time period under analysis, starting from 70 percent, then 75 percent, and reaching 81 percent in 1991-96. A similarity with the ICT case is that the growth of the contribution of non-specialists was consistently higher than the growth in materials patenting by specialists sectors as can be seen in Table 5.4. Among non-specialists, large contributors to new materials patents are the chemicals, electrical/electronics and photography and photocopy industries.[5] The greatest increases in patenting were seen in the photography and photocopy, computers and chemicals industries. Among specialist sectors, i.e., the materials, metals, paper and rubber and plastics industries, patenting performances were not distinctive.

Table 5.4   Percentage distribution in the contribution of specialists and non-specialists to materials technology patents obtained by all firms

	1980-85/1986-90	1986-90/1991-96	1980-85/1991-96
Non-specialists	57%	47%	130%
Specialists	22%	8%	32%

Source: Elaborations on the SPRU database.

Patterns detected in the drugs and bioengineering group show that specialists sectors, i.e. the pharmaceutical industry, the food, drink and tobacco industry and the chemicals industry, dominate the production of this technology with a share of about 90 percent of all patents granted. We also note that specialists' patenting growth is higher in the 1980s, whereas non-specialists perform comparatively better in the early 1990s as shown in Table 5.5. How-

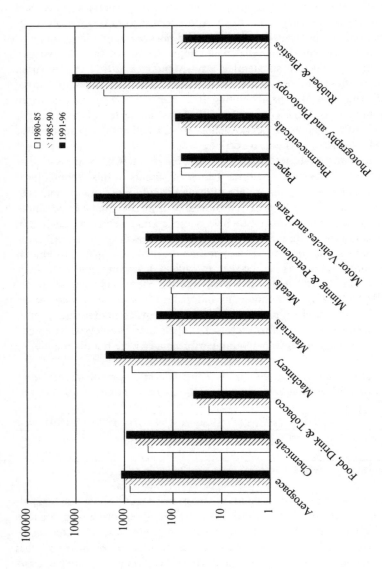

Source: Elaborations on the SPRU database.

Figure 5.2 The number of patents within ICT obtained by firms in non-specialist sectors (log-scale)

136

ever, the greatest overall increase in patenting happened among non-specialist industries.

Table 5.5 Growth in drugs and bioengineering patents obtained

	1980-85/1986-90	1986-90/1991-96	1980-85/1991-96
Non-specialists	124%	160%	199%
Specialists	131%	146%	191%

Source: Elaborations on the SPRU database.

Table 5.5 suggests furthermore that non-specialist patenting in drugs and bioengineering grew relatively more from 1980-85 to 1991-96 (last column) and seemed to have accelerated between 1986-90 and 1991-96. Non-specialist industries that contribute the most to the non-specialist sector patent are the photography and photocopy, mining and petroleum and the metals industries.[6] The highest growth rates in patenting between 1986-90 and 1991-96 were felt in mining and petroleum, photography and photocopy, metals, electrical/electronics, machinery and the computer industries.[7]

4.5 Comparing Growth and Growth Differentials between Technology Groups

What are the parallels between the rates of variation of different technological groups? Such information can indicate which technologies tend to be developed together by multi-technology firms. In Table 5.6 we correlate the growth observed in patent counts by the different industries and find several statistically significant correlations. We see that between 1980-85 and 1991-96 growth tends to be positively correlated between technological fields that have some art-based similarities, which can hide a danger of spurious correlation. However, it is interesting to note that the strongest correlations involve two of our key technologies for technological diversification: materials and fine chemicals, ICT and electrical technology. It is also interesting to see that the growth in the new field of drugs and bioengineering seems detached from possible interrelations with other technological groups.

The data suggests that the 'new economy' technologies of ICT and materials co-evolve with the old. There is no evidence that the growing technological opportunities emerging in these fields have destroyed the relevance of established fields of competence. At the same time, the accelerating growth of drugs and bioengineering appears disconnected from the rest of the technological groups, which is in line with its revolutionary character. The radical breakthroughs in the life sciences, particularly in the area of molecular biology and molecular genetics, date from the early 1970s and revolutionized the

Table 5.6 Correlation between patent growth by technological groups between 1980-85 and 1991-96

	Chemi-cals	Fine chem	Drugs & bio	Materials	Mechanical	Transport	ICT	Electrical
Chemicals	—	0.489	0.311	0.699**	0.528	0.008	0.247	0.38
Fine chem		—	0.496	0.887**	-0.04	-0.155	-0.062	0.005
Drugs & bio			—	0.303	-0.193	-0.209	-0.218	-0.224
Materials				—	0.322	-0.030	0.271	0.469
Mechanical					—	0.702**	0.373	0.629*
Transport						—	0.163	0.332
ICT							—	0.838**
Electrical								—

Notes:
* Correlation is significant at the 0.05 level (2-tailed).
** Correlation is significant at the 0.01 level (2-tailed).
Source: Elaborations on the SPRU database.

138

route to new drug discovery. Not until the early 1980s did the applications of these radical new technologies start to develop seriously (Sharp and Senker, 1999). New applications for biotechnology outside the pharmaceutical industry are becoming apparent every day, for example, in wine making or the cork industry.

Creative accumulation appears to be the result, but the story does not have to end here. Trying to detect signs of substitution tendencies between technologies is a more subtle matter. We designed a complementary analysis in which we tried to assess the way in each of the technology components of the different industries varied across time periods. For a given industrial sector the volume of patents in each technological group can grow but at different rates, so that certain components of the competence portfolio can systematically gain weight in relation to others. Basically, if a technological group tends to enlarge as a component of an industry's technological portfolio this can mean that the technology is surpassing another technological field in terms of importance in the hierarchy of competencies in which the industry is active, given that propensities to patent in different patent classes remain constant. Using the terminology of Granstrand et al. (1997) this means that a certain technology can move from being marginal or niche to become a core technological field where the industry is increasingly committed and competent. Our aim is to detect these movements.

For each industry we computed the structure of the technology portfolios and found the percentage point change between 1980-85 and 1991-96. We then correlated the changes in technological groups. We found only two statistically significant correlations, both negative. The growth in the drugs and bioengineering component of technology portfolios was found to be negatively correlated with fine chemicals technology at the 0.05 level, two-tailed test ($\rho = -0.647$). The other significant correlation, now at the 0.01 level, two-tailed, is between ICT and electrical technology ($\rho = -0.681$). In other words, the ICT and drugs and bioengineering components of technology portfolios register a rise in their share of total patents that is associated with a diminishing share of the other two older technologies. This is certainly evident in the case of ICT. As seen above, ICT and electrical patents are growing together, but the rise of ICT is coupled with the fact that electrical technology is losing ground in the average technology portfolio.

5. THE CHANGING COMPOSITION OF TECHNOLOGICAL DIVERSIFICATION

The role and importance of technologies differs across industries. There are, nevertheless, some regularities emerging in the process of technological diversification over time. The results show how ICT, new materials and drugs and bioengineering all exert a powerful influence on practically all sectors, not only on the industries that are specifically devoted to selling artefacts primarily based on them or produced with their assistance. An implication of this is that the technological diversification phenomenon has been changing. What is the nature of this change?

Over time, multi-technology companies kept changing their capabilities while still maintaining their previous heterogeneous, or incoherent, technological profiles. The literature mostly argues that technology profiles are industry-specific, but is more ambivalent as to whether there should be any process of technological convergence between industries. However, the major point that emerges from the patterns observed in the US Patent and Trademark Office data is that 'old-tech' sectors are showing signs of renewing their patent portfolios with new technologies. Our empirical exploration shows an accelerating pattern of convergence when companies from different industries patent outside their traditional fields of technological expertise. This is in line with previous findings using patents (Fai and von Tunzelmann, 2001a) and fits with the tendencies of development of the major international networks of inter-firm alliances (Hagedoorn, Giuri and Mariani, 2000). Although the period covered by the data is not sufficient to test long wave arguments, our findings support the view that the new technological paradigms gradually influence all industrial sectors (Freeman and Louçã, 2001).

We find evidence of complementarity between pairs of technology groups as they grow together and are accumulated by companies. Nevertheless, as new technologies climb up the list of technologies patented by industries when they patent outside their 'core technical fields', the question arises as to whether there is some kind of creative rearrangement of the importance of capabilities in the distributed competences of the profiles of companies. It may be that new technologies increasingly replace old ones in some key co-ordinating roles of corporate technology systems.[8] At the present level of analysis, we can only suggest very indirect ways of testing such a hypothesis.

The analysis focused primarily on technologies, rather than industries. We adopted the notion of corporate coherence used to refer to related diversification at the product level and adapted it to refer explicitly to the corporate knowledge base. We sought to develop an understanding of the behaviour of technological profiles across industries over time. The patterns show that, by the 1990s, patenting in ICT, new materials and drugs and bioengineering became an important issue for non-specialists. Results are especially strong for ICT. All industries, except the paper industry, have increased the share of ICT patents in their technology portfolio, in particular computers, the electrical/electronics sector, photograph and photocopy, machinery, metals, motor vehicles and parts and materials industries.[9] A quarter of ICT patents come from outside ICT sectors. The world's largest innovative companies have not remained passive as the ICT tide has advanced. But what explains the fact that the cluster of ICT-related technologies is not only utilized, but also increasingly developed by 'old economy' sectors? One hypothesis is that ICT has the potential to 'fuse' with many different technologies and that the resluting new technologies are likely to play a particular role in creating new areas of technological interconnectedness in the current paradigm (Cantwell and Santangelo, 2000).[10] This might have implications not only for product design and process improvement but also for the ability of the firm to manage the competitive forces it faces.

Technological capabilities are also more widespread than is usually recognized in the cases of new materials technology and drugs and bioengineering. As in the case of ICT, non-specialist sectors performed relatively better than specialists in the rate of growth of new patents during the 17 years under analysis. Again, beneath these technological trends there are industry-specific regularities that it is useful to differentiate but the basic insight is that industries augmenting the share of drugs and bioengineering in their portfolios are essentially not the same as those augmenting the share of materials technology, except photocopy and photography, electrical/electronics and the computer industries. As in the case of ICT, the generation of cutting-edge capabilities in new material and drugs and bioengineering by non-specialist companies remains a captivating stylized fact of the late twentieth century. How can we explain in detail this 'active diffusion' process of generic, revolutionary or general-purpose technologies?

In our tentative approach to this question, we are compelled to frame the phenomenon of the evolving corporate technological profiles in the context of a larger historical transition between techno-economic paradigms. Changes are rapid for such a short period and are presumably encouraged by high technological opportunities and associated profit prospects (Dalum et al., 1999). It is more difficult to speculate about the micro-motives that contribute to attract industries from their path-dependent technological trajectories. We suggest two related interpretations.

Firstly, as specific new technologies become a vital element of the innovative and productive system, the governance of that system will start to depend critically on the knowledge of the principles of the new technologies. Sophisticated knowledge and numerous patent claims emerge therefore as strategic assets that companies use with the intention of managing technological and productive relations with other players of the national (and international) system of innovation and the web of relations in which the firm is embedded. Intellectual advantage can be used to manage relations with innovative suppliers, but also with rivals, buyers, potential entrants, producers of substitute products, universities, government labs, regulators, etc. One remaining source of advantage is internal R&D activity, which enables the large innovative organization to gain a degree of autonomy in generating advanced technological capabilities in the newly important fields. In this sense, R&D can have a third face, since it can enable the company to co-ordinate its competitive and collaborative environments. The discussion around multi-technology firms as systems integrators and knowledge brokers promises interesting insights (Pavitt, Chapter 4, this volume).[11]

Secondly, one way to explain the persistent, but changing, incomplete technological coherence of established industrial giants is to probe the potential reasons as to why a variety of internal capabilities may play an important role in the reproduction of organizations. Knowledge of key technologies may be critical for large firms to sustain themselves as central knots in a web of technological and economic relations. However, long term corporate survival implies renewing technological and organizational capabilities and this means keeping technological options open as they are costly to develop and the evolution of the business environment is uncertain. The managerial implication is that tolerance of activities at the margin and willingness to experiment within the boundaries of firm is a way to keep stretching the understanding of possibilities and prevent old competence configurations becoming rigidities (de Geus, 1997). As Hodgson (1999: 26) puts it in his description of the so-called 'impurity principle', every socio-economic system relies on at least one 'structurally dissimilar subsystem' in order to function. Following these ideas, a more organizational line of research would assess the specific mechanisms by which technological incoherence or impurity facilitates corporate learning and renovation.

The last topic of this section has to be methodology. There is always the possibility that the patterns extracted from the dataset are due to spurious turbulence in the patent indicator. Recent research on patenting practice (Cohen et al., 2000; Hicks et al., 2001; Jaffe, 2000) does not point to variations on propensities to patent that would make the observed shifts in patenting a function of non-systematic behavior of companies, industries or countries. Our figures do not include software data. However, the inclusion of such data would probably only make the patterns we found for ICT even more pronounced.[12] In order to conduct a careful empirical analysis we gained extra leverage against the limitations of the database by reclassifying the patent classes into new groups. This provided a way of performing sensitivity analysis and filtering the most robust empirical regularities. Last but not least, in the appreciation of patterns of evolution, we preferred to rely mostly on descriptive statistics.

6. CONCLUSION

This work has sought to track changes in the composition of corporate techno-logical portfolios in the last two decades of the twentieth century. In doing so we discovered a period of transition in the development of the technological diversification trend. The multi-technology phenomenon is in itself probably an aspect of a broader process of change, i.e. the transition to a knowledge economy. The importance of this research lies in the fact that to understand the future organization of economic innovation we must necessarily start by understanding the changes that have occurred in the very recent past.

We presented suggestive evidence about the unevenness of technological diversification and found such diversification to be directed more towards some technologies than others throughout successive time periods. Our empir-ical study points to an increasing generation of 'new technology' patents by non-specialists, including 'old-technology'/'old-economy' companies. By the 1990s cutting-edge knowledge about ICT, drugs and bioengineering and new materials is no longer exclusive to specialist sectors. In particular, the perva-siveness of the cutting-edge ICT capabilities in non-ICT industries should not be underestimated.[13] This diffusion of key technologies suggests a link between multi-technology trends in the organization of knowledge and inno-vation and the rise of a new techno-economic paradigm.

The dissemination of capabilities in new materials and drugs and bioengi-neering across non-specialist industries is a complex phenomenon that is not easily explained. Undoubtedly, there are industry-specific regularities beneath basic technological trends that are useful to differentiate. In order to discuss this dynamic puzzle, we tentatively suggest two hypotheses worth researching in the future: the third face of R&D and the strategic rationale behind techno-logical incoherence.

The first hypothesis stresses the role of multi-technological knowledge for orchestrating a web of relationships with other actors, such as suppliers, part-ners, universities and public institutions. R&D not only constitutes a source of inventions and a basis for the absorption of technical knowledge developed elsewhere, it also brings power in socio-economic interactions. Diversified, cutting-edge and proprietary technological knowledge strengthens the compa-ny's position in strategic negotiations with other players of sectoral, national and international systems of innovation. Thus, the third face of R&D is rela-tional as it facilitates the coordination of a network of actors in the company's advantage.

The second idea is that internal diversity in capabilities can increase the chances of survival and success in a complex and ever-changing environment. A distributed set of technological competencies is also costly to integrate, both in terms of different components in new artefacts and in terms of making

multidisciplinary teams work together smoothly. There is a cost side to technological diversification that should also constitute an object for further
research. An interesting avenue for exploration is the extent to which new
organizational arrangements, or social technologies, are evolving to cope with
the dynamics of the changing corporate knowledge bases.

The existence of interrelations between different technologies is yet another challenging topic in terms of empirical analysis. Our limited incursion into
the matter suggests that some features of the process of technological diversification indicate the subordination of some technologies by others in corporate technology systems. Attempts to understand the multiple dimensions of
technological diversification are likely to continue to shed light on broader
patterns of innovation and structural transformation. Results of these efforts
will certainly appeal to managers and policy makers.

NOTES

1. The process leading to this paper is indebted to Keith Pavitt. His provocative views, useful
    advice and encouragement constituted a major source of inspiration in this work. Keith
    loved to engage in debates, my wish is that he would have found the views expressed here
    interesting enough to contend with. Nick von Tunzelmann, Ed Steinmueller, Pari Patel and
    Alfonso Gambardella provided precious comments on earlier stages of this research. I am
    grateful to the participants of the DRUID Summer Conference 2002 for their discussions.
    Jens Christensen, Keld Laursen, Peter Maskell, Dan Ward and Isabel Salavisa offered help-
    ful suggestions in the revision process. The use of SPRU's, University of Sussex, database is
    gratefully appreciated. The author is a member of DINÂMIA, a research unit of ISCTE
    University, School of Labour and Business Studies. The usual disclaimer applies.
2. A detailed description of the database can be found in Patel (1999).
3. Elsewhere (Mendonça, 2002), we have considered this group as a residual ICT family with
    the strict purpose of using it to add 'noise' to ICT and check if the patterns still hold.
4. See, for example, Griliches (1990) and Patel and Pavitt (1995).
5. These sectors explain 84 percent of non-specialist ICT patents in 1991-96.
6. These sectors explain 71 percent of non-specialist materials technology patents in 1991-96.
7. These sectors explain 71 percent of non-specialist patents in drugs and bioengineering in
    1991-96.
8. Detailed industry-by-industry analysis of patenting growth is not carried out for 1980-85
    and 1991-96 due to the existence of small numbers in the first sub-period, which distort
    inter-temporal comparisons.
9. Digitization of the engine control system and its climbing up the hierarchy of the technolog-
    ical subsystems that make a modern jet able to fly and carry its tasks represents a vivid
    example (Prencipe, 2000).
10. In the future, studies will probably need to be more careful in relation to photocopy and pho-
    tography, because a case can be made to include at least part of the industry (photography)
    in the ICT sector due to the drastic shift occurring in its knowledge base in our short time
    frame.
11. Yet another, more sociological hypothesis, is to consider the potentially facilitating role of
    ICT in the process of creation of diversified knowledge research networks. This possibility
    would lead to reflections about trans-disciplinary community formation and the dynamics of
    virtual collaboration. Although this may be an interesting avenue for further research, these
    topics lie outside the present scope of analysis.

12. A related opportunity for investigation is the connection between the increasing vertical dis-integration in the innovative stages of complex products industries and the development of markets for technology. Markets for technology are an increasingly important institution in the way innovation is organized in contemporary societies. See, for example, Arora et al. (2001).
13. This would be the case for the pharmaceuticals sector due to the innovative use of computer simulation technology (Nightingale, 2000).

REFERENCES

Acha, V. and S. Brusoni (2002), 'Knowledge on Wheels: New Lessons from the Tire Industry', paper presented at the DRUID Summer Conference 2002 on the 'Industrial Dynamics of the New and Old Economy: Who is Embracing Whom', Copenhagen, Denmark, 6-8 June 2002.

Arora, A., A. Fosfuri and A. Gambardella (2002), 'Markets for technology and their implications for corporate strategy', *Industrial and Corporate Change*, 10 (2), 419-51.

Brusoni, S., A. Prencipe and K. Pavitt (2001), 'Knowledge Specialization, Organizational Coupling and the Boundaries of the Firm: Why do Firms Know More than they Make?', *Administrative Science Quarterly*, 46, 597-621.

Cantwell, J. and C. Noonan (2001), 'Technological Relatedness and Corporate Diversification: 1890-1995', paper presented at DRUID's Nelson & Winter Conference, 12-15 July 2001, Aalborg, Denmark.

Cantwell, J. and G.D. Santangelo (2000), 'Capitalism, Profits and Innovation in the new Techno-economic Paradigm', *Journal of Evolutionary Economics*, 9, 131-57.

Chandler Jr., A.D. and H. Daems (1980), 'Introduction', in A.D. Chandler Jr. and H. Daems (eds), *Managerial Hierarchies: Comparative Perspectives on the Rise of the Modern Industrial Enterprise*, Cambridge, Mass.: Harvard University Press, pp. 1-8.

Christensen, J.F. (2000), 'Building Innovative Assets and Dynamic Coherence in Multi-technology Companies', in N.J. Foss and P. Robertson (eds), *Resources, Technology and Strategy: Explorations in the Resource-based Perspective*, London, UK: Routledge, pp. 123-52.

Cohen, W., R. Nelson and J. Walsh (2000), 'Protecting their Intellectual Assets: Appropriability Conditions and Why US Manufacturing Firms Patent (or Not)', NBER Working Paper Series 7552.

Dalum, B., C. Freeman, R. Simonetti, N. von Tunzelmann, and B. Verspagen (1999), 'Europe and the Information and Communication Technologies Revolution', in J. Fagerberg, P. Guerrieri and B. Verspagen (eds), *The Economic Challenge for Europe: Adapting to Innovation Based Growth*, Cheltenham, UK, Northampton, MA, USA: Edward Elgar.

de Geus, A. (1997), *The Living Company*, Cambridge: Harvard Business School.

Dosi, G., D. Teece and S. Winter (1992), 'Toward a Theory of Corporate Coherence: Preliminary Remarks', in G. Dosi, R. Gianneti and P.A. Toninelli (eds), *Technology and Enterprise in Historical Perspective*, Oxford, UK: Clarendon Press.

Fai, F. and J. Cantwell (1999), 'Firms as the Source of Innovation and Growth: the Evolution of Technological Competence', *Journal of Evolutionary Economics*, 9 (3), 331-66.

Fai, F. and N. von Tunzelmann (2001a), 'Industry-specific Competencies and Converging Technological Systems: Evidence from Patents', *Structural Change and Economic Dynamics*, 12, 141-70.

Fai, F. and N. von Tunzelmann (2001b), 'Scale and Scope in Technology: Large Firms 1930/1990', *Economics of Innovation and New Technology*, 10 (4), 255-88.

Foss, N.J. and J. Christensen (2001), 'A Market-process Approach to Corporate Coherence', *Managerial and Decision Economics*, 22, 213-26.

Freeman, C. and F. Louçã (2001), *As Time Goes By: From the Industrial Revolutions to the Information Revolution*, Oxford, UK: Oxford University Press.

Gambardella, A. and F. Malerba (1999), 'The Organization of Innovative Activity in Europe: Toward a Conceptual Framework', in A. Gambardella and F. Malerba (eds), *The Organization of Economic Innovation in Europe*, Cambridge: Cambridge University Press.

Gambardella, A. and S. Torrisi (1998), 'Does Technological Convergence imply Convergence in Markets?: Evidence from the Electronics Industry', *Research Policy*, 27, 445-64.

Granstrand, Ö. (1998), 'Towards a Theory of the Technology-based Firm', *Research Policy*, 27, 465-89.

Granstrand, Ö. (2000), 'The Economics of Mul-tech: A Study of Multi-technology Corporations in Japan, Sweden and the US', background paper submitted to the Dynacom project, mimeo.

Granstrand, Ö. and S. Sjölander (1990), 'Managing Innovation in Multi-technology Corporations', *Research Policy*, 19, 35-60.

Granstrand Ö. and S. Sjölander (1992), 'Internationalisation and Diversification of Multi-technology Corporations', in Ö. Granstrand, L. Håkanson and S. Sjölander (eds), *Technology Management and International Business: Internationalisation of R&D and Technology*, Chichester: John Wiley and Sons.

Granstrand, Ö., P. Patel and K. Pavitt (1997), 'Multi-technology Corporations: why they have "Distributed" rather "Distinctive core" Competencies', *California Management Review*, 39, 8-25.

Griliches, Z. (1990), 'Patent Statistics as Economic Indicators: A Survey', *Journal of Economic Literature*, 27, 1661-707.

Hagedoorn, J., P. Giuri and M. Mariani (2000), 'On Technological Diversification and Strategic Alliances', mimeo.

Hicks, D., T. Breitzman, D. Olivastro and K. Hamilton (2001), 'The Changing Composition of Innovative Activity in the US – A Portrait based on Patent Analysis', *Research Policy*, 30, 681-703.

Hodgson, G. (1999), *Economics and Utopia: Why the Learning Economy is Not the End of History*, London and New York: Routledge.

Jaffe, A.B. (2000), 'The US Patent System in Transition: Policy Innovation and the Innovation Process', *Research Policy*, 29, 531-57.

Lawson, C. (1997), 'Towards a Competence Theory of the Region', ESRC Centre for Business Research, University of Cambridge, Working Paper no. 81.

Mendonça, S. (2002), 'The ICT Component of Technological Diversification: Is there an underestimation of ICT capabilities among the world's largest companies?', SPRU Electronic Working Paper Series, no. 82.

Narin, F. and D. Olivastro (1988), 'Technology Indicators based on Patents and Patent Citations', in A. van Raam (ed.), *Handbook of Quantitative Studies of Science and Technology*, Amsterdam: North Holland, pp. 465-95.

Nelson, R (1991), 'Why Firms Differ, and How does it Matter?', *Strategic Management Journal*, Winter, 61-74.

Nightingale, P. (2000), 'Economies of Scale in Experimentation: Knowledge and Technology in Pharmaceutical R&D', *Industrial and Corporate Change*, 9, 315-59.

Patel, P. (1999), 'Measurement and Analysis of Technological Competencies of Large Firms', draft report Dynacom project.

Patel, P. and K. Pavitt (1994), 'Technological Competencies in the World's Largest Firms: Characteristics, Constraints and Scope for Managerial Choice', STEEP Discussion Paper no. 13.

Patel, P. and K. Pavitt (1995), 'Patterns of Economic Activity: Their Measurement and Interpretation', in P. Stoneman (ed.), *Handbook of Economics of Innovation and Technical Change*, Blackwell: Oxford.

Patel, P. and K. Pavitt (1997), 'The Technological Competencies of the World's Largest Firms: Complex and Path-dependent, but not much Variety', *Research Policy*, 26, 141-56.

Pavitt, K. (1998a), 'Introduction', in *Technology, Management and Systems of Innovation*, Cheltenham, UK and Northampton, MA, USA: Edward Elgar.

Pavitt, K. (1998b), 'Technologies, Products and Organisation in the Innovating Firm: What Adam Smith tells us and Joseph Schumpeter doesn't', *Industrial and Corporate Change*, 7, 433-52.

Prencipe, A. (2000), *Divide and Rule: Firm Boundaries in the Aeroengine Industry*, PhD Dissertation, SPRU, University of Sussex.

Sharp, M. and J. Senker (1999), 'European Biotechnology: Learning and Catching up', in A. Gambardella and F. Malerba (eds), *The Organization of Economic Innovation in Europe*, Cambridge: Cambridge University Press, pp. 269-302.

Teece, D. and G. Pisano (1994), 'The Dynamic Capabilities of Firms: An Introduction', *Industrial and Corporate Change*, 3, 537-56.

von Tunzelmann, G.N. (1998), 'Localized Technological Search and Multi-technology Companies', *Economics of Innovation and New Technology*, 6, 231-55.

APPENDIX

Table 5A.1   The SPRU patent classes

1. Inorganic Chemicals
2. Organic Chemicals
3. Agricultural Chemicals
4. Chemical Processes
5. Hydrocarbons, mineral oils, fuels and igniting devices
6. Bleaching Dyeing and Disinfecting
7. Drugs and Bioengineering
8. Plastic and rubber products
9. Materials (inc. glass and ceramics)
10. Food and Tobacco (processes and products)
11. Metallurgical and Metal Treatment processes
12. Apparatus for chemicals, food, glass, etc.
13. General Non-electrical Industrial Equipment
14. General Electrical Industrial Apparatus
15. Non-electrical specialized industrial equipment
16. Metallurgical and metal working equipment
17. Assembling and material handling apparatus
18. Induced Nuclear Reactions: systems and elements
19. Power Plants
20. Road vehicles and engines
21. Other transport equipment (exc. aircraft)
22. Aircraft
23. Mining and wells machinery and processes
24. Telecommunications
25. Semiconductors
26. Electrical devices and systems
27. Calculators, computers, and other office equipment
28. Image and sound equipment
29. Photography and photocopy
30. Instruments and controls
31. Miscellaneous metal products
32. Textile, clothing, leather, wood products
33. Dentistry and Surgery
34. Other – (Ammunitions and weapons, etc.)

Table 5A.2   Correspondence between industry and 'core technical fields'

Industry (i.e., principal product group)	'Core technical field'
Aerospace	Aircraft; General Non-electrical Industrial Equipment; Power Plants
Chemicals	Organic Chemicals; Agricultural Chemicals; Drugs & Bioengineering
Electrical/Electronics	Telecommunications; Semiconductors; Electrical Devices; Computers; Image & Sound Equipment
Food, Drink & Tobacco	Food & Tobacco; Chemical Processes; Drugs & Bioengineering
Machinery	General Non-electrical Industrial Equipment; Metallurgical & Metal Working Equipment; Chemical Apparatus; Vehicles Engineering; Mining Machinery; Specialized Machinery
Materials	Materials
Metals	Metallurgical & Metal Treatment Processes; Materials; Metallurgical & Metal Working Equipment
Mining & Petroleum	Organic Chemicals; Inorganic Chemicals; Mining Machinery
Motor Vehicles & Parts	Vehicles Engineering; General Non-electrical Industrial Equipment; Other transport Equipment
Paper	Materials; Specialized Machinery
Pharmaceuticals	Organic Chemicals; Drugs & Bioengineering
Photography & Photocopy	Photography & Photocopy; Instruments & Controls
Rubber & Plastics	Plastics & Rubber Products; Materials

Source: Adapted from Patel (1999).

6. Digital Information Systems and Global Flagship Networks: How Mobile is Knowledge in the Global Network Economy?

Dieter Ernst

1. INTRODUCTION

There is a widespread belief, formalized by agglomeration and innovation economists and network sociologists, that knowledge is stickier in space (i.e. less mobile) than finance or production facilities (for example, Markusen, 1996; Archibugi and Michie, 1995; Breschi and Malerba, 2001). It is argued that this is true in particular for higher-level, mostly tacit forms of 'organizational knowledge' required for learning and innovation. This chapter demonstrates that, in the emerging global network economy, we need to reconsider and amend the 'stickiness-of-knowledge' proposition.

A central argument of this chapter is that two inter-related transformations in the organization of international business may gradually reduce constraints to international knowledge diffusion : the evolution of cross-border forms of corporate networking practices, especially global flagship networks (GFNs), and the increasing use of digital information systems (DIS) to manage these networks. GFNs expand inter-firm linkages across national boundaries, increasing the need for knowledge diffusion, while DISs enhance not only information exchange, but also provide new opportunities for the sharing, and joint utilization and creation of knowledge.

A GFN covers both intra-firm and inter-firm transactions and forms of coordination: it links together the flagship's own subsidiaries, affiliates and joint ventures with its subcontractors, suppliers, service providers, as well as partners in strategic alliances. While equity ownership is not essential, network governance is distinctively asymmetric. Global corporations (the 'network flagships') construct these networks to gain quick access to skills and capabilities at lower-cost overseas locations that complement the flagships' core competencies. Furthermore, flagships need to transfer technical and managerial knowledge to local suppliers. This is necessary to upgrade the suppliers' technical and managerial skills, so that they can meet the technical specifications of the flagships. Initially this primarily involved operational skills and procedures required for routine manufacturing and services. Over time, knowledge sharing also incorporates higher-level, mostly tacit forms of 'organizational knowledge' required for learning and innovation (Ernst and Kim, 2002a). The more dispersed and complex these networks, the more demanding their coordination requirements. Knowledge sharing is the necessary glue that keeps these networks growing (Ernst, 2002a). In short, knowledge exchange penetrates new geographic areas, and the contents of knowledge become more complex.

The use of DIS as a management tool can enhance the scope for knowledge sharing among multiple network participants at distant locations. But these changes will occur only gradually, as a long-term, iterative learning process, based on search and experimentation (Ernst, forthcoming, a). The digitization of knowledge implies that it can be delivered as a service and built around open standards. This has fostered the specialization of knowledge creation, giving rise to a process of modularization, very much like earlier modularization processes in hardware manufacturing. Under the heading of 'e-business', a new generation of networking software provides a greater variety of tools for representing knowledge, including low-cost audio-visual representations. Those programs also provide flexible information systems that support not only information exchange among dispersed network nodes, but also the sharing, utilization and creation of knowledge among multiple network participants at remote locations (Jørgensen and Krogstie, 2000). New forms of remote control are emerging for manufacturing processes, quality, supply chains and customer relations. Equally important are new opportunities for the joint production across distant locations of knowledge support services (for example, software engineering and development, business process outsourcing, maintenance and support of information systems, as well as skill transfer and training).

While much of this is still at an early stage of 'trial-and-error', international business now faces a huge potential for extending knowledge exchange across organizational and national boundaries. Large bodies of theoretical and applied work exist on the individual topics of GFN, DIS, and international knowledge diffusion. Their mutual interaction however is still mostly uncharted territory. This chapter attempts to link together the above three areas of research, as a first step towards an appreciative theory, as defined in Nelson's (1995) thought-provoking review of economic growth theory.

We first introduce a stylized model of forces that drive the development of GFNs. We then look at the economic structure and peculiar characteristics of the flagship network model that fosters the new mobility of knowledge. We explore how two distinctive characteristics of GFNs that are enhanced by DIS, shape the scope for international knowledge diffusion: a rapid yet concentrated dispersion of value chain activities, and, simultaneously, their integration into hierarchical networks. Finally, we identify prerequisites for effective knowledge diffusion through GFNs. We highlight opportunities, pressures and incentives that may result from network participation, and explore how they affect the absorptive capacity of network suppliers.

2. FORCES DRIVING GLOBAL FLAGSHIP NETWORKS

A defining characteristic of the global network economy is the transition from vertically integrated 'multinational corporations' (MNCs), with their focus on stand-alone, equity-controlled overseas investment projects, to 'global flagship networks' (GFNs) which integrate their geographically dispersed supply, knowledge and customer bases (Ernst, forthcoming, b). This contrasts with centuries of economic history where MNCs were the main drivers of international production (for example, Braudel, 1992; Wilkins, 1970). Typically, the focus of MNCs has been on the penetration of protected markets through tariff-hopping investments, and on the use of assets developed at home to exploit international factor cost differentials, primarily for labour (for example, Dunning, 1981). This has given rise to a peculiar pattern of international production: stand-alone offshore production sites in low-cost locations are linked through triangular trade with the major markets in North America and Europe (for example, Dicken, 1998).

What forces have driven the shift in industrial organization from MNCs to GFNs? To answer this question, we highlight three inter-related explanatory variables: institutional change through liberalization; changes in competition and industrial organization; and information and communications technologies that gave rise to digital information systems (DIS).

2.1 Institutional Change: Liberalization

Liberalization dates back to the early 1970s: it thrived in response to the breakdown of fixed exchange rate regimes and the failure of Keynesianism to cope with pervasive stagflation. To a large degree, liberalization has been initiated by government policies. But there are also other actors that have played an important role: financial institutions; rating agencies; supra-national institutions like bi-lateral or multi-lateral investment treaties and regional integration schemes, like the EU or NAFTA. In some countries with decentralized devolution of political power, regional governments can also play an important role.

Liberalization imposes far-reaching changes on the economic institutions, i.e. the rules of the game that structure economic interactions. These institutions shape the allocation of resources, the rules of competition and firm behaviour. Liberalization affects all aspects of institutions, but at different speeds. North (1996, p.12) distinguishes formal rules (statute law, common law, regulations), informal constraints (conventions, norms of behaviour and self-imposed codes of conduct), and the enforcement characteristics of both. While liberalization will first affect formal rules, informal constraints and enforcement mechanisms are more difficult to change. This implies that there is no homogeneous model of liberalization, but many different and often hybrid forms.

Liberalization covers four main areas: trade, capital flows, foreign direct investment (FDI) policies and privatization. While each of these has generated separate debates in the literature, they hang together. Earlier success in trade liberalization has sparked an expansion of trade and FDI, increasing the demand for cross-border capital flows. This has increased the pressure for a liberalization of capital markets, forcing more and more countries to open their capital accounts. In turn this has led to a liberalization of FDI policies, and to privatization tournaments.

The overall effect of liberalization has been a considerable reduction in the cost and risks of international transactions and a massive increase in international liquidity. Global corporations (the network flagships) have been the primary beneficiaries: liberalization provides them with a greater range of choices for market entry between trade, licensing, subcontracting, franchising, etc. *(locational specialization)* than otherwise; it provides better access to external resources and capabilities that a flagship needs to complement its core competencies *(vertical specialization)*; and it has reduced the constraints for a geographic dispersion of the value chain *(spatial mobility)*.

2.2 Competition and Industrial Organization

As liberalization has been adopted as an almost universal policy doctrine, this has drastically changed the dynamics of competition. Again, we reduce the complexity of these changes and concentrate on two impacts: a broader geographic scope of competition; and a growing complexity of competitive requirements. Competition now cuts across national borders – a firm's position in one country is no longer independent from its position in other countries (for example, Porter, 1990). This has two implications. The firm must be present in all major growth markets *(dispersion)*. It must also integrate its activities on a worldwide scale in order to exploit and coordinate linkages between these different locations *(integration)*. Competition also cuts across sector boundaries and market segments: mutual raiding of established market segment fiefdoms has become the norm, making it more difficult for firms to identify market niches and to grow with them.

This has forced firms to engage in complex strategic games to pre-empt a competitor's move. This is especially the case for knowledge-intensive industries like electronics (Ernst, 2002b). Intense price competition needs to be combined with product differentiation, in a situation where continuous price wars erode profit margins. Of critical importance, however, is speed-to-market: getting the right product to the largest volume segment of the market right on time can provide huge profits. Being late can be a disaster, and may even drive a firm out of business. The result has been an increasing uncertainty and volatility, and a destabilization of established market leadership positions (Richardson, 1996; Ernst, 1998).

This growing complexity of competition has changed the determinants of location, as well as industrial and firm organization. Take first location decisions: while both market access and cost reductions remain important, it has become clear that they have to be reconciled with a number of equally important requirements that encompass: the exploitation of uncertainty through improved operational flexibility (for example, Kogut, 1985; and Kogut and Kulatilaka, 1994); a compression of speed-to-market through reduced product development and product life cycles (for example, Flaherty, 1986); learning and the acquisition of specialized external capabilities (for example, Antonelli, 1992; Kogut and Zander, 1993; Zander and Kogut, 1995; Zanfei, 2000; Dunning, 2000); and a shift of market penetration strategies from established to new and unknown markets (for example, Christensen, 1997).

Equally important are changes in industrial organization. No firm, not even a dominant market leader, can generate all the different capabilities internally that are necessary to cope with the requirements of global competition. Competitive success thus critically depends on vertical specialization: a capacity to selectively source specialized capabilities *outside* the firm that can range from simple contract assembly to quite sophisticated design capabilities. This requires a shift from individual to increasingly collective forms of organization, from the multidivisional (M-form) functional hierarchy (for example, Williamson, 1975 and 1985; Chandler, 1977) of 'multinational corporations' to the networked global flagship model.

The electronics industry has become the most important breeding ground for this new industrial organization model. Over the last decades, a massive process of vertical specialization has segmented an erstwhile vertically integrated industry into closely interacting horizontal layers (Grove, 1996). Until the early 1980s, IBM personified 'vertical integration': almost all ingredients necessary to design, produce and commercialize computers remained internal to the firm. This was true for semiconductors, hardware, operating systems, application software, and sales & distribution. Above all, 'IBM was famous (some would say notorious) for the power of its sales force… (and distribution system)' (Sobel, 1986, p. 37).

Since the mid-1980s, vertical specialization became the industry's defining characteristic. Most activities that characterized a computer company were now being farmed out to multiple layers of specialized suppliers, giving rise to rapid market segmentation and an ever finer specialization within each of the above five main value chain stages. This has given rise to the co-existence of complex, globally organized product-specific value chains (for example, for microprocessors, memories, board assembly, PCs, networking equipment, operating systems, applications software, and sales & distribution). In each of these value chains GFNs compete with each other, but may also cooperate (Ernst, 2002a). The number of such networks and the intensity of competition vary across sectors, reflecting their different stages of development and their idiosyncratic industry structures.

2.3 Information and Communication Technology: Digital Information Systems

An important initial catalyst of vertical specialization was the availability of standard components, which allowed for a change in computer design away from centralized (IBM mainframe) to decentralized architectures (PC, and PC-related networks) (for example, Langlois, 1992). More recently, the use of DIS to manage these networks has accelerated this process. For the manufacturing of electronics hardware, the use of DIS facilitated geographic dispersion. This is now being mirrored by similar developments for software and electronic design and engineering.

We first need to highlight important transformations in the use of DIS as a management tool. From a machine to automate transaction processing, the focus has shifted to the extraction of value from information resources, and then further to the establishment of Internet-enabled flexible information infrastructures that can support the extraction and exchange of knowledge across firm boundaries and national borders. A combination of technological and economic developments is responsible for this transformation.

On the technology side, the rapid development and diffusion of cheaper and more powerful information and communication technologies (for example, Sichel, 1997, and Flamm, 1999) has considerably reduced transaction costs. In addition, the move towards more open standards in DIS architecture (UNIX, Linux and HTML) and protocols (TCP/IP) enabled firms to integrate their existing intranets and extranets on the Internet, which, by reducing cost and by multiplying connectivity, dramatically extended their reach across firm boundaries and national borders.

Compared to earlier generations of DIS, the Internet appears to provide much greater opportunities to share knowledge with a much greater number of people faster, more accurately, and in greater detail, even if they are not permanently co-located (Ernst, 2000b, 2001a, 2001b). The most commonly used technologies today facilitate *asynchronous interaction*, such as e-mail or non-real time database sharing. But as data transfer capacity ('bandwidth') increases, new opportunities are created for using technologies that facilitate *synchronous interaction* such as real-time data exchange, video-conferencing, as well as remote control of manufacturing processes, product quality and inventory, maintenance and repair, and even prototyping. This has created new opportunities for extending knowledge exchange across organizational and national boundaries, hence magnifying the scope for vertical specialization. Equally important, wireless Internet-based technologies have increased the mobility of DIS.

On the economic side, vertical specialization, particularly pronounced in the electronics industry, poses increasingly complex information requirements (for example, Chen, 2002; Macher, Mowery and Simcoe, 2002). As firms now have to deal with constantly changing, large numbers of specialized suppliers, they need flexible and adaptive information systems to support these diverse linkages. These requirements are becoming ever more demanding, as flagships attempt to integrate their dispersed production, knowledge and customer bases into global and regional networks. DIS now need to provide new means to improve global supply chain management and speed-to-market. DIS also need to provide for effective communication between design and manufacturing, and for the exchange of proprietary knowledge. The semiconductor industry provides examples for both developments (for example, Macher, Mowery and Simcoe, 2002): vertical specialization gives rise to the separation of design ('fabless design') and manufacturing ('silicon foundry'). This creates very demanding requirements for knowledge exchange between multiple actors at distant locations, say a design house in Silicon Valley and a silicon foundry in Taiwan's Hsinchuh Science Park. Vertical separation of design and production of semiconductor devices in turn has created a vibrant trade in 'intellectual property rights' among specialized design firms that create, license and trade 'design modules' for use in integrated circuits.

In addition, far-reaching changes in work organization have fundamentally increased the requirements for information management and for the exchange of knowledge. The transition from Fordist 'mass production' to 'mass customization' requires a capacity to constantly adapt products or services to changing customer requirements, 'sensing and responding' to individual customer needs in real time (Bradley and Nolan, 1998). This necessitates dynamic, interactive information systems, and a capacity to rapidly adjust the organization of firms and corporate networks to disruptive changes in markets and technology. Third, real-time resource allocation, performance monitoring and accounting become necessary, due to the short-term pressures of the financial system (quarterly reports) and due to the shortening life cycles of products and technologies. Fourth, to cope with ever more demanding competitive requirements, firms have to continuously adapt their organization and strategy, hence the demand for flexible DIS.

Following Brynjolfsson and Hitt (2000), we argue that the impact of DIS on economic performance is mediated by a combination of intangible inputs as well as intangible outputs that act as powerful catalysts for organizational innovation. Intangible inputs include, for instance, the development of new software and databases; the adjustment of existing business processes; and the recruitment of specialized human resources and their continuous upgrading. Of equal importance are intangible outputs that would not exist without DIS, like speed of delivery, the flexibility of response to abrupt changes in demand and technology, and organizational innovations, like 'just-in-time' (JIT), 'mass customization', the built-to-order (BTO) production model, integrated supply chain management (SCM), and customer-relations management (CRM).

After a while, these induced organizational changes may lead to productivity growth, by reducing the cost of coordination, communications and information processing. Most importantly, these organizational changes may enable firms 'to increase output quality in the form of new products or in improvements in intangible aspects of existing products like convenience, timeliness, quality and variety.' (Brynjolfsson and Hitt, 2000, p.4). In short, we are talking about a complex process that involves a set of inter-related ('systemic') changes (Milgrom and Roberts, 1990): by combining DIS with changes in work practices, strategies, and products and services, a firm transforms its organization as well as its relations with suppliers, partners and customers.

Once we adopt such a framework, it becomes clear that firms that participate in GFNs can reap substantial benefits from using DIS as a management tool. There is ample scope for cost reduction across all stages of the production process, both for the flagship company and local suppliers. Procurement costs can be reduced by means of expanded markets and increased competition through Internet-enabled online procurement systems. Another cost-reducing option is to shift sales and information dissemination to lower-cost on-line channels.

The transition to Internet-based information systems can drastically accelerate speed-to-market by reducing the time it takes to transmit, receive and process routine business communications such as purchase orders, invoices and shipping notifications. There is much greater scope for knowledge management: documents and technical drawings can be exchanged in real time, legally recognized signatures can be authenticated, browsers can be used to access the information systems of suppliers and customers, and transactions can be completed much more quickly.

A further advantage can be found in the low cost of expanding an Internet-based information system. While establishing a network backbone requires large up-front fixed investment costs (purchasing equipment, laying new cable, training), the cost of adding an additional user to the network is negligible. The value of the network thus increases with the number of participants ('network externalities'). In addition, the Internet and related organizational innovations provide effective mechanisms for constructing flexible infrastructures that can link together and coordinate knowledge exchange between distant locations (Hagstrøm, 2000; Pedersen et al., 1999; Antonelli, 1992).

This has important implications for organizational choices and locational strategies of firms. In essence, Internet-enabled DIS foster the development of leaner, meaner and more agile production systems that cut across firm boundaries and national borders. The underlying vision is that of *networks of networks* that enable a global network flagship to respond quickly to changing circumstances, even if much of its value chain has been dispersed. DIS, especially the open-ended structure of the Internet, substantially broadens the scope for vertical specialization. It allows global flagships to shift from partial outsourcing, covering the nuts and bolts of manufacturing, to systemic outsourcing that includes knowledge-intensive support services, such software production, electronic design services, business process outsourcing, maintenance and repair of information systems, as well as skill transfer and training (Ernst, 2002c).

3. THE FLAGSHIP NETWORK MODEL

3.1 Theoretical Foundations

Until recently, these fundamental changes in the organization of international production have been largely neglected in the literature, both in research on knowledge spillovers through FDI, and in research on the internationalization of corporate R&D. This is now beginning to change. There is a growing acceptance in the literature that in order to capture the impact of globalization on industrial organization and upgrading, the focus of our analysis needs to shift away from the industry and the individual firm to the international dimension of business networks (for example, Bartlett and Ghoshal, 1989; Gereffi and Korzeniewicz, 1994; Ernst, 1997; Rugman and D'Cruz, 2000; Birkinshaw and Hagstrøm, 2000; Borrus et al., 2000; Pavitt, 2002; Ernst and

Ozawa, 2002). A focus on the evolution of cross-border corporate networks allows us to identify what is 'new' about the global network economy.

Trade economists have recently discovered the importance of changes in the organization of international production as a determinant of trade patterns (for example, Feenstra, 1998; Jones and Kierzskowski, 2001; Navaretti et al., 2002). Their work demonstrates that (i) production is increasingly 'fragmented', with parts of the production process being scattered across a number of countries, hence increasing the share of trade in parts and components; and (ii) countries and regions which have been able to become a part of the global production network are the ones which have industrialized the fastest. And leading growth economists (for example, Grossman and Helpman, 2002) are basing their models on a systematic analysis of global sourcing strategies.

Our model of GFNs builds on this work, but uses a broader concept that emphasizes three essential characteristics: (i) *scope:* GFNs encompass all stages of the value chain, not just production; (ii) *asymmetry:* flagships dominate control over network resources and decision-making; and (iii) *knowledge diffusion:* the sharing of knowledge is the necessary glue that keeps these networks growing.

A focus on international knowledge diffusion through an extension of firm organization across national boundaries distinguishes our concept of GFN from network theories developed by sociologists, economic geographers and innovation theorists, which focus on localized, mostly inter-personal networks (for example, Powell and Smith-Doerr, 1994). The central problem of these theories is that industries now operate in a global rather than a localized setting (Ernst et al., 2001). Important complementarities exist however with work on global commodity chains (GCC) (for example, Gereffi and Korzeniewicz, 1994). A primary concern of the GCC literature has been to explore how different value chain stages in an industry (i.e. textiles) are dispersed across borders, and how the position of a particular location in such a GCC affects its development potential through access to economic rents (for example, Gereffi and Kaplinsky, 2001; Henderson et al., 2001). Strong complementarities also exist with research on computer-based flexible information infrastructures which frequently uses the terms 'extended enterprise' or 'virtual enterprise', where the first stands for more durable network arrangements, and the latter for very short-term ones (for example, Pedersen et al., 1999; Jørgensen and Krogstie, 2000; and various issues of the electronic journal *virtual-organization.net*).

As for the dynamics of network evolution, our approach complements the transaction cost approach to networks and vertical disintegration, which centres on the presumed efficiency gains from these organizational choices (for example, Williamson, 1985; Milgrom and Roberts, 1990). However, the latter approach skips some of the more provocative chapters in the economic history of the modern corporation. Chandler's vibrant histories (for example 1962 and 1990) show that the quest for profits and market power via increased through-put and speed of coordination were more important in explaining hierarchy than the traditional emphasis on transaction costs. This implies that the analysis of the determinants of institutional form must move beyond a narrow focus on transaction costs to the broader competitive environment in which firms operate. It is time to bring back into the analysis market structure and competitive dynamics, as well as the role played by knowledge and innovation. Like hierarchies, GFNs not only promise to improve efficiency, but can permit flagships to sustain quasi-monopoly positions, generate market power through specialization, and raise entry barriers; they also enhance the network flagships' capacity for innovation (Ernst, 1997; Borrus et al., 2000).

3.2 Network Characteristics

GFNs differ from MNCs in three important ways which need to be taken into account in the study of knowledge diffusion (Ernst, forthcoming, b). First, these networks cover both intra-firm and inter-firm transactions and forms of coordination: a GFN links together the flagship's own subsidiaries, affiliates and joint ventures with its subcontractors, suppliers, service providers, as well as partners in strategic alliances. A network flagship like IBM or Intel breaks down the value chain into a variety of discrete functions and locates them wherever they can be carried out most effectively, where they can improve the flagship's access to resources and capabilities, and where they are needed to facilitate the penetration of important growth markets.

Second, GFNs differ from MNCs in that a great variety of governance structures is possible. These networks range from loose linkages that are formed to implement a particular project and that are dissolved after the project is finished, so-called 'virtual enterprises' (for example, Pedersen et al., 1999, p.16), to highly formalized networks, 'extended enterprises', with clearly defined rules, common business processes and shared information infrastructures. What matters is that formalized networks do not require common ownership: these arrangements may, or may not involve control of equity stakes.

Third, 'vertical specialization' ('outsourcing' in business parlance) is the main driver of these networks (Ernst, 2002b). GFNs help flagships to gain quick access to skills and capabilities at lower-cost overseas locations that complement the flagships' core competencies. As the flagship integrates geographically dispersed production, customer and knowledge bases into global production networks, this may well produce transaction cost savings. Yet, the real benefits result from the dissemination, exchange and outsourcing of knowledge and complementary capabilities.

Increasingly, the focus of outsourcing is shifting from assembly-type manufacturing to knowledge-intensive support services, like supply chain management, engineering services and new product introduction. Outsourcing may also include design and product development. This indicates that GFNs also differ from traditional forms of subcontracting: much denser interaction between design and production and other stages of the value chain require substantially more intense exchange of information and knowledge. Network flagships increasingly rely on the skills and knowledge of specialized suppliers to enhance their core competencies.

Two distinctive characteristics of GFNs that are enhanced by DIS shape the scope for international knowledge diffusion: a rapid yet concentrated dispersion of value chain activities, and, simultaneously, their integration into hierarchical networks.

3.3 Concentrated Dispersion

GFNs typically combine a rapid geographic dispersion with spatial concentration on a growing but still limited number of specialized clusters. To simplify, we distinguish two types of clusters (Ernst, forthcoming, a): 'centres of excellence' which combine unique resources, such as R&D and precision mechanical engineering, and 'cost and time reduction centres' which thrive on the timely provision of lower-cost services. Different clusters face different constraints to knowledge diffusion, depending on their specialization, and on the product composition of GFNs. The dispersion of clusters differs across the value chain: it increases, the closer one gets to the final product, while dispersion remains concentrated especially for high-precision and design-intensive components.

Let us look at some indicators in the electronics industry, a pace setter of the flagship network model (Ernst, 2002b). On one end of the spectrum is final PC assembly which is widely dispersed to major growth markets in the US, Europe and Asia. Dispersion is still quite extended for standard, commodity-type components, but less so than for final assembly. For instance, flagships can source keyboards, computer mouse devices and power switch supplies from many different sources, both in Asia, Mexico and the European periphery, with Taiwanese firms playing an important role as intermediate supply chain co-ordinators. The same is true for printed circuit boards. Concentration of dispersion increases, the closer we move toward more complex, capital-intensive precision components: memory devices and displays are sourced primarily from 'centres of excellence' in Japan, Korea, Taiwan and Singapore; and hard disk drives from a Singapore-centred triangle of locations in South-East Asia. Finally, dispersion becomes most concentrated for high-precision, design-intensive components that pose the most demanding requirements on the mix of capabilities that a firm and its cluster need to master: microprocessors, for instance, are sourced from a few globally dispersed affiliates of Intel, two American suppliers, and one recent entrant from Taiwan.

In other words, geography continues to matter, even when DIS and high-velocity transportation are used. Rapid cross-border dispersion thus coexists with agglomeration. GFNs extend national clusters across national borders. This implies three things: first, some stages of the value chain are internationally dispersed, while others remain concentrated. Second, the internationally dispersed activities typically congregate in a limited number of overseas clusters. And third, agglomeration economies continue to matter, hence the path-dependent nature of development trajectories for individual specialized clusters. In short, the new mobility of knowledge remains constrained in space: while cross-border exchange of knowledge has penetrated new geographic areas, it remains limited to a finite number of specialized clusters.

3.4 Integration: Hierarchical Networks

A GFN integrates diverse network participants who differ in their access to and in their position within such networks, and hence face very different opportunities and challenges. This implies that these networks do not necessarily give rise to less hierarchical forms of firm organization (as predicted, for instance, in Bartlett and Ghoshal, 1989, and in Nohria and Eccles, 1992). GFNs typically consist of various hierarchical layers, ranging from network flagships that dominate such networks, due to their capacity for system integration (Pavitt, 2002), down to a variety of usually smaller, local specialized network suppliers.

The flagship is at the heart of the network: it provides strategic and organizational leadership beyond the resources that, from an accounting perspective, lie directly under its management control (Rugman, 1997). The strategy of the flagship company thus directly affects the growth, the strategic direction and network position of lower-end participants, like specialized suppliers and subcontractors. The latter, in turn, 'have no reciprocal influence over the flagship strategy' (Rugman and D'Cruz, 2000, p. 84). The flagship derives its strength from its control over critical resources and capabilities that facilitate innovation, and from its capacity to coordinate transactions and knowledge exchange between the different network nodes.

Flagships retain in-house activities in which they have a particular strategic advantage; they outsource those in which they do not. It is important to emphasize the diversity of such outsourcing patterns (Ernst, 1997). Some flagships focus on design, product development and marketing, outsourcing volume manufacturing and related support services. Other flagships outsource as well a variety of high-end, knowledge-intensive support services. This includes, for instance, trial production (prototyping and ramping-up), tooling and equipment, benchmarking of productivity, testing, process adaptation, product customization and supply chain coordination. It may also include design and product development.

3.5 Diversity of Flagships: OEMs versus CMs

To move this model a bit closer to reality, we distinguish two types of global flagships: i) Original equipment manufacturers (OEM) that derive their market power from selling global brands, regardless of whether design and production is done in-house or outsourced; and ii) 'contract manufacturers' (CM) that establish their own GFN to provide integrated manufacturing and global supply chain services (often including design) to the OEM. Cisco provides an interesting example of a global brand leader that has pushed vertical specialization to the extreme. Cisco outsources much of its manufacturing and support services, including important elements of R&D (Bunnell and Brate, 2000). Cisco's GFN connects the flagship to 32 manufacturing plants worldwide. These first-tier international suppliers are formally independent, but they go through a lengthy process of certification to ensure that they meet Cisco's demanding requirements.

The 'New Economy' boom in the US has accelerated a long-standing trend toward vertical specialization in the electronics industry: outsourcing based on contract manufacturing became the 'panacea of the '90s' (Lakenan et al., 2001, p.3), a 'New American Model of Industrial Organization' (Sturgeon, 2002). Two inter-related transformations need to be distinguished: supply contracts and M&A (Ernst, 2002c). Global brand leaders like Dell, the 'original equipment manufacturers' (OEMs), increasingly subcontract manufacturing and related services to US-based global 'contract manufacturers' (CMs), like Flextronics. However, equally important is the fact that the very same CMs have acquired existing facilities of OEMs, as the latter are divesting internal manufacturing capacity, seeking to allocate capital to other activities that are expected to generate higher profit margins, such as sales and marketing, and product development.

Contract manufacturers (CM) have rapidly increased in importance since the mid-1990s. For the eight largest global contract manufacturers, capital expenditures grew 11-fold from 1996 to 2000 (50 percent CAGR), and revenues increased by almost 400 percent (81 percent CAGR) (Hoover's Corporate database). The percentage of total electronics production being done by contract manufacturers is estimated to be around 22 percent (courtesy of Technology Forecasters, Inc., Alameda, CA, 15 April 2002).

During the 1990s, global brand leaders (OEMs) have put up for sale a growing number of their overseas facilities and in some cases, whole chunks of their global production networks. OEMs from North America like HP, Dell, Compaq, Motorola, Intel, IBM, Lucent, Nortel were first in pursuing such divestment strategies. But European OEMs (for example, Philips, Ericcson, Siemens) and, more recently, Japanese ones (for example, NEC, Fujitsu, Sony) have followed suit. CMs have aggressively seized this opportunity: through acquisition and capacity expansion they have developed, within a few years, their own GFNs which now complement the networks established by the global brand leaders (OEMs). For the three leading CM players, these global networks are now larger than those developed by the leading OEM: Solectron has factories in 70 countries, Flextronics has 62 plants worldwide, and the recently merged Sanmina/SCI has 100 factories around the world (Ernst, 2002c). This has created increasingly complex, multi-tier 'networks of networks' that juxtapose global ties among the two types of large global players (the OEMs and CMs), as well as intense regional ties with smaller firms (the local network suppliers), as argued, for instance, in Almeida and Kogut (1997).

A focus on complex, multi-tier 'networks of networks' distinguishes our analysis from Sturgeon's modular production network model (2002). In that model, nothing can stop continuous outsourcing through contract manufacturing: global CMs and OEMs '... co-evolve in a recursive cycle of outsourcing and increasing supply-base capability and scale, which makes the prospects for additional outsourcing more attractive' (Sturgeon, 2002, p.6). In contrast, our analysis emphasizes that global contract manufacturing is a highly volatile industry. While powerful forces push for outsourcing, this process is by no means irreversible. Major OEMs retain substantial internal manufacturing operations; they are continuously evaluating the merits of manufacturing products or providing services internally versus the advantages of outsourcing (Ernst, forthcoming, a).

4. PREREQUISITES FOR KNOWLEDGE DIFFUSION

In short, the combined forces of DIS and GFNs are gradually reducing constraints to international knowledge diffusion. Yet, this occurs in complex ways: a rapid yet concentrated dispersion of value chain activities, and, simultaneously, their integration into hierarchical and complex 'networks of networks' limits the new mobility of knowledge to a finite number of specialized clusters (Ernst, forthcoming, c). What needs to be done to translate the new opportunities into effective knowledge diffusion to local network suppliers?

We first distinguish 'local suppliers' in terms of their network position and capabilities. We then highlight opportunities: GFNs can act as a conduit for knowledge diffusion for state-of-the-art management approaches as well as product and process technologies, including the required tacit knowledge.

Finally, we introduce the missing link in our argument: local suppliers are exposed to a combination of pressures and incentives from network flagships to upgrade their capabilities.

4.1 Local Suppliers

Local suppliers differ substantially in their capacity to benefit from the new mobility of knowledge. Greatly simplifying, we distinguish two types of local suppliers: higher-tier and lower-tier suppliers. 'Higher-tier' suppliers, like for instance Taiwan's Acer group (Ernst, 2000b), play an intermediary role between global flagships and local suppliers. They deal directly with global flagships (both OEMs and CMs); they possess valuable proprietary assets (including technology); and they have sufficient resources to upgrade their absorptive capacities. Some of these higher-tier suppliers have even developed their own mini-GFN (Chen, 2002). With the exception of hard-core R&D and strategic marketing that remain under the control of the OEM, the lead supplier must be able to shoulder all steps in the value chain. It must even take on the coordination functions necessary for global supply chain management.

'Lower-tier' suppliers are the weakest link in the GFNs. Their main competitive advantages are low cost and speed, and flexibility of delivery. They are typically used as 'price breakers' and 'capacity buffers', and can be dropped at short notice. This second group of local suppliers rarely deals directly with the global flagships; they interact primarily with local higher-tier suppliers. Lower-tier suppliers normally lack proprietary assets; their financial resources are inadequate to invest in training and R&D; and they are highly vulnerable to abrupt changes in markets and technology, and to financial crises.

4.2 Opportunities

GFNs cannot work without some sharing of knowledge. First, flagships need to transfer technical and managerial knowledge to the local suppliers. This is necessary in order to upgrade the suppliers' capabilities, so that they can meet the technical specifications of the flagships. It has been argued that flagship-dominated business networks can be a boon rather than a bane for knowledge transfer (Rugman and D'Cruz, 2000). Their asymmetric distribution of resources, power and decision-making can facilitate trust and credible commitments, enhancing stability, coherence and organizational learning. This, it is argued, reduces the risks that flagships encounter when sharing technology.

Second, once a network supplier successfully upgrades its capabilities, this creates an incentive for flagships to transfer more sophisticated knowledge, including engineering, product and process development. This reflects the increasingly demanding competitive requirements that we referred to earlier.

In the electronics industry for instance, product life-cycles have been cut to six months, and sometimes less (Ernst, 2002b). Overseas production thus frequently occurs soon after the launching of new products. This is only possible if flagships share key design information more freely with overseas affiliates and suppliers. Speed-to-market requires that engineers across the different nodes of a GFN be plugged into the flagship's product development process almost from the beginning.

For higher-tier local network suppliers, this necessitates an early involvement in product design and prototype development; access to proprietary technical and marketing information on end users' requirements and on competitors' products; informal sharing of technical information and ideas between the flagship and different network nodes; and knowledge exchange through informal, transnational peer group networks (Ernst and Lundvall, 2000; Ernst, 2000a; Saxenian, 2002).

DIS, and especially the Internet, generate new opportunities for improving communication routines, blending old forms of communication (for example, face-to-face) with new forms (for example, on-line). This facilitates the integration of local suppliers into the flagship's design process. Of course, the Internet is no substitute for traditional modes of communication. However, it facilitates knowledge exchange without co-location, *provided* that the agents involved know each other through earlier face-to-face informal conversations. Once this basis exists, the Internet provides previously unavailable opportunities for knowledge exchange among distant locations.

4.3 Pressures and Incentives

Diffusion is completed only when transferred knowledge is internalized and translated into specific capabilities of local suppliers (for example, Kim, 1997, and Ernst et al., 1998). Important constraints exist that can derail this process (Lam, 1998; Ernst et al., 2002). Of critical importance is the absorptive capacity (Cohen and Levinthal, 1990) of the local suppliers, i.e. their resources, capabilities and motivations (Ernst and Kim, 2002a). The absorptive capacity is shaped by pressures imposed by network flagships, and by the existing incentives. The flagships can exert considerable pressure on local suppliers, by threatening to drop them from the networks whenever they fail to provide the required services of a world-class quality at a low price.

Under certain conditions, these pressures can catalyse local suppliers into concerted upgrading efforts. In response to intensifying global competition, the flagships' outsourcing requirements have become more demanding. Typically, suppliers are selected on the basis of three criteria: a solid financial standing; high ratings on a quarterly scoreboard measuring performance in delivery, quality etc.; and speed of response. The latter is of critical importance: suppliers are expected to respond within hours with a price, a delivery time, and a record of their recent performance with regard to reliability and product quality. This implies that local suppliers can only upgrade or perish.

To stay in the network, local suppliers must constantly upgrade their absorptive capacity by investing in their skills and knowledge base. Adequate incentives are required to sustain these investments. For instance, the flagship may reduce the perceived risk of such investments through a reasonably long-term commitment. That commitment could provide the supplier with a stable source of income to finance the investment. The flagship may also offer access to superior market and technology information which may reduce the supplier's risks involved in the investment decision. These are fairly demanding requirements which not all networks meet.

There is a clear need for government policies and support institutions that enable local suppliers to exploit the opportunities and pressures that result from network participation, and that induce flagships to provide the above incentives. Realistically, the focus of such policies has to be on the promotion of local suppliers (as illustrated for instance by countries like Denmark, Taiwan and Singapore). Most governments (with the exception of quasi-continental economies like China, India and Brazil) are simply too weak to influence flagship behaviour. However, there is room for policies to exploit existing differences in flagship behaviour. It is now well established that nationality of ownership of network flagships, home country institutions and product mix (specialization) explain why GFNs differ in their governance structures, and hence in the incentives they provide for capability-upgrading investment by local suppliers (Ernst and Ravenhill, 1999; Borrus et al., 2000).

5. CONCLUSIONS

This chapter demonstrates that we need to reconsider and amend the 'stickiness-of-knowledge' proposition in the emerging global network economy. Two inter-related transformations in the organization of international business are gradually reducing constraints to international knowledge diffusion: the evolution of cross-border forms of corporate networking practices, especially global flagship networks (GFNs), and the increasing use of digital information systems (DIS) to manage these networks. The chapter presents robust evidence, based on research in information industries, that GFNs expand inter-firm linkages across national boundaries, increasing the need for knowledge diffusion, while DIS enhance not only information exchange, but also provide new opportunities for the sharing, and joint utilization and creation of knowledge. We also demonstrate that GFNs may provide new opportunities, pressures and incentives for local suppliers to upgrade their capabilities, *provided* appropriate policies and support institutions are in place.

The approach that I have chosen focuses on international knowledge diffusion through an extension of firm organization across national boundaries. We explore how two distinctive characteristics of GFNs, which are enhanced by DIS, shape the scope for international knowledge diffusion: a rapid yet concentrated dispersion of value chain activities, and, simultaneously, their integration into hierarchical networks. We demonstrate that the new mobility of knowledge is an unintended consequence of the evolution of global flagship networks. The more dispersed and complex these networks, the more demanding their coordination requirements. Hence, knowledge sharing is the necessary glue that keeps these networks growing.

In short, we propose to focus the economic study of international knowledge diffusion on the dynamics of these networks. This will allow us to identify what is 'new' about the global network economy. Vertical specialization is the main driver of these networks. The use of DIS fosters the development of leaner, meaner and more agile production systems that cut across firm boundaries and national borders. It allows global flagships to shift from *partial* outsourcing, covering the nuts and bolts of manufacturing, to *systemic* outsourcing that includes knowledge-intensive support services. The underlying vision is that of a network of networks which enables a global network flagship to respond quickly to changing circumstances, even if much of its value chain has been dispersed.

But vertical specialization does not imply that the 'Visible Hand' of large manufacturing firms will become invisible (as argued, for instance, in Langlois, 2001), giving rise to a resurgence of market forces. The necessary complement to vertical specialization, and the resultant geographic dispersion, are large global corporations (the network flagships) that can act as system integrators for the diverse, multi-layered global flagship networks that have evolved as a result of vertical specialization (see also Pavitt, 2002). In short, while the trend toward vertical specialization is real, there are also important limits and countervailing forces that the study of international knowledge diffusion needs to explore.

REFERENCES

Almeida, P. and B. Kogut (1997), 'The Exploration of Technological Diversity and the Geographic Localization of Innovation', *Small Business Economics*, 9, 21-31.
Antonelli, C. (ed.) (1992), *The Economics of Information Networks*, Amsterdam: Elsevier North Holland.

Archibugi, D. and J. Michie (1995), 'The Globalisation of Technology: A New Taxonomy', *Cambridge Journal of Economics*, 19, 121-40.

Bartlett, C.A. and S. Ghoshal (1989), *Managing Across Borders: The Transnational Solution*, Boston: Harvard Business School Press.

Bell, Martin and Keith Pavitt (1993), 'Technological Accumulation and Industrial Growth: Contrasts Between Developed and Developing Countries', *Industrial and Corporate Change*, 2 (2), 215-24.

Birkinshaw, J. and P. Hagstrøm (eds) (2000), *The Flexible Firm. Capability Management in Network Organizations*, Oxford: Oxford University Press.

Borrus, M., D. Ernst and S. Haggard (eds) (2000), *International Production Networks in Asia. Rivalry or Riches?*, London: Routledge.

Bradley, S P. and R.L. Nolan (eds) (1998), *Sense and Respond: Capturing Value in the Network Era*, Boston: Harvard Business School Press.

Braudel, F. (1992), *The Perspective of the World, Civilization and Capitalism. 15th-18th Centuries*, 3, Berkeley: University of California Press.

Breschi, S. and F. Malerba (2001), 'The Geography of Innovation and Economic Clustering: Some Introductory Notes', *Industrial and Corporate Change*, 10 (4), 817–34.

Brynjolfsson, E. and L.M. Hitt (2000), 'Beyond Computation: Information Technology, Organizational Transformations and Business Performance', manuscript, Sloan School of Management, MIT, July.

Bunnell, D. with A. Brate (2000), *Making the Cisco Connection*, New York: John Wiley & Sons.

Chandler, A.D. (1977), *The Visible Hand: the Managerial Revolution in American Business*, Cambridge, US: Harvard University Press.

Chandler, A. D. and J.W. Cortada (2000), 'The Information Age: Continuities and Differences', chapter 9, in A. D. Chandler, and J.W. Cortada (eds), *A Nation Transformed by Information*, Oxford and New York: Oxford University Press, pp. 281-300.

Chen, Shin-Horng (2002), 'Global Production Networks and Information Technology: The Case of Taiwan,' *Industry and Innovation*, special issue 'Global Production Networks', 9 (3), guest editors: D. Ernst and Linsu Kim, 249-65.

Christensen, C. M. (1997), *The Innovator's Dilemma: When New Technologies Cause Great Firms to Fail*, Boston: Harvard Business School Press.

Cohen, Wesley M. and Daniel A. Levinthal (1990), 'Absorptive Capacity: A New Perspective on Learning and Innovation', *Administrative Science Quarterly*, 35 (1), 128-52.

Dicken, P. (1998), *Global Shift: Transforming the World Economy*, 3rd edition, New York: Guilford Press.

Dunning, J. (1981), *International Production and the Multinational Enterprise*, London: George Allen & Unwin.

Dunning, J. (ed.) (2000), *Regions, Globalization and the Knowledge-Based Economy*, Oxford: Oxford University Press.

Ernst, D. (1997), *From Partial to Systemic Globalization. International Production Networks in the Electronics Industry*, report prepared for the Sloan Foundation project on the Globalization in the Data Storage Industry, *The Data Storage Industry Globalization Project Report 97-02*, Graduate School of International Relations and Pacific Studies, University of California at San Diego.

Ernst, D. (1998), 'High-Tech Competition Puzzles. How Globalization Affects Firm Behavior and Market Structure in the Electronics Industry', *Revue d'Economie Industrielle*, 85, 9-30.

Ernst, D. (2000a), 'Inter-Organizational Knowledge Outsourcing: What Permits Small Taiwanese Firms to Compete in the Computer Industry?', *Asia Pacific Journal of Management*, 17 (2), 223-55.

Ernst, D. (2000b), 'Placing the Networks on the Internet: Challenges and Opportunities for Knowledge Creation in Developing Asia', paper presented at the Second Asia Academy of Management Conference, 15-18 December 2000, Shangri-La Hotel, Singapore, forthcoming in B.A. Lundvall and K. Smith (eds), *Knowledge Creation in the Learning Economy*, Cheltenham, UK and Northampton, MA, USA: Edward Elgar.

Ernst, D. (2001a), 'The Internet, Global Production Networks and Knowledge Diffusion. Challenges and Opportunities for Developing Asia', in Pacific Telecommunications Council, *PTC2001: From Convergence to Emergence: Will the User Rule?*, proceedings of the 2001 Annual Pacific Telecommunications Council Conference, 14-18 January 2001, Honolulu, Hawaii.

Ernst, D. (2001b), 'The Evolution of a Digital Economy. Research Issues and Policy Challenges', *Economia e Politica Industriale*, XXVIII (110), 127-39.

Ernst, D. (2002a), 'Global Production Networks and the Changing Geography of Innovation Systems. Implications for Developing Countries', *Economics of Innovation and New Technologies*, XI (6), 497-523.

Ernst, D. (2002b), 'The Economics of Electronics Industry: Competitive Dynamics and Industrial Organization', in William Lazonick (ed.), *The International Encyclopedia of Business and Management (IEBM)*, *Handbook of Economics*, London: International Thomson Business Press.

Ernst, D. (2002c), 'Global Production Networks in East Asia's Electronics Industry and Upgrading Perspectives in Malaysia', study prepared for the *East Asian Prospects Study*, Development Economics Research Group, World Bank, Washington DC, to appear in S. Yusuf (ed.), *Upgrading East Asia's Industries*, 2, Oxford University Press, 2003.

Ernst, D. (forthcoming, a), 'The New Mobility of Knowledge: Digital Information Systems and Global Flagship Networks', in R. Latham and S. Sassen (eds), *Digital Formations in a Connected World*, Princeton University Press, 2003.

Ernst, D. (forthcoming, b), *Global Digital Business Networks – A New Divide in Industrial Organization*, Oxford: Oxford University Press.

Ernst, D. (forthcoming, c), 'Global Production Networks and Industrial Upgrading – Malaysia's Electronics Industry', in J. Kidd and F.J. Richter (eds), *Trust and Anti-Trust in Cross-Cultural Alliances*, published for the World Economic Forum, Palgrave, London, 2003.

Ernst, D. and Linsu Kim (2002a), 'Global Production Networks, Knowledge Diffusion and Local Capability Formation', *Research Policy*, special issue in honour of Richard Nelson and Sydney Winter, 31 (8/9), 1417-29.

Ernst, D. and Linsu Kim (2002b), 'Introduction: Global Production Networks, Information Technology and Knowledge Diffusion', in *Industry and Innovation*, special issue 'Global Production Networks', 9 (3), 147-53.

Ernst, D. and Bengt-Åke Lundvall (2000), 'Information Technology in the Learning Economy – Challenges for Developing Countries' in Erich Reinert (ed.), *Evolutionary Economics and Spatial Income Inequality*, Cheltenham, UK and Northampton, MA, USA: Edward Elgar.

Ernst, D. and D. O'Connor (1992), *Competing in the Electronics Industry. The Experience of Newly Industrialising Economies*, Paris: Development Centre Studies, OECD.

Ernst, D. and T. Ozawa (2002), 'National Sovereign Economy, Global Market Economy, and Transnational Corporate Economy', *Journal of Economic Issues*, XXXVI (2), 547-55.

Ernst, D. and John Ravenhill (1999), 'Globalization, Convergence, and the Transformation of International Production Networks in Electronics in East Asia', *Business and Politics*, I (1), 35-62.

Ernst, D., J. Fagerberg and J. Hildrum (2002), 'Do Global Production Networks and Digital Information Systems Make Knowledge Spatially Fluid?', *East-West Center Working Paper, Economics Series*, No. 40, February.

Ernst, D., T. Ganiatsos and Lynn Mytelka (1998), *Technological Capabilities and Export Success: Lessons from East Asia*, London: Routledge.

Ernst, D., P. Guerrieri, S. Iammarino and C. Pietrobelli (2001), 'New Challenges for Industrial Districts: Global Production Networks and Knowledge Diffusion', chapter 6, in P. Guerrieri, S. Iammarino and C. Pietrobelli (eds), *The Global Challenge to Industrial Districts. Small and Medium-Sized Enterprises in Italy and Taiwan*, Cheltenham, UK and Northampton, MA, USA: Edward Elgar.

Feenstra, R. (1998), 'Integration of Trade and Disintegration of Production in the Global Economy', *The Journal of Economic Perspectives*, 12 (4), 31-50.

Flaherty, Theresa (1986), 'Coordinating International Manufacturing and Technology', in Michael Porter (ed.), *Competition in Global Industries*, Boston: Harvard Business School Press, pp. 83-110.

Flamm, K. (1999), 'Digital Convergence? The Set-Top Box and the Network Computer', chapter 12, in: J.A. Eisenach and T.M. Lenard (eds), *Competition, Innovation and the Microsoft Monopoly: Antitrust in the Digital Market Place*, Boston: Kluwer Academic Publishers.

Gereffi, G. and R. Kaplinsky (eds) (2001), *The Value of Value Chains*, special issue of IDS Bulletin, 32 (3).

Gereffi, Gary and Miguel Korzeniewicz (eds) (1994), *Commodity Chains and Global Capitalism*, Westport, US: Praeger.

Ghoshal, S. and C. A. Bartlett (1990), 'The Multinational Corporation as an Interorganizational Network', *Academy of Management Review*, 15 (4), 603-25.

Grossman, G. and E. Helpman (2002), 'Integration versus Outsourcing in Industry Equilibrium', *The Quarterly Journal of Economics*, 117 (1), 85-120.

Grove, A.S. (1996), *Only the Paranoid Survive. How to Exploit the Crisis Points that Challenge Every Company and Career*, New York and London: Harper Collins Business.

Hagstrøm, P. (2000), 'New Wine in Old Bottles: Information Technology Evolution in Firm Strategy and Structure', in J. Birkinshaw and P. Hagstrøm (eds), *The Flexible Firm. Capability Management in Network Organizations*, Oxford: Oxford University Press, 194-206.

Henderson, J., P. Dicken, M. Hess, N. Coe and H. Wai-Chung Yeung (2001), 'Global Production Networks and the Analysis of Economic Development', manuscript, Manchester Business School, University of Manchester.

Jones, R. and H. Kierzskowski (2001), 'A Framework for Fragmentation', in S. Arndt and H. Kierzkowski (eds), *Fragmentation – New Production Patterns in the World Economy*, Oxford: Oxford University Press, 17-34.

Jørgensen, H.D. and J. Krogstie (2000), 'Active Models for Dynamic Networked Organisations', Working Paper, Institute of Computer & Information Sciences, Norwegian University of Science and Technology. Available from <hdj.jok@ informatics.sintef.no>.

Kim, Linsu (1997), *Imitation to Innovation. The Dynamics of Korea's Technological Learning*, Boston: Harvard Business School Press.

Kogut, B. (1985), 'Designing Global Strategies: Profiting from Operational Flexibility', *Sloan Management Review*, Autumn, 27-38.

Kogut, B. and N. Kulatilaka (1994), 'Operating Flexibility, Global Manufacturing, and the Option Value of a Multinational Network', *Management Science*, 40 (1), 123-39.

Kogut, B. and U. Zander (1993), 'Knowledge of the Firm and the Evolutionary Theory of the Multinational Corporation', *Journal of International Business Studies*, 24 (4), 625-45.

Lakenan, B., D. Boyd and E. Frey (2001), 'Why Cisco Fell: Outsourcing and its Perils', *Strategy + Business*, Booz-Allen &Hamilton, Issue 24, 3rd Quarter, 54-65.

Lam, A. (1998), 'The Social Embeddedness of Knowledge: Problems of Knowledge-Sharing and Organisational Learning in International High-Tech Ventures', *DRUID Working Paper 98-7*, Department of Business Studies, Aalborg University.

Langlois, R.N. (1992), 'External Economies and Economic Progress: The Case of the Microcomputer Industry', *Business History Review*, 66 (Spring), 1-50.

Langlois, R.N. (2001), 'The Vanishing Hand: The Modular Revolution in American Business', (mimeo), University of Connecticut.

Lerner, J. and J. Tirole (2000), 'The Simple Economics of Open Source', manuscript, Harvard Business School, December 29.

Litan, R.E. and A.M. Rivlin (2001), *The Economic Payoff from the Internet Revolution*, Washington: Brookings Institution Press.

Macher, J.T., D.C. Mowery and T.S. Simcoe (2002), 'eBusiness and the Semiconductor Industry value Chain: Implications for Vertical Specialization and Integrated Semiconductor Manufacturers', *Industry and Innovation*, special issue 'Global Production Networks', 9 (3), guest editors: D. Ernst and Linsu Kim, 155-81.

Maltz, A.B. et al. (2000), 'Lessons from the Semiconductor Industry. The International Sematech Semiconductor Logistics Forum Study', *Supply Chain Management Review*, November/ December.

Markusen, A. (1996), 'Sticky Places in Slippery Space: A Typology of Industrial Districts', *Economic Geography*, 72, 293-313.

Milgrom, P. and J. Roberts (1990), 'The Economics of Modern Manufacturing: Technology, Strategy, and Organization', *The American Economic Review*, 80 (3), 511-28.

Navaretti, G.B., J.I. Haaland and A. Venables (2002), *Multinational Corporations and Global Production Networks: The Implications for Trade Policy*, Brussels: Directorate General for Trade, European Commission, March.

Nelson, Richard (1995), 'The Agenda for Growth Theory: A Different Point of View', IIASA Working Paper.

Nohria, N. and R.G. Eccles (1992), *Networks and Organizations: Structure, Form, and Action*, Boston: Harvard Business School Press.

Nolan, R.L. (2000), 'Information Technology Management since 1960', in A.D. Chandler, and J.W. Cortada (eds), *A Nation Transformed by Information*, Oxford and New York: Oxford University Press.

North, D. C. (1996), 'Institution, Organizations, and Market Competition', keynote address to the Sixth Conference of the International Joseph Schumpeter Society, Stockholm, 2-5 June.

Pavitt, K. (2002), 'Are Systems Designers & Integrators "Post-Industrial" Firms?', in A. Prencipe, A. Davies and M. Hobday (eds), *Systems Integration and Firm Capabilities*, Oxford: Oxford University Press.

Pedersen, J.D., M. Tølle and J. Vesterager (1999), *Global Manufacturing in the 21st Century. Final Report on Models*, report prepared for ESPRIT under contract # 26509, European Commission, Brussels, 30 November.

Porter, M. (1990), *The Competitive Advantage of Nations*, London, Basingstoke: Macmillan Press.

Powell, W. and L. Smith-Doerr (1994), 'Networks and Economic Life', in N. Smelser and R. Swedber (eds), *The Handbook of Economic Sociology*, Princeton: Princeton University Press.

Richardson, G.B. (1996), 'Competition, Innovation and Increasing Returns', *DRUID Working Paper* #96-10, Department of Business Studies, Aalborg University, July.

Rugman, A. M. (1997), 'Canada: Globalization, Competitiveness and Government Policy in a Regional Market', in J. H. Dunning (ed.), *Governments, Globalization and International Business*, London: Oxford University Press.

Rugman, A.M. and J. R. D'Cruz (2000), *Multinationals as Flagship Firms. Regional Business Networks*, Oxford and New York: Oxford University Press.

Saxenian, A. (2002), 'Transnational Communities and the Evolution of Global Production Networks: The Cases of Taiwan, China and India', *Industry and Innovation*, 9 (2), special issue on 'Global Production Networks, Information Technology and Local Capabilities', guest editors: D. Ernst and Linsu Kim, 183-202.

Sichel, D.E. (1997), *The Computer Revolution. An Economic Perspective*, Washington: Brookings Institution Press.

Sobel, R. (1986), *IBM vs. Japan. The Struggle for the Future*, New York: Stein & Day.

Sturgeon, T. (2002), 'Modular Production Networks: A New American Model of Industrial Organization', *Industrial and Corporate Change*, 11 (3), 451-96.

UNCTAD (1993), *World Investment Report, 1993: Transnational Corporations and Integrated International Production*, Geneva.

UNCTAD (1999), *World Investment Report 1999. Foreign Direct Investment and the Challenge of Development*, Geneva.

Weber, S. (2001), 'The Political Economy of Open Source Software', BRIE Working Paper No. 140, Department of Political Science, University of California, Berkeley.

Wilkins, M. (1970), *The Emergence of Multinational Enterprise*, Cambridge, US: Harvard University Press.

Williamson, O.E. (1975), *Markets and Hierarchies: Analysis and Antitrust Implications*, New York: The Free Press.

Williamson, O.E. (1985), *The Economic Institutions of Capitalism. Firms, Markets, Relational Contracting*, New York and London: The Free Press.

Zander, U. and B. Kogut (1995), 'Knowledge and the Speed of the Transfer and Imitation of Organizational Capabilities: An Empirical Test', *Organizational Science*, 5 (1), 76-92.

Zanfei, A. (2000), 'Transnational firms and the changing organisation of innovative activities', *Cambridge Journal of Economics*, 24, 515-42.

PART III

7. Digital Dynamics and Types of Industry Convergence:[*] The Evolution of the Handheld Computers Market

Nils Stieglitz

1. INTRODUCTION

One recurrent theme in the discussion about the salient features of the new digital economy is the claim that industries like telecommunications, computing and entertainment are converging and could one day evolve into one huge multimedia industry (Collis et al., 1997, *The Economist*, 2000a). The notion of industry convergence goes back to Rosenberg (1963) and his study of the early evolution of the US machine tool industry. A separate, specialized machine tool industry emerged in the mid-1800s as similar mechanical skills like drilling, grinding, polishing etc. were applied to diverse final products and industries. Rosenberg (1963) termed this process technological convergence, because different industries increasingly relied on the same set of technological skills in their production processes. Product markets which were apparently unrelated from a market perspective became closely related from a technological point of view. Examples of such technologically convergent industries in the 19th century are firearms, sewing machines and bicycles.

Sahal (1985) and Dosi (1988) have developed similar conceptions of technology-related industry convergence. They argue that certain technological paradigms spread their effects across various industries and induce innovative activities even in once stagnant markets. Key modern-day examples are digital electronics technologies like semiconductors and their impact on the computer, telecommunications and consumer electronics industries.[1]

Not surprisingly, this idea of industry convergence figures prominently in the management literature on corporate strategy and industry dynamics. Both Porter (1985) and Hamel and Prahalad (1994) independently argue that technological innovations may change the boundaries of traditional industries. As a result, different existing products are often becoming closer substitutes, since their functions are increasingly unified and bundled in innovative products (Katz, 1996; Yoffie, 1997). Thus, industry convergence not only implies the convergence of technologies but also of products. The strategic response to this 'new competitive landscape' (Bettis and Hitt, 1995) is an increased reliance on corporate networks and strategic alliances (Gomes-Casseres, 1996) and the migration and diversification of firms into convergent industries (Wirtz, 2001).

Despite this common interest in the issue of industry convergence, there has been little cross-fertilization between evolutionary economics and the strategic management literature. The diversity of definitions and of opinions about what industry convergence really means certainly does not help. While the notion of industry convergence is often used to characterize industrial dynamics in the new digital economy, it is seldom clearly defined (Katz, 1996). As a result, industry convergence often means different things to different authors. If industry convergence is to be more than a popular buzzword, the concept needs more analytical clarity.

Consequently, in section 2, four types of industry convergence are defined and related to the existing body of literature. The developed taxonomy allows us to identify and disentangle different drivers of industrial convergence. In section 3, the taxonomy is applied to the handheld computer industry in the 1990s and beyond. A handheld computer or Personal Digital Assistant (PDA) is a compact, palm-sized computing device. One of its defining product characteristics is the user's ability to hold the device in one hand while entering data with the other hand. Other key product characteristics are an expandable set of personal organizing software (calendar, address book etc.) and other programs and the ability to communicate with complementary devices like personal computers, fax machines and mobile phones. Thus, handheld computing lies at the core of the digital economy's emerging multimedia sector. We show that different types of industry convergence shaped corporate strategies and competitive dynamics in this particular industry at one point or another, making the handheld computer industry a particularly interesting case for studying industry convergence. Section 4 makes some main propositions and concludes.

2. CONVERGENCE DEFINED

In trying to specify the notion of industry convergence, it is useful first to reflect upon what is actually meant when talking about industries and markets. Traditionally, an industry is defined by the substitutability of the traded products (Geroski, 1998), and products can be considered substitutes if they satisfy the same needs (Abbott, 1955). Lancaster (1966) perceives a product as a bundle of multiple product characteristics. Consumers do not derive their utility from the product as such but from the embodied mixture of product characteristics. As a result, substitutes are products that share common characteristics, even if the exact mixture or specification of the product characteristics may vary. Consequently, the boundary of an industry is determined by grouping products with similar characteristics. Moreover, to derive or to increase the utility of a product, the joint use of this and other products may be required, for example a video recorder and a video cassette, or a CD player, an amplifier and speakers. Therefore, products can not only be substitutes, but complements as well.

Besides this demand-side approach to defining industries, there is also a small stream of literature which tries to tackle the issue from the supply side. Building on the resource-based view of the firm, Bettis (1998) claims that a firm competes against other firms with similar resources, not just against firms producing substitutable products. Industries could therefore be defined as groups of firms with similar resource bases. Hence, it is possible to define an industry from both the demand side (products) and the supply side (resources, technologies).

According to the Merriam-Webster (2000) dictionary, convergence signifies the movement towards the same point or the meeting of two or more elements. Thus, industry convergence involves the 'meeting' of at least two industries. Since industries can be defined by both demand and supply criteria, we can make a distinction between technology-based convergence from the supply side and product-based convergence from the demand side.

Technologically convergent industries produce different goods and services with similar technological capabilities. Two generic types of technology-based convergence are possible. The first type involves a new technology replacing different technologies in established industries. We term this type of technology-based convergence 'technology substitution'. In the second case, various technologies previously associated with different industries are fused or integrated, thereby giving rise to entirely new industries (Kodama, 1992, Iansiti, 1997). For this type of convergence we shall use Iansiti's (1997) notion of 'technology integration'.[2]

Industries characterized by product-based convergence offer new substitutable products or complementary product characteristics (Greenstein and Khanna, 1997). In the former case, an established product from one industry evolves to integrate product features that are similar to those of another product in a different industry. We shall label this type of product-based convergence 'product substitution'. In the latter case, two formerly unrelated products are turned into complements. We call this type of product-based convergence 'product complementarity'.[3]

The taxonomy is summarized in Figure 7.1.[4]

	Substitutes	Complements
Technology-based convergence	Technology substitution	Technology integration
Product-based convergence	Product substitution	Product complementarity

Figure 7.1 Types of industry convergence

Industry convergence is an inherently dynamic process which can be conceptualized as consisting of three distinct stages. In the first stage, two existing industries are unrelated from the viewpoint of both the supply and the demand side. A process of convergence is then triggered by an outside event, for example by the invention of a new technology. In the second stage, the industries converge, implying changes in industry boundaries, market structures and corporate strategies. Finally, in the third stage, the industries are related from a technological or product market perspective, and industry structures may stabilize, or new processes of convergence may evolve.

In order to further characterize each of these generic types of industry convergence, we employ a framework, advanced by Saviotti and Metcalfe (1984) and Saviotti (1996), which integrates the supply and demand characteristics of products and industries. A particular product can be represented by its technology and product characteristics respectively (Figure 7.2).

The technological characteristics X_1, X_2, ...X_N comprise the knowledge base required to transform inputs and labour into a particular product. The product exhibits a mixture of certain characteristics C_1, C_2, ...C_N which are used by the buyers to satisfy certain needs. The product characteristics offered by a firm crucially depend on the technologies utilized in the development and production of the product. In sections 2.1 and 2.2, the different types of convergence will be further discussed and specified by using this framework.

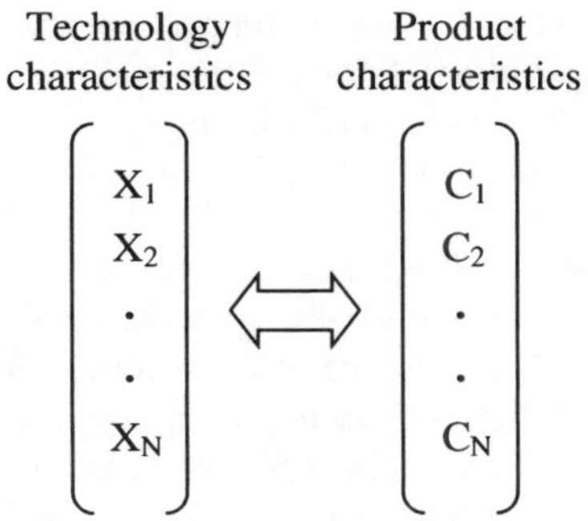

Technology   Product
characteristics   characteristics

$$
\begin{pmatrix} X_1 \\ X_2 \\ \cdot \\ \cdot \\ X_N \end{pmatrix} \Longleftrightarrow \begin{pmatrix} C_1 \\ C_2 \\ \cdot \\ \cdot \\ C_N \end{pmatrix}
$$

Source: Adapted from Saviotti, 1996.

Figure 7.2 The technology and product characteristics of a product

2.1 Technology-Based Convergence

Technology-based convergence implies that unrelated product markets become related from a technological point of view, because they begin to share the same technologies. Below, we shall give a 'stylized' outline of how two industries that use different technologies to produce the products A and B eventually become technologically convergent through either technology sub-stiution or integration (cf. Figure 7.3).

Technology substitution

Technology substitution is triggered by the introduction of a new process technology X_Z. The adoption of this technology in the production of product A and B represents a technological substitution of hitherto existing process technologies in these industries. Unlike all other forms of industry convergence, process innovation thus drives technology substitution. Consequently, as depicted in the left-hand side of Figure 7.3, the product characteristics of A or B are not affected. Technology substitution is characterized by the development and diffusion of the new technology. Eventually, the older technologies X_M and X_{M+1} are replaced, and the former unrelated industries become related from a technological point of view. For incumbent firms, technology substitution implies a technological discontinuity, since a part of their technological capabilities is rendered obsolete (Tushman and Anderson, 1986).

Empirically more prevalent is the case in which process innovations not only make the production of existing goods cheaper, but also transform the trade-offs associated with the bundling of product characteristics and their individual performance (Rosenberg, 1982). Thus the invention, development and diffusion of X_Z lead to a complex innovation process in which both the underlying technological capabilities and product characteristics in the two industries undergo modification and improvement. Such a process is typically associated with changes in market structures and corporate strategies in established industries.

Despite the technology-based convergence of the industries, their horizontal boundaries are not usually affected by technology substitution. What often changes, however, is the degree of vertical integration. Because the new technology does not build on the existing technological capabilities of incumbent firms, entrants or firms from different industries are often a primary source of innovation. Since the new technology can be applied in more industries, firms are able to specialize in its development and commercialization. This leads to the emergence of a specialized supplier industry upstream from the traditional industries, and correspondingly, an increasing tendency among incumbents to outsource their process technologies (Rosenberg, 1963; Pavitt, 1984; Rao, 1999).

This type of industry convergence is identical to Rosenberg's (1963) classic notion of technological convergence. As sketched in the introduction, industries like firearms (A) and sewing machines (B) became technologically convergent, since mechanical technologies like precision grinding (X_Z) replaced older technologies (X_M, X_{M+1}) dedicated to those industries and mostly developed by incumbent firms. In the wake of technological substitution, a specialized machine-tool industry emerged.

Technological substitution also lies at the heart of the new digital economy.[5] Since the 1970s, digital technologies have been widely diffused in many

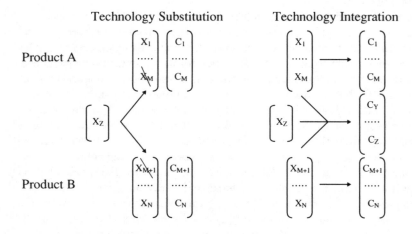

Figure 7.3 Types of technology-based convergence

established industries such as the machine tool industry, telecommunications, consumer electronics and financial services (Gambardella and Torrisi, 1998; Helpman, 1999). Older, analogue technologies have become and are still being replaced by new digital technologies. By the early 1980s, a specialized information technology sector had evolved, supplying both itself and other industries with hard- and software (Mowery, 1996; Chandler 2001).

Technology integration
Like technology substitution, technology integration may be triggered by the development of a new technology X_Z. While the new technology replaces existing technologies in technology substitution, technology integration creates the opportunity to combine the new with the existing technologies X_M and X_{M+1} to produce an entirely new product C (cf. right-hand side of Figure 7.3). An example is the development of the handheld computer in the early 1990s. Advances in handwriting recognition technology (X_Z) enabled companies from the telecommunications, computers and consumer electronics industries to offer the first handheld computers (C) by combining this technology and various existing technologies (X_M, X_{M+1}).

Since technology integration draws, at least in part, on existing technologies, established firms are able to utilize their technological capabilities, possibly in combination with new externally developed technologies, as a springboard for entering the emerging new industry (Teece et al., 1994; Bower 2002). Their pre-entry experience with established technologies could give them a competitive advantage over new entrants (Klepper and Simons, 2000; Helfat and Lieberman, 2002). However, a new entrant may be a serious threat to incumbents if it not only possesses a new distinct technological capability (X_Z) but also is an early mover in the emerging new industry.

The competitive dynamics of technological integration are shaped by two learning processes. Firstly, the creation of the entirely new product requires an entrepreneurial process of product and business development. Producers and users have to discover the basic characteristics constituting the product and how value is derived from them (Suarez and Utterback, 1995; Adner and Levinthal, 2000). This reflects a search for a dominant product design. Secondly, the existing technological capabilities have to be amended and integrated in order to be able to develop and produce the new product and enhance its quality over time (Kodama, 1992; Iansiti, 1997). This process of technological learning is particularly important if technological convergence is triggered by an entirely new technology X_Z. As Iansiti and West (1997, p. 69) point out, these two learning processes are interrelated because 'if a company selects technologies that don't work well together, it can end up with a product that is hard to manufacture, is late getting to market, and does not fulfil its envisioned purpose'.

2.2 Product-Based Convergence

In the case of product-based convergence, unrelated product markets become related from a market point of view. They begin to share similar or complementary product characteristics, leading to product substitution or product complementarity respectively (cf. Figure 7.4).

Product substitution

Product substitution leads to a (greater) substitutability between formerly unrelated products as they (increasingly) come to share the same product characteristics. As sketched in the left-hand side of Figure 7.4, product B is developed to also include a new characteristic C_M, making it a (partial) substitute of product A. Once again, this type of industry convergence is often sparked by a new technological capability (X_Z) that enables the changes in product characteristics.

Products become closer substitutes the more product characteristics they share. The industrial dynamics of product substitution involve increasing cross-industry competition in which firms from two or more industries expand their existing products by incorporating features from the other industry's products. Correspondingly, besides having to assimilate the new technology X_Z, firms in both industries also have to adopt existing technologies of the other industry.[6] This means that product substitution is often followed and accompanied by technology-based convergence as the technological features of firms in both industries converge. In the extreme case, the industries merge into one larger industry with similar technologies and product characteristics. This larger industry, however, tends to be characterized by several market segments and strategic groups of firms that still carry the traits of their former industries (see Christensen on Internet services, Chapter 8, this volume).

In contrast to technology integration, the learning process associated with product substitution takes its departure in existing dominant designs and firms can more incrementally build on and extend their existing products to develop convergent product offerings. The subsequent redrawing of industry boundaries may, however, lead to renewed uncertainty and ambiguity for established firms (Greenstein and Khanna, 1997). Firms have to discover who their new competitors and customers are, what bundles of product characteristics customers want and which new capabilities to build.

An example of convergence through product substitution is the dynamic relationship between the markets for mainframes and minicomputers in the 1970s and early 1980s (Bresnahan and Greenstein, 1999). Mainframes (product A) were used for general purposes, while minicomputers (product B) were employed for conducting highly specialised and repetitive single tasks. Accordingly, they differed substantially in terms of product characteristics and

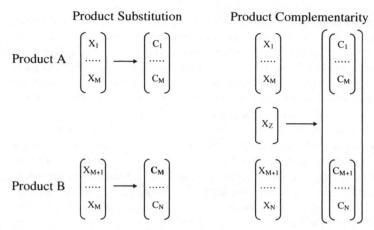

Figure 7.4 Types of product-based convergence

were considered distinct product markets. Technological innovations in semiconductors (X_Z) led to increased computing power for minicomputers which allowed their employment for more complex, general purpose tasks (C_M). The result was increased competition between mainframe and minicomputer manufacturers.

Product complementarity

Industry convergence through product complementarity means that existing products that were once used independently become complementary from a user perspective. Again, this type of product-related convergence is often caused by technological development and the creation of a standard interface (X_Z) which creates the opportunity to jointly use the two existing products (cf. right-hand side of Figure 7.4). Successful product complementarity leads to a situation in which two (or more) products deliver a higher value if used together.

While the new technology or standard (X_Z) is not needed to produce the products A or B individually, its task is to provide the 'glue' to align the two products. Some kind of standard or technical interface is necessary to govern the complementary use of the products (Katz, 1996; Yoffie, 1997). In some cases, only a new standard is required to trigger product complementarity, but usually new standards also imply new or adapted technologies. Consequently, product complementarity is being shaped by how and what kind of standards and technologies emerge.

Thus, for example, the development of the computer language HTML (X_Z) led to the development of HTML-based browser programs that allowed users to access Internet services easily via a PC (A) and existing telephone networks

(B). PCs and phones were formerly distinct products serving different needs, that is data processing and voice communication respectively. It was only after the commercial diffusion of the Internet that computers and telephone networks came to be widely perceived as complementary products in both business and households. Much the same is currently happening in the handheld computer industry. Due to rapid advances in wireless telecommunication technologies, online services can increasingly be accessed via PDAs.

Unlike product substitution, product complementarity does not lead to technology-based convergence, since incumbents do not have to attain the technologies underlying the product features of the complementary product. This is not to say that product complementarity has no impact on the established products. Often, product innovations are triggered by product complementarity, because the old products can be used in novel contexts. The Internet, for example, sparked a wave of product innovations in computer hardware and software, but also in telecommunications. Product complementarity thus has a major impact on industry dynamics and corporate strategies in the established industries.

These categories of industry convergence are fairly generic and represent abstract ideal types in the sense of Weber (1988). Empirical processes of industry convergence often combine two or more types of industry convergence and are paralleled by other sorts of innovative activities which have nothing to do with convergence. For example, a defining moment for the digital economy was the commercial advent of the Internet (see Kenney, Chapter 2, this volume). The subsequent product complementarity between personal computers and telecommunications propelled innovations in the two industries. At the same time, rapid advances in computing power and semiconductor technologies continued, but these innovations were carried on independently of the dynamics of industry convergence. In addition, several types of convergence may be shaping industry dynamics and corporate strategy in a particular market. For instance, technology-based convergence could bring about a process of product substitution because firms in different industries acquire similar technological capabilities. It is the main proposition of this chapter that the suggested typology of industry convergence allows the identification and disentanglement of different drivers of change in converging markets, and provides a basic framework for analysing complex patterns of industry convergence. This will be attempted with respect to the handheld computer case in the next section.

3. INDUSTRY CONVERGENCE: THE CASE OF HANDHELD COMPUTERS

Most prior studies of industry convergence have analysed industry convergence based on technology substitution (see, for example, Rosenberg, 1976; Gambardella and Torrisi, 1998; Duysters and Hagedoorn, 1998; Rao, 1999). Technology substitution is a pervasive phenomenon in the digital economy, and it forms the background of our case study of the handheld computer industry; however, our focus here will be on other types of industry convergence that have been comparatively neglected in the literature.

In the late 1990s, the handheld computer industry was among the fastest growing markets of the digital economy. In 2000, nearly 11 million PDAs were shipped worldwide and market growth was a stunning 112 per cent (Hamilton, 2001). The handheld computer industry has been influenced by different types of convergence at different stages in its evolution. As will be discussed in greater detail below, the formative years were characterized by technology integration since different technologies from consumer electronics, computers and telecommunications were integrated in the development of handheld computers. However, the competitive landscape has been transformed by new forms of industry convergence since the early 2000s. Handheld computers are becoming substitutes for mobile phones, implying a convergence process of product substitution between the handheld computer industry and the mobile phone industry. A process of product complementarity is accelerating this development, as multimedia online services and handheld computers are evolving into complementary products.

3.1 The Evolution of the Handheld Computer Industry: An Overview

A handheld computer's basic hardware consists of a microprocessor, a solid-state memory, a liquid crystal display (LCD), an input device, batteries and various input/output ports and extension slots. Psion, a former software company, developed the first handheld computer in 1984 (Potter, 1998). Psion's Organiser was basically a programmable calculator with a database and a simple calendar. The first generation of handheld computers, appropriately called electronic organizers, was heavily inspired by pen and paper organizers. Early imitators were, among other consumer electronics companies, Casio and Sharp who both entered the emerging market in 1988. By 1991, Casio and Sharp had together gained a worldwide market share of 90 per cent (Consumer Reports, 1991, p. 768). The same year Hewlett-Packard entered the industry while Psion launched the Series 3, a major revision of its earlier model. For the next two years, Hewlett-Packard and Psion were Casio's and Sharp's main competitors.

A second generation of handheld computers was brought onto the market in 1993. Established firms like Apple, AT&T, Motorola and Sony developed 'Personal Digital Assistants', a term coined by Apple CEO Sculley in 1992. Compared to the earlier electronic organizers, the PDAs had vastly expanded product features, and all of them used handwriting recognition as the input device. However, the second generation PDAs turned out to be commercial failures, and all the new entrants had again left the industry by 1998. In contrast, the early pioneers Casio, Hewlett-Packard, Psion and Sharp prospered by incrementally expanding the features during these years, but overall industry growth was less than industry observers had predicted for the emerging handheld computer market.

A revival of the PDA was expected when Microsoft launched a handheld computer version of its successful Windows operating system, Windows CE, in late 1996 (Bennahum, 1995; Bournellis, 1996). Microsoft did not become a handheld computer company itself, but licensed its operating system to PDA makers. New entrants who licensed Windows CE were Philips, Hitachi and LG Electronics, and Casio and Hewlett-Packard adopted the operating system for new versions of their handhelds. Despite the powerful technological and marketing capabilities of these firms, Windows CE-based PDAs only gained a 20 percent share of the US market in 1997 (Butter and Pogue, 2002, p. 171).

Instead, the Pilot handheld computer came to dominate the market, with a US market share of well over 70 percent in 1997. The Pilot was developed by the software company Palm Computing. Before deciding to design its own handheld computer, Palm had been a specialized supplier of application software and handwriting recognition technology for PDAs. With the Pilot, Palm established what quickly became the dominant design of handheld computers, and a driver for rapid industry growth. Handspring, a spin-off founded by former key employees at Palm, grew to become Palm's main competitor in 1999 (Butter and Pogue, 2002, pp. 234-41). Another threat to Palm's dominance was the introduction of Microsoft's PocketPC operating system, a substantially revised version of Windows CE, in 2000. Compaq's iPaQ became the most successful PocketPC-based handheld, reaching a worldwide market share of 13 percent in 2001. The same year, Palm's market share dropped to 57 percent, down from 64 percent in 2000.

3.2 Technology Integration in the Formative Years of the Handheld Computer Industry

Technology integration shaped the early phases of the handheld computer industry in the late 1980s and early 1990s. Technologies that had their roots in different industries were combined in the development of the first waves of PDAs. Thus, for example, LCD displays and power management technologies

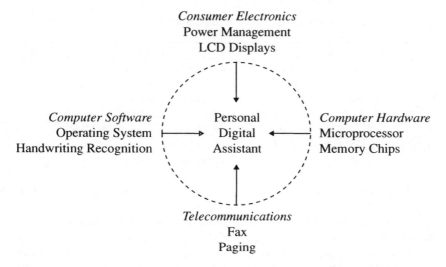

Figure 7.5 Technology integration in the handheld computer industry

emanated from the consumer electronics industry, while the computer industry provided semiconductors, memory chips and operating system software (Figure 7.5).

The formative years of the handheld computer industry were characterized by two major waves of market entry. In both waves, established large firms from consumer electronics, computers and telecommunications played leading roles. They could largely draw on their existing technological capabilities and components to develop their products. This was obviously the case with the two major consumer electronics entrants, Casio and Sharp. Sharp had pioneered the development of electronic calculators and LCD displays in the 1970s and was the largest supplier of LCDs in the late 1980s (Fransman, 1995; Chandler, 2001, pp. 67-71). Likewise, Casio relied on its experience in calculators, watches and handheld television receivers. Their pre-entry technological experience and existing complementary assets (Teece, 1986; Christensen, 1995) like brand reputation and distribution, especially in the US and Japanese markets, gave them an early competitive advantage over innovative start-up entrants like Poqet Computer Corporation, a Fairchild spin-off, or Psion, a former software company, that launched the very first handheld computer (Table 7.1). Founded in 1980, Psion had developed computer games prior to the launch of the Organiser and thus had only a very narrow technological base. Hewlett-Packard's entry was based primarily on the company's existing technological capabilities, especially in the design of scientific calculators. Hewlett-Packard had pioneered the scientific handheld calculator in

Table 7.1   Major market entries in the handheld computer industry, 1984-92

Entry year	Entrants	Product	Original Industry	Year of exit?
1984	Psion	*Organiser*	Computer Software	2001
1988	Casio	*Boss*	Consumer Electronics	
	Sharp	*Wizard*	Consumer Electronics	
1989	Atari	*Portfolio*	Computer Hardware	1996
	Poqet	*Poqet PC*	Start-up	1996
1991	Hewlett-Packard	*LX 95*	Calculators, Computer Hardware	

1973 and was the market leader in programmable calculators in the 1980s (Resnick, 1992; Roberts, 1992).

Due to limited functionality, widespread adoption of handheld computers failed to materialize in the wake of the first wave of entrants. These early models relied on tiny keyboards that made entering data a cumbersome process. However, the technological problems associated with the user interface came to act as a focusing device (Rosenberg, 1976, p. 125) for further innovation efforts in the industry.

In the early 1990s, pen-based computing associated with handwriting recognition was predicted to become a major new breakthrough technology for personal computers. GriD, a Tandy division, had introduced the first pen-based tablet computer in 1988 (Butter and Pogue, 2002, pp. 6-9). In 1991, IBM, NCR and Toshiba announced plans to bring pen-based tablet computers to the market, and venture capitalists financed many start-ups developing pen-based computing technologies (*The Economist*, 1990). Furthermore, following the path paved by Apple's MacOS operating system, software companies like Microsoft, GeoWorks and General Magic were developing graphical user interfaces that would simplify user interaction (Wright and Caron, 1991; Rogers, 1992). Lastly, the continuous rapid advances in computing power made it possible to add ever more functions to desktop computers, laptops and, eventually, to handheld devices (Linderholm et al., 1992).

These technological opportunities were mainly developed in the personal computer industry, but they created the foundation for a new wave of product innovations and market entry in handheld computing. This wave took off in 1993 and consisted of firms diversifying from personal computers, consumer electronics and telecommunications (Gomes-Casseres and Leonard-Barton, 1997; Bayus et al., 1997). Entrants included Apple, AT&T, Motorola, Tandy and Sony (Table 7.2).[7] Despite very innovative products, these second-wave innovations became commercial failures, and all involved firms left the handheld computer industry during the subsequent five years.

Table 7.2 Main market entries of second-generation PDAs, 1993-94

Entry year	Entrants	Product	Original Industry	Exit year
1993	AT&T	*EO440*	Telecommunications	1994
	Apple	*Newton*	Computer Hardware	1998
	Tandy and Casio	*Zoomer*	Consumer Electronics	1995
	Amstrad	*PenPad*	Consumer Electronics	1996
1994	IBM and BellSouth	*Simon*	Computer Hardware, Telecommunications	1996
	Motorola	*Envoy, Marco*	Computer Hardware	1996
	Sony	*MagicLink*	Consumer Electronics	1996

Technology integration is associated with a distinct pattern of industry dynamics and corporate strategy. Firstly, technology integration requires technological learning of how to align different kinds of technological knowledge developed in different industries. Secondly, the technology integration implies entrepreneurial endeavours, the creation of an entirely new product and the search for a dominant design. Each of the dynamics will be discussed below in connection to the emergence of the handheld computer industry.

Technological learning and strategic alliances

Technology integration implies the fusion of technologies from different industries. With two exceptions, none of the entrants had in-house access to all the technologies required to develop their products. They therefore formed strategic alliances with firms from other industries.[8] The exceptions were the early movers Sharp and Casio, whose models relied exclusively on internal technological capabilities. For instance, Sharp's Wizard electronic organizer was based on LCD displays and semiconductors originally developed for Sharp's long-standing product line of calculators. As new technological opportunities were created in the computer industry and handheld computers became technologically more complex, Casio and Sharp turned to strategic alliances to gain access to the increasing range of technologies.

These alliances were largely knowledge-using rather than knowledge-developing (Mowery et al., 1998), even if the existing technologies had to be modified for use in a handheld device (Gomes-Casseres and Leonard-Barton, 1997). For example, Casio and Tandy collaborated to develop the Zoomer PDA in 1993. Their partners were GeoWorks who modified their GEOS operating system, originally developed for home computers, while Palm Computing, a Tandy spin-off, provided the handwriting recognition software originally devised for the GridPad pen-based computer.

The integration of internal capabilities and external technologies was particularly important in the development of two highly innovative products introduced by Apple and AT&T. Apple created the concept of a 'Personal Digital Assistant' with its Newton PDA, which drew extensively on its in-house capabilities in hardware and software design. For handwriting recognition, Apple entered a knowledge-developing alliance with ParaGraph International. The low power consumption CPU was developed by ARM in close co-operation with Apple. For other technologies, Apple entered knowledge-using alliances with, among others, Sharp (LCD screens, manufacturing), Toshiba (CD-ROMs) and US West (communication services). Likewise, AT&T built the EO 440 PDA around its already developed Hobbit microprocessor with the help of GO Corporation (handwriting recognition), Matsushita (manufacturing) and Sharp (LCD display).

Product learning, pre-entry experience and the search for a dominant design

In convergence through technological integration, another key learning area is associated with business and product development, since producers and users have to find out what features and design constitute a valuable product. The early entrants tested very different concepts of a PDA.[9] Each of these were heavily influenced by the firms's pre-entry experiences. The early designs of Sharp, Casio and Hewlett-Packard basically were basically programmable calculators with a database. With the Newton, Apple developed a highly innovative product that was, in essence, a mobile information processor. Its design and features were inspired by the personal computer. Apple planned to generate most of its profit from selling application software for the Newton. Accordingly, like many firms in the computer industry, Apple freely licensed its hardware technology (McGahan et al., 1997). In contrast, AT&T's participation in the development of the EO 440 led to the creation of a personal communicator with very strong communication features based on a built-in fax/modem (*Popular Electronics*, 1994). Profits were expected to come from proprietary communication services.

The second generation of PDAs, introduced in 1993 and 1994, were all valiant failures. These models were bulky, slow and expensive. Handwriting recognition, as the only input device, was technologically advanced but error-prone and unreliable for serious day-to-day use. They thus failed to fully integrate the various technologies and deliver effective functionality to the customer (Bayus et al., 1997). The pre-entry experiences of these firms appear to have been liabilities, rather than assets in this particular industry, because they led to flawed design decisions (Leonard-Barton, 1992). Market growth came from the first-generation entrants, Sharp, Casio, Hewlett-Packard and Psion, whose combined market-share was more than 70 percent in 1994, despite the large influx of new firms the year before. These early pioneers already had a dynamic learning base on which to build industry-specific capabilities when the second generation competitors entered the market. They based product design on their existing models and added new features with each new product generation (Bennahum, 1995). The four early movers are still important players in the handheld computer industry.

From 1996 onwards, industry growth exploded (Figure 7.6). This was due neither to the first nor second generation PDAs, but can largely be attributed to the introduction of the Pilot PDA in April 1996. With the Pilot, the start-up company Palm Computing established the dominant design of a PDA.[10] Prior to the development of the Pilot, Palm had been a key partner of Casio and Tandy in the development of the Zoomer. As a specialized supplier, it had provided the handwriting recognition technology and application software. After the commercial failure of the Zoomer, the handheld computer market was too small to keep Palm afloat as a specialized supplier and Palm's management decided to develop its own PDA (Butter and Pogue, 2002, pp. 66-9).

Despite its narrow technology base, Palm possessed critical capabilities in handwriting recognition, operating systems and connectivity software. The residual technologies required to build a handheld were largely accessible through off-the-shelf products (for example, a Motorola processor and an outdated Toshiba memory chip).[11] For hardware design and production, Palm cooperated with, respectively, Palo Alto Design Group and Flextronics, a manufacturer with long-standing experience in consumer electronics.[12] In this way, Palm exploited the window of opportunity opened by technological integration despite its narrow range of technological capabilities.

PDA Sales worldwide 1993-2002

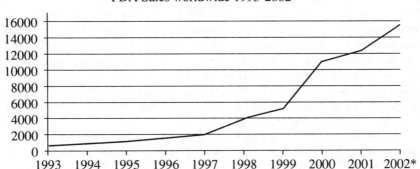

Note: * 2002 expected.
Source: Gartner Dataquest.

Figure 7.6 Units sold in the handheld computer industry

Furthermore, Palm's product design was not constrained by existing experience and routines developed in other industries. Its involvement in the Zoomer project was an important learning experience. A major weakness of the Zoomer and other second generation PDAs remained handwriting recognition. Palm drew the right lessons and developed the Graffiti technology for the Pilot. Unlike other approaches to handwriting recognition, Graffiti did not try to interpret the handwriting of the user, but forced the user to adopt a stylized alphabet. Thereby, Graffiti proved to be more reliable and faster than other, more ambitious, handwriting recognition technologies. Despite the lack of communication features and without sophisticated software bundles, the Pilot was successful because, in the words of one reviewer (Himowitz, 1996, p. 224), it is a 'gadget that does a few things very well'. The second generation PDAs thus did not fail because they tried 'too little, too early', as Bayus et al. (1997) claim, but because they tried too much, too early.[13]

3.3 Product Complementarity between Handheld Computers and Online Services

While many second-generation PDAs contained data communication features like fax, e-mail and rudimentary Internet access, these product characteristics were not key features of a handheld computer. Since 2000, this has been changing. Increasingly, PDAs can be used to access Internet services. A real boost to data communications is expected to come from new wireless telecommunication standards like GPRS (General Packet Radio Standard) and especially the UMTS (Universal Mobile Telecommunications System) standard that has been introduced since 2002 (*The Economist*, 2000b; Maitland et al., 2002). Other important emerging network technologies are Bluetooth and 802.11b (Kenedy, 2002; *The Economist*, 2002). All these wireless telecommunications technologies offer a higher bandwidth than the current GSM (Global System for Mobile Telecommunications) standard. They make possible the complementary use of multimedia online services and cellular phones, but also of PDAs. Consequently, PDAs and online services are converging as complementary products, since the emerging wireless technologies create the prospect of making multimedia data communications an integral feature of a PDA, not just an expensive add-on.

As a result, industry dynamics have become increasingly influenced by this process of product complementarity. As outlined in Section 2, a prerequisite for product complementarity is the emergence of a standard that enables the complementary use of formerly distinct products. We look first at how these standards evolve in the handheld computer industry. Secondly, we discuss the impact of product complementarity on product development of handheld computers.

Product complementarity and standards in handheld computing

Currently, the handheld computer industry is influenced by competing standards at two levels. In wireless communication, it is still not clear which of the many incompatible standards will prevail in the market. Many telecommunications firms who expected UMTS to become the future standard have seen their very optimistic expectations shattered as other wireless technologies, like GPRS and Bluetooth, have matured and become commercially feasible (Fransman, 2002). However, PDA makers are barely able to influence this. They will have to more or less passively adapt to whatever de facto standard emerges.

The second standards issue relates to the operating system on which PDAs and other wireless multimedia devices will rely (Neel and Leon, 2001). At the moment, the main contenders in the handheld computer industry are Palm and Microsoft (Yoffie and Kwak, 2001). Palm has made its operating system PalmOS an open standard, thereby encouraging many independent software companies to develop software for PalmOS-based PDAs. Palm and its primary licensee, Handspring, have a dominant, but declining market share in the PDA market. According to Aberdeen Group (2002), the two firms had a combined worldwide market share of 79 percent in 2000. This large installed user and developer base remains Palm's prime competitive advantage. Microsoft licenses its proprietary operating system to PDA makers like Casio and Compaq. While not very successful in the beginning, Microsoft and its licensees have won market shares since 2000, especially in the market for corporate users (Hamilton, 2001). Palm's worldwide market share sharply dropped from 64 percent in 2000 to 57 percent in 2001. Microsoft's licensees increased their market share from 10 to over 20 percent. The recent success is largely attributed to the much enhanced wireless communications and multimedia features of Microsoft's PocketPC operating system (Nobel, 2000). These features enable the product complementarity between PocketPC-based PDAs with wireless online services, making PocketPC the preferred product for corporate clients and high-end users.

Product development

Product complementarity leads to changes in the features of existing products. In the handheld computer industry, all companies are currently attempting to broaden the multimedia capabilities of their devices and improve the wireless communications features.[14]

For example, Palm released its first wireless, Internet-enabled handheld in 1999 and a handheld with a colour LCD display in early 2000. One of its latest models introduced in 2002, the Palm i705, features instant messaging and 'always on' e-mail technology. For these communication services, Palm has entered a strategic alliance with online service provider AOL. Furthermore,

Palm has built up its own wireless network for Internet access, Palm.net, with the assistance of BellSouth. In 2002, Palm has introduced a Bluetooth extension card for its PDAs that has been developed together with start-up company Broadcom. Palm has also entered alliances with Texas Instrument and Toshiba to develop wireless technologies and applications. Similarly, Handspring expanded its in-house capabilities in data communications with the acquisition of BlueLark Systems in 2000. BlueLark had developed the Blazer browser which can access not only Internet content explicitly designed for mobile access but also standard HTML sites. Moreover, Handspring's Visor PDA features an innovative expansion slot makes it possible to expand the Visor's multimedia functionality with add-on modules, including, among others, wireless modems, MP3 players, Bluetooth cards and GPS (Global Positioning System) location-tracking systems. These modules are developed by independent firms.

3.4 Product Substitution: the Development of 'Smart Cell Phones'

The new wireless communications technologies are also fuelling a process of product substitution. Consumers can access mobile online services either through their cellular phones or their PDAs. This development leads to a higher substitutability of cell phones and PDAs (Sabat, 2002, p. 531). This convergence dynamics has been reinforced by advances in miniaturization achieved in the development and production of mobile phones. This has made the combination of voice communication and features of a PDA in a single device technically viable. As outlined in Section 2, the established dominant designs are the point of departure for convergence processes towards product substitution. New product designs evolve from there. Firms have to discover exactly what mixture of features users want in convergent products. The result is experimentation and renewed industry ambiguity.

Product evolution

Early attempts at developing 'smart cell phones' were the Simon PDA developed by IBM and BellSouth and Nokia's Communicator, both introduced in 1996 (Clarke, 1995). These devices had very rudimentary organizing features and could not be considered substitutes for a PDA. But this is now changing. Mobile phone companies Kyocera, Samsung, Motorola and Nokia and PDA maker Handspring have all released smart phones in late 2001, with many more models following in 2002 (Crockett, 2001; Thornton and Aquino, 2002). These products combine the salient product characteristics of a PDA and of a mobile phone into one compact design. To develop convergent products, the established firms build on their existing technological capabilities and product designs.

Nokia has been an early mover (Steinbock, 2001). In 1996, Nokia released the Communicator, an early cell phone/PDA hybrid. While not very successful commercially, it initiated Nokia's ongoing involvement in the development of hybrid phones and was thus an important learning experience. In 1998, Nokia was a founding member of Symbian, a joint venture set up by Ericsson, Motorola and PDA maker Psion (*Business Europe*, 1999; Baker, 2000). Symbian was formed to promote Psion's EPOC operating system, originally developed for Psion's handhelds, as the standard operating system for wireless communication. In 2001, Nokia released the latest Communicator smart phone, the 9210, with great success in Europe (Livingstone, 2002). Motorola and a joint venture formed by Ericsson and Sony also released Symbian-based smart phones in 2001 and 2002. With Psion's expertise and the backing of many cell phone makers, the Symbian operating system is a strong contender for Palm and Microsoft in the emerging market segment of operating systems for smart phones.

In the PDA market, Handspring is pursuing a convergence strategy by diversifying into cellular phones (Butter and Pogue, 2002, pp. 302-23). In late 2000, Handspring shipped the VisorPhone module for its Visor PDA. Developed together with Belgian company Option International, the VisorPhone adds voice and data communications to the Visor. In late 2001, Handspring released a smart phone, the Treo. The built-in communication module of the Treo was developed by the French firm Wavecom (Fyffe, 2001). For the 3G-enabled version of the Treo, Handspring is co-operating with the telecommunications companies Sprint and Airprime.

Industry ambiguity

As illustrated in the case of PDAs and mobile phones, product substitution leads to a redrawing of industry boundaries and, hence, to a renewed uncertainty about competitors, customers and suppliers for all firms in the two industries. It is far from clear how large the demand for genuinely convergent products really is (Frontline Solutions, 2002). Many customers who only want a cell phone for voice communication will be unwilling to pay a higher price for integrated PDA functions. Accordingly, many firms are reluctant to jump on the convergence bandwagon. For example, Palm has so far refused to develop smart phones, focusing on wireless data communication instead (Nelson et al., 2000; Butter and Pogue, 2002, pp. 301-3). Palm's only stakes in the market segment for hybrid products are licences for their operating system to Kyocera and Samsung. In this way, Palm is focusing its strategic effort on handheld computers, expecting smart phones to remain a niche market. Handspring, on the other hand, is clearly pursuing an active convergence strategy. Thereby, Handspring not only competes against traditional PDA makers, but also against innovative mobile phone companies. Handspring is currently broadening its range of technological capabilities to integrate voice communications. Palm's and Handspring's learning trajectories diverge as a result. It remains to be seen how successful the hybrid products will become and how large the market segment for these convergent offerings will turn out to be.

4. CONCLUSIONS: PATTERNS OF INDUSTRY CONVERGENCE

The emergence of a digital economy has clearly put industry convergence on centre stage in understanding industrial dynamics. As we have seen, there are different forms of industry convergence, and they shape industry dynamics in different ways. Technology substitution, barely touched upon in this chapter, lies at the heart of the digital economy. Unlike other forms of industry convergence, process innovations take the helm in technological substitution. Since digital technologies are applicable to a range of industries, firms are able to specialize in their commercialization. This leads to the creation of supplier industries upstream from traditional markets as Christensen shows in his chapter on the Internet service industry.

This contrasts with industry convergence based on technology integration. Technology integration usually leads to the creation of new products largely based on existing technologies. Associated with technology integration are two dynamic learning processes involving both business and product development and the underlying 'fusion' of technologies. These trial-and-error processes are the key drivers of industry dynamics in technology integration. In the handheld computer industry, a start-up company was able to draw the right conclusions from these learning experiences. Besides controlling key technologies, Palm was able to access and integrate missing technological capabilities through off-the-shelf products and, to a lesser extent, strategic alliances. Despite the widespread entry of established firms from computers, telecommunications and consumer electronics, Palm emerged as the dominant firm.

Product complementarity is a whole different story. Here existing products in established markets, rather than existing technologies, form the starting points for industry convergence. Established firms draw on their existing technological and complementary capabilities to cope with product complementarity. Standards and the corresponding technologies are needed to enable product complementarity. Industry outsiders often develop these enabling technologies. In the handheld computer industry, important technologies to make wireless online access possible are provided by new firms like BlueLark and Broadcom. PDA makers do not have much influence on the development and diffusion of wireless telecommunications standards. In contrast, the battle for the dominant operating system for 'intelligent cell phones' could be decided in the handheld computer industry.

In product substitution, different products converge to become closer substitutes. Firms pursue convergence through product substiution by expanding their established products with new product features from products in other industries. These firms tend to build on their existing technological and complementary capabilities in developing hybrid products. Over the years, Nokia has incrementally extended the Communicator's organizing features, while Handspring started from its Visor PDA. Handspring first developed an external add-on phone and later a built-in voice communication module. In the wake of this product evolution, the boundaries of the established markets are becoming ambiguous, leading to increased competition and a renewed uncertainty about competitors, users and suppliers.

Consequently, different types of industry convergence have to be distinguished because they differ in their underlying patterns of industry dynamics. The case study of the handheld computer industry has tried to shed some light on these different dynamics of industry convergence. The proposed taxonomy is only a very first step towards a more thorough analysis of these patterns. To develop these ideas further, the taxonomy could be linked with the literature on sectoral systems of innovation (Malerba and Orsenigo, 2000; Marsili, 2001; Malerba, 2002). Using sectoral systems of innovation as a conceptual backdrop, various determinants of industrial convergence could be more systematically analysed.

An important open question to be studied is the dynamic interplay between the different forms of industry convergence. In the handheld computer industry, the creation of product complementarity with wireless communications generates opportunities and incentives for product substitution, since access to multimedia online services makes smart phones more attractive. In the digital economy, large companies in particular expand and diversify their technology bases as Mendonça demonstrates in his contribution to this book (Chapter 5). These broader technology bases may form the starting point for industry convergence of different types, since large firms control technologies from different fields and industries. For example, in the handheld computer industry, Sharp and Casio drew extensively on their existing capabilities in various technological fields. These firms were looking for new ways to apply their diversified technological capabilities and, eventually, created an entirely new industry.

The developed taxonomy allows for the identification and analysis of these complex constellations by highlighting the different roles played by the various forms of convergence. However, our understanding of the dynamic interdependencies between the different types of convergence remains limited, and much more theoretical and empirical work is needed.

NOTES

*   An earlier version of this chapter was presented at the DRUID Summer Conference 2002 in Copenhagen. It has benefited from many helpful comments by Keith Pavitt, Peter Maskell, Elmar Gerum, Jonas Kjær, Michael Olesen and especially Jens Frøslev Christensen. All remaining errors are mine.

1. Such technologies are what Bresnahan and Trajtenberg (1995) term general-purpose technologies. See Carlsson in this book (Chapter 1) for a review of historical examples of general-purpose technologies and the particular case of computers and the Internet.

2. I am indebted to Jens Frøslev Christensen for pointing out the link between industry convergence and Iansiti's (1997) notion of technological integration and for suggesting the labelling of the different types of industry convergence developed in this chapter.

3. Substitution and integration of technologies or products of course also take place within a single industry and without any associated industry convergence. In this chapter, however, we shall only use the terms as related to industry convergence. Hence, to keep things simple, we will speak of technology substitution instead of 'industry convergence through technology substitution' and so on.

4. For a similar representation, see Pennings and Puranam (2001). They differentiate between demand side and supply side convergence. Demand side convergence is caused by growing similarity of needs across groups of consumers or the de-regulation of industries. The result is greater substitutability between different groups of consumers ('substitution') or the bundling of different products in a single architecture ('complementarity'). An example of demand substitution is the globalization of markets, while the bundling of hard- and software illustrates demand complementarity. Technological change leads to supply side convergence. In the case of 'supply side substitution', different technologies become similar in the sense that they can satisfy the same set of needs. Examples are digital imaging and photography technologies. Different technologies are brought together to create new kinds of technology in 'supply side complementarity', for example optoelectronics.

5. Important differences exist between the evolution of the machine tool industry and of the computer industry. In the former case, the new knowledge that eventually led to technology substitution was initially developed by machine-using firms, and specialized suppliers emerged in co-operation with and close vicinity to the user firms (Rosenberg, 1963). This contrasts with the emergence of the computer industry, in which a few firms like IBM and Sperry Rand developed the new knowledge, while the user firms had to adapt to and adopt the new technologies (Chandler, 2001). However, in both cases dynamic learning processes between technology producers and users were crucial, and these differences in the sources of knowledge largely arise from the different technological regimes of computers and machinery (Marsili, 2001).

6. The extent to which firms must adopt the technological capabilities of the other industry critically depends on the existence of off-the-shelf technologies and standardized interfaces (Demsetz, 1991; Baldwin and Clark, 1997). If these exist, firms only have to develop a general understanding of the technologies in order to be able to successfully integrate the technologies (see Pavitt, Chapter 4, this volume). This is relevant for all types of industry convergence.

7. See *Popular Electronics* (1994) and Bayus et al. (1997) for the PDAs introduced in 1993 and 1994.

8. *Red Herring* (1993) and Halfhill (1993) list the major strategic alliances involved in developing second-generation PDAs. See McGahan, Vadasz and Yoffie (1997) and especially Gomes-Casseres and Leonard-Barton (1997) for a much more detailed analysis.

9. Sakakibara et al. (1995) provide an in-depth discussion of the different product development approaches to second-generation PDAs.

10. In September 1995, before the launch of the Pilot, Palm Computing was acquired by US Robotics, which in June 1999 was bought by 3COM. In March 2000, after a successful IPO, Palm again became an independent company. See Butter and Pogue (2002) for a history of Palm.

11. Baldwin and Clark (1997) discuss the crucial role of off-the-shelf technologies for innovation strategies in general and for Palm's case in particular. With the decision to develop its own PDA, Palm became an architect (Baldwin and Clark, 1997) or system integrator (see Pavitt, Chapter 4, this volume), because Palm now defined product interfaces via the hardware design and especially PalmOS, the operating system developed by Palm.
12. With 65 plants worldwide, Flextronics is one of the world's leading contract manufacturers that have established themselves as global flagship networks (see Ernst, Chapter 6, this volume). Flextronics does not only offer manufacturing services to its clients, but design and supply chain services as well.
13. Unlike, for example, Apple's Newton, Palm's Pilot was expressly designed to complement a personal computer. Accordingly, it had only limited, but tightly integrated features. Its main applications – calendar, address manager, to-do list and memo pad – could be launched instantly by pressing a button. Newton, on the other hand, offered a very sophisticated file management and many more programs than the Pilot, but they were much slower than Pilot's applications. Moreover, the synchronization between a desktop PC and the Pilot was made easy by a specially designed device and Palm's own connectivity software. Newton users, on the other hand, had to buy an additional device. Newton's handwriting recognition, while technologically advanced, was nevertheless error-prone and too unreliable for serious day-to-day use. The Newton was very bulky compared to the shirt-pocked sized Pilot. Lastly, the Pilot was a lot cheaper ($300 in 1996) than the Newton ($700 in 1993).
14. In on-line services, content providers like CNN and Internet portals like Yahoo are also adapting their products. They offer modified, scaled-down versions of their regular Internet content for access via a PDA or a cell phone. But these offerings probably will be a transitory phenomenon, as the third generation wireless communication standards will eventually be introduced and fast wireless Internet access will become widely available. For an account of mobile Internet strategies of online service providers, see Feldmann (2002).

REFERENCES

Abbot, Lawrence (1955), *Quality and Competition*, New York: Columbia University Press.

Aberdeen Group (2002), Various press releases, download under www.aberdeen.com.

Adner, R. and D. A. Levinthal (2000), 'Technology Speciation and the Path of Emerging Technologies', in Gary S. Day and Paul J.H. Schoemaker (eds), *Wharton on Managing Emerging Technologies*, New York, Chichester: John Wiley, 57-74.

Baker, S. (2000), 'Why Psion is still in the game', *Business Week*, 04/03/2000 (3675), 46-7.

Baldwin, C.Y. and K.B. Clark (1997), 'Managing in an Age of Modularity', *Harvard Business Review*, 75 (5), 84-93.

Bayus, B.L., S. Jain and A.G. Rao (1997), 'Too Little, too Early: Introduction Timing and New Product Performance in the Personal Digital Assistant Industry', *Journal of Marketing Research*, 33, 50-63.

Bennahum, D. (1995), 'The return of the PDA', *MC: Marketing Computers,* 15 (2), 34-42.

Bettis, R.A. (1998), 'Comment on "Redefining Industry Structure for the Information Age" by J.L. Sampler', *Strategic Management Journal*, 19, 357-62.

Bettis, R.A. and M.A. Hitt (1995), 'The New Competitive Landscape', *Strategic Management Journal*, 16, 7-19.

Bournellis, C. (1996), 'Handhelds based on Windows CE start the rush', *Electronic News*, 42 (2144), 1-3.

Bower, J.L. (2002), 'Not all M&As are alike – and that matters', *Harvard Business Review*, 80 (2), 93-101.

Bresnahan, T.F. and S. Greenstein (1999), 'Technological Competition and the Structure of the Computer Industry', *Journal of Industrial Economics*, XLVII (1), 1-40.

Bresnahan, T.F. and M. Trajtenberg (1995), 'General Purpose Technologies: Engines of Growth?', *Journal of Econometrics*, 65, 63-108.

Business Europe (1999), 'The Symbian Gamble', *Business Europe*, 39 (5), 1-3.

Butter, Andrea and David Pogue (2002), *Piloting Palm*, New York: John Wiley.

Chandler, Alfred D. (2001), *Inventing the Electronic Century*, New York: Free Press.

Christensen, C.M., F.F. Suarez and J.M. Utterback (1998), 'Strategies for Survival in Fast-Changing Industries', *Management Science*, 44, 207-20.

Christensen, J.F. (1995), 'Asset Profiles for Technological Innovation', *Research Policy*, 24, 727-45.

Clarke, M. (1995), 'Nokia Smart Phones take on a PDA Role', *Electronic Engineering Times*, 2/20/95 (836), 14.

Collis, D.J., P.W. Bane and S.P. Bradley (1997), 'Winners and Losers: Industry Structure in the Converging World of Telecommunications, Computing, and Entertainment', in David B. Yoffie (ed.), *Competing in the Age of Digital Convergence*, Boston: Harvard Business School Press, 159-99.

Consumer Reports (1991), 'Need Organizing?', *Consumer Reports*, November 1991, 768-74.

Crockett, R.O. (2001), 'It's a phone, it's a handheld, it's ...', *Business Week*, 11/12/2001(3757), 134.

Demsetz, H. (1991), 'The Theory of the Firm Revisited', in Oliver E. Williamson and S.G. Winter (eds), *The Nature of the Firm: Origins, Evolution, and Development*, Oxford: Oxford University Press, pp. 159-77.

Dosi, G. (1988), 'Sources, Procedures and Microeconomic Effects of Innovation', *Journal of Economic Literature*, 36, 1126-71.

Duysters, G. and J. Hagedoorn (1998), 'Technological Convergence in the IT Industry: The Role of Strategic Technological Alliances and Technological Competencies', *International Journal of the Economics of Business*, 5, 355-68.

The Economist (1990), 'Digital Quill', *The Economist*, 316 (7672), 88.

The Economist (2000a), 'The Great Convergence Gamble, *The Economist*, 357 (8200), 67-8.

The Economist (2000b), 'The Wireless Gamble', *The Economist*, 357 (8192), 19-21.

The Economist (2002), 'Watch this Airspace', *The Economist*, 363 (8278), 14-22.

Feldmann, V. (2002), 'Competitive Strategy for Media Companies in the Mobile Internet', *Schmalenbach Business Review*, 54, 351-71.

Fransman, Martin (1995), *Japan's Computer and Communications Industry: The Evolution of Industrial Giants and Global Competitiveness*, Oxford, UK: Oxford University Press.

Fransman, Martin (2002), *Telecoms in the Internet Age – From Boom to Bust to...?*, Oxford, UK: Oxford University Press.

Frontline Solutions (2002), 'Handheld Manufacturers must keep Innovating says Yankee Group', *Frontline Solutions Europe*, 11 (5), 34-5.

Fyffe, S. (2001), 'Handspring Combines PDA with Cell Phone', *Electronic News*, 47 (43), 6.

Gambardella, A. and S. Torrisi (1998), 'Does technological convergence imply convergence in markets? Evidence from the electronics industry', *Research Policy*, 27, 445-63.

Geroski, P.A. (1998), 'Thinking creatively about markets', *International Journal of Industrial Organization*, 16, 677-95.

Gomes-Casseres, Benjamin (1996), *The Alliance Revolution*, Cambridge, MA: Harvard University Press.

Gomes-Casseres, B. and D. Leonard-Barton (1997), 'Alliance Clusters in Multimedia', in David P. Yoffie (ed.), *Competing in the Age of Digital Convergence*, Boston: Harvard Business School Press, 325-69.

Greenstein, S. and T. Khanna (1997), 'What does Industry Convergence Mean?', in David B. Yoffie (ed.): *Competing in the Age of Digital Convergence*, Boston: Harvard Business School Press, 201-26.

Halfhill, T.R. (1993), 'PDAs arrive but aren't quite here yet', *Byte*, 18(10), 66-86.

Hamel, Gary and C.K. Prahalad (1994), *Competing for the Future*, Boston: Harvard Business Press.

Hamilton, A. (2001), 'PDA wars: Round Two', *Time*, 04/02/2001, 40-41.

Helfat, C.E. and M.B. Lieberman (2002), 'The Birth of Capabilities: Market Entry and the Importance of Pre-history', *Industrial and Corporate Change*, 11, 725-60.

Helpman, Elhanan (ed.) (1999), *General Purpose Technologies and Economic Growth*, Cambridge, MA: MIT Press.

Himowitz, M. (1996), 'Why Users Love the Pilot', *Fortune*, 134 (9), 224-6.

Iansiti, M. (1997), *Technology Integration*, Boston: Harvard Business School Press.

Iansiti, M. and J. West (1997), 'Technology Integration: Turning Great Research into Great Products', *Harvard Business Review*, 75 (3), 69-79.

Katz, M.L. (1996), 'Remarks on the Economic Implications of Convergence', *Industrial and Corporate Change*, 3, 1079-95.

Kenedy, K. (2002), 'Bluetooth seen as a Connectivity Option for PDAs', *Computer Reseller News*, 4/29/2002 (993), 43-4.

Klepper, S. and K.L. Simons (2000), 'Dominance by Birthright: Entry of Prior Radio Producers and Competitive Ramifications in the US Television Receiver Industry', *Strategic Management Journal*, 21, 997-1016.

Kodama, F. (1992), 'Technology Fusion and the New R&D', *Harvard Business Review*, 70 (4), 70-78.

Lancaster, K.J. (1966), 'A New Approach to Consumer Theory', *Journal of Political Economy*, 14, 133-56.

Leonard-Barton, D. (1992), 'Core Capabilities and Core Rigidities: A Paradox in Managing New Product Development', *Strategic Management Journal*, 13, 111-25.

Linderholm, O., S. Apiki and M. Nadeau (1992), 'The PC gets more Personal', *Byte*, 17 (7), 128-38.

Livingstone, B. (2002), 'Symbian Cell-through', *InfoWorld*, 24 (12), 24.

Maitland, C.F., J.M. Bauer and R. Westerveld (2002), 'The European Market for Mobile Data: Evolving Value Chains and Industry Structures', *Telecommunications Policy*, 26, 485-504.

Malerba, F. (2002), 'Sectoral Systems of Innovation and Production', *Research Policy*, 31, 247-64.

Malerba, F. and L. Orsenigo (2000), 'Knowledge, Innovative Activities and Industrial Evolution', *Industrial and Corporate Change*, 9, 289-314.

Marsili, Orietta (2001), *The Anatomy and Evolution of Industries*, Cheltenham, UK and Brookfield, US: Edward Elgar.

McGahan, A.M., L.L. Vadasz and D.B. Yoffie (1997), 'Creating Value and Setting Standards', in David B. Yoffie (ed.), *Competing in the Age of Digital Convergence*, Boston: Harvard University Press, 227-64.

Merriam-Webster (2000), *Webster's Third New International Dictionary*, Springfield: Merriam-Webster.

Mowery, David C. (ed.) (1996), *The International Computer Software Industry*, New York: Oxford University Press.

Mowery, D.C., J.E. Oxley, J.E. and B.S. Silverman (1998), 'Technological Overlap and Interfirm Cooperation: Implications for the Resource-based View of the Firm', *Research Policy*, 28, 507-23.

Neel, D. and M. Leon (2001), 'Embedded Chaos', *infoworld*, 23 (46), 42-5.

Nelson, M.G., N. Turek, A.M. Williams and M.E. Thyfault (2000), 'A Market Left to its own Devices', *InformationWeek*, 11/13/2000 (812), 295-303.

Nobel, C. (2000), 'Palm gearing up for a wireless battle', *eWeek*, 17 (43), 37-8.

Pavitt, K. (1984), 'Patterns of Technical Change: Towards a Taxonomy and a Theory', *Research Policy*, 13, 343-73.

Pennings, J.M. and P. Puranam, P. (2001), 'Market Convergence & Firm Strategy: New Directions for Theory and Research', Paper presented at the ECIS Conference, Eindhoven, Netherlands, 20-23 September 2001.

Popular Electronics (1994), 'The ABC's of PDA's', *Popular Electronics*, 11 (3), 51-65.

Porter, Michael E. (1985), *Competitive Advantage*, New York: Free Press.

Potter, D. (1998), 'Entrepreneurship: Psion and Europe', *Business Strategy Review*, 9, 15-20.

Rao, P.M. (1999), 'Convergence and Unbundling of Corporate R&D in Telecommunications: is Software taking the Helm?', *Telecommunication Policy*, 23, 83-93.

Red Herring (1993), 'PDA hype is greater than reality', *Red Herring*, 2 (7), 22-31.

Resnick, R. (1992), 'Palmtop Strategies', *Compute!*, 14 (10), 83-6.

Roberts, T. (1992), 'Hewlett-Packard HP 95LX', *Compute!*, 14 (9), 8-10.

Rogers, M. (1992), 'Windows of opportunity', *Newsweek*, 119 (17), 63.

Rosenberg, N. (1963), 'Technological Change in the Machine Tool Industry, 1840-1910', *The Journal of Economic History*, 23, 414-46.

Rosenberg, Nathan (1976), *Perspectives on Technology*, Cambridge, UK: Cambridge University Press.

Rosenberg, Nathan (1982), *Inside the Black Box*, Cambridge, UK and New York: Cambridge University Press.

Sabat, H.K. (2002), 'The Evolving Mobile Wireless Value Chain and Market Structure', *Telecommunications Policy*, 26, 505-35.

Sahal, D. (1985), 'Technological Guideposts and Innovation Avenues', *Research Policy*, 14, 61-82.

Sakakibara, K., C. Lindholm and A. Ainamo (1995), 'Product Development Strategies in Merging Markets: The case of Personal Digital Assistants', *Business Strategy Review*, (Winter 1995), 23-38.

Saviotti, Paolo (1996), *Technological Evolution, Variety and the Economy*, Cheltenham, UK and Brookfield, US: Edward Elgar.

Saviotti, P. and S. Metcalfe (1984), 'A Theoretical Approach to the Construction of Technological Output Indicators', *Research Policy*, 13, 141-51.

Steinbock, Dan (2001), *The Nokia Revolution*, New York: Amacom.

Suarez, F.F. and Utterback, J.M. (1995), 'Dominant Designs and the Survival of Firms', *Strategic Management Journal*, 16, 415-31.

Teece, D.J. (1986), 'Profiting from Technological Innovation', *Research Policy*, 15, 285-305.

Teece, D.J., G. Dosi, R. Rumelt and S. Winter (1994), 'Understanding Corporate Coherence: Theory and Evidence', *Journal of Economic Behavior and Organization*, 23, 1-30.

Thornton, C. and G. Aquino (2002), 'Next-Generation PDAs', *PCWorld*, April, 85-94.

Tushman, M. and P. Anderson (1986), 'Technological Discontinuities and Organizational Environments', *Administrative Science Quarterly*, 31, 439-65.

Weber, Max (1988) *Gesammelte Aufsätze zur Wissenschaftslehre*, Tübingen: UTB.

Wirtz, B. (2001), 'Reconfiguration of Value Chains in Converging Media and Communications Markets', *Long Range Planning*, 34, 489-507.

Wright, J. and J. Caron, 'A New Generation of Interfaces', *Datamation*, 37 (13), 89-92.

Yoffie, D.B. (1997), 'Introduction: CHESS and Competing in the Age of Digital Convergence', in David B. Yoffie (ed.), *Competing in the Age of Digital Convergence*, Boston: Harvard Business School Press, 1-35.

Yoffie, D.B. and M. Kwak (2001), 'Mastering Strategic Movement at Palm', *MIT Sloan Management Review*, 43 (1), 55-63.

8. Innovation, Entrepreneurship and Industrial Dynamics in Internet Services[1]

Jens Frøslev Christensen

1. INTRODUCTION

The Internet can be viewed as a general-purpose technology that gives rise to a wide array of new products, processes and services (Brynjolfsson and Kahin, 2000; Mowery and Simcoe, 2002). Bo Carlsson, in his contribution to this book (Chapter 1), takes this idea one step further arguing that the combination of digitization and the Internet seems to have much broader applicability than previous general-purpose technologies. It not only affects the manufacturing industries but also, and even more so, the service industries which account for an increasing and dominating share of the overall economy. This chapter seeks to expand our understanding of precisely how the Internet has created the basis for innovation and entrepreneurship in Internet-related business services. Our main concerns are to identify the evolutionary dynamics of Internet services and to analyse whether and in what respects these dynamics differ from those typical of manufacturing industries.

Internet-related business development can roughly be divided into three groups of entrepreneurs and innovators (for a more differentiated outline of the US Internet business, see Martin Kenney, Chapter 2 in this book). One group has been involved in innovations of completely new products or services dedicated to developing the Internet and enabling easy and cheap access to and use of it by non-professional mass customers. These include suppliers of the basic network infrastructure and its individual parts and components (e.g. Cisco), of browsers and search engines (i.e. Netscape, Yahoo), and of access to the Internet, e-mail and other standard services (Internet service providers such as AOL and Tiscali). Another, and much larger group of entrepreneurial agents was from the start engaged in competitive relations with 'old economy' industries and firms. They were the swarms of dot.coms that raided virtually all sectors of the economy, armed with radical visions of 'disintermediating' the traditional distribution and marketing channels, in the hopes of reducing transaction costs and improving customization and overall customer comfort. They were born in confrontation with the old ways of doing business and were quickly perceived as posing serious competitive threats against incumbents in most industries. Even though very few of the dot.coms survived and even fewer have become commercially viable, at the height of the dot.com hype they created a strong sense of concern and urgency among 'old economy' companies: they had to respond!

The third category of entrepreneurial actors, the Internet consulting firms or Web agencies, envisioned the huge prospects of assisting 'old economy' companies in making this response. They became the second swarm of Internet-related entrepreneurs – although much smaller than the dot.com swarm. In contrast to the dot.coms they earned money from the very beginning. They were the New Economy consultancies for the Old Economy firms, exploiting the fact that the latter (i) perceived an urgent need to jump onto the Internet bandwagon, (ii) were prospering from the macroeconomic boom, hence were able to pay, and (iii) had no professional knowledge of the Internet.

This was the point of departure for the formation of an Internet business services industry, hereafter termed the Internet services (IS) industry.[2] It is part of a broader sector of knowledge-intensive business services, such as consultancy, training, R&D and computing services, which have long been among the economy's most rapidly growing sectors (OECD, 1999). They play a significant role in resolving the difficulties many firms have in incorporating new technologies (such as the Internet) that are not core to their own R&D strategies, and in adapting to globalization and new demands for complex coordination and communication (OECD, 2000, p. 44). Within just about six years the IS industry has experienced massive waves of entrepreneurial entry, several boundary transformations as new types of services have emerged, excessive cycles of mergers and acquisitions, alliance building, divestitures and exits.

Hitherto, most business studies of Internet-related business dynamics have focused on either the first group of technical innovators (e.g. Mowery and Simcoe, 2002) or the second group of dot.coms or incumbents that offer innovative services with disintermediating prospects (Brousseau, 2002), or with prospects of complementing existing sales and distribution channels with Web-based channels (BRIE-IGCC E-Economy Project, 2001). The early IS pioneers created a new market and established themselves as new 'intermediators' between the traditional IT-firms, including the providers of corporate software systems, and customer firms and organizations in demand of Internet-related solutions. They innovated new service concepts in close interaction with their customers, of whom the most important ones belonged to the category of large 'old economy' companies, that is, the overwhelming majority of well-established firms outside the professional Internet-related sectors. These corporate customers early on provided a privileged market platform for the services firms to experiment, learn and mature the technologies. Later on, as the corporate customers became more knowledgeable about their user requirements, they became critical lead-users for the service providers (von Hippel, 1988).

According to a study from IDC (2001) the Internet services industry experienced excessive growth rates during the late 1990s, implying a near doubling of annual spending between 1997 and 1999, and despite the evolving 'Internet depression' since mid-2000, IDC forecasted annual global growth rates of 26.5 percent from 2000 to 2005. While the US market took the lead towards the end of the 1990s, Western Europe has since caught up with comparably high growth rates. Within just a few years Internet services grew to become a multi-billion dollar market with estimated worldwide spendings of US$ 37 billion by 2002 (18 billion in the US, 11 billion in Western Europe and 8 billion in the rest of the world).

The chapter first gives an overall outline of the dynamics shaping and reconfiguring the IS industry. We do this by describing the co-evolution between corporate customers' Internet needs and the innovation of new Internet services (section 2), and by describing the evolving competitive terms associated with the entry of new strategic groups (section 3) and the changing patterns of strategic positioning (section 4). After the empirical account, we discuss to what extent three well-established frameworks for understanding industry dynamics in manufacturing sectors also apply to the IS industry (section 5). These are the life cycle framework, the economic organization framework on vertical integration and specialization and the appropriability framework. Finally, we conclude the chapter with a short discussion of what may be distinctly new in the industrial dynamics of Internet services.

2. THE EVOLUTION OF INTERNET USE AND SERVICE GENERATIONS[3]

Throughout the chapter we use the abbreviation OEC ('Old Economy' Companies) to signify the main customers of Internet services firms, acknowledging that also public sector organizations have played important customer roles.

The corporate opportunities for Internet use have gradually expanded from being an instrument to supplement existing, and create new communication and marketing channels to becoming a comprehensive means of improving a company's performance. Table 8.1 shows a stage model providing a simplified understanding of the firm-based learning processes associated with the evolution of corporate Internet use from the mid-1990s. The stages are not mutually exclusive but have tended to develop in a cumulative and partly overlapping fashion.

In *Stage 1*, OECs use the Internet as a means of communication through (i) e-mail supplementing and substituting telephone, fax and postal mail, and (ii) homepages as a remedy to provide standardized corporate communication to external stakeholders. Combined, e-mail and the homepage constitute a new means of corporate communication and marketing (Hagel and Armstrong, 1997, p. 215). Internet services reflecting these needs prevailed from around 1994/95 to around 1998. By the mid-1990s the further potentials of the Internet had not yet unfolded, and most OECs were either not aware of, or not thoroughly convinced of, the promise held by the Internet. Therefore, these new services were created in a context of great design uncertainty by experimenting and entrepreneurial Web agencies in search of the 'true' Internet needs of the OECs.

In *Stage 2*, OECs' use of the Internet develops to become a remedy also for *internal communication*. This stage reflects the IT professionals' ambitions to take advantage of the technical opportunities of the Internet. Through the implementation of intranets, extranets and different types of administrative and information systems, it becomes possible to diffuse and exchange proprietary information within the organization and with its external partners at a scope and speed previously unthinkable (Earl, 2000). While Stage 1 signifies a radically new medium for external communication, Stage 2 is rather associated with incremental development from traditional IT systems to Web-enabled systems. However, the eventual innovative significance of this development has probably been at least as great as the significance of the Internet use for external communication. Services to create and implement Internet-enabled information systems emerged in the mid-1990s and became an important part of Internet services around 1998/99.

In *Stage 3* users realize the potentials of conducting commerce through the Internet. Thus, the Internet comes to be perceived as a completely new transaction mode challenging the traditional channels (Brousseau, 2002; Smith et al., 2000). From around 1997/98 the prospect of cost savings became a strong driver for implementing e-commerce (Kenney and Curry, 1999). An even stronger driver was the competitive threats that by then began to confront the countless OECs from the aggressive dot.com ventures popping up everywhere. In other words, e-commerce became widely perceived as a radical innovation promising (and threatening) to largely make existing distribution channels obsolete. The services linked to this stage provide advice on e-business strategies and implementation of e-commerce systems.

Table 8.1 The evolution of corporate use of Internet technology

Stages in corporate use of the Internet	Stage 1: External communication (1994/95-)	Stage 2: Internal communication (1995/96-)	Stage 3: E-commerce (1997/98-)	Stage 4: Off/on-line business alignment (1998/99-)	Stage 5: Corporate system integration (1999-)
Focus	E-mail and Web-based promotion	Administrative information and support systems	On-line order processing	Re-design of business procedures	Technical functionality/ integration
Perception	A new communication and promotion media	Tool for internal information exchange/control	A new transaction media	A support for corporate objectives	Connecting internal and external stakeholders
Key business functions involved	PR, media or marketing departments	IT and marketing departments	Sales/distribution/e-business departments	Most business functions	Most business functions

Note: The table tries to align 'stylized facts' based on a diverse set of information.
Source: Inspired by Earl (2000).

As OECs escalate their use of the Internet for business transactions, they realize that Internet activities should not be isolated from the rest of their business processes (Brousseau, 2002; Porter, 2001). In other words, they recognize the need for congruity between their on-line and off-line business processes and strategies (Earl, 2000; Srivastava and Dutta, 2001). This is the focus of *Stage 4* in OECs' Internet use. Companies begin to re-evaluate and redesign their business processes in order to improve overall efficiency in sales, distribution, logistics, production etc. These user needs became particularly prevalent during the last years of the 1990s only shortly after, or simultaneously with, Stage 3. Services of Stage 4 involve assisting OECs in formulating on-line strategies and operating routines, in ensuring that these are consistent with the strategies and routines of other business functions, and in guiding the consequential changes in organization and business processes.

Stage 5 reflects the emergent need to establish an overall Internet-based infrastructure that allows the *technical* integration of, on the one hand, external and internal corporate systems, and, on the other hand, of front-end and back-end technologies[4] (ComputerResellerNews, 2000; Srivastava and Dutta, 2001). The challenges here are underlined by the fact that most large companies have implemented a comprehensive portfolio of enterprise software systems and databases of different generations, parts of which are functionally outdated, not properly maintained, not Web-enabled, and not mutually compatible (Sonderegger et al., 1998). Technical systems integration services gained prominence in the corporate market for Internet services from around the turn of the millennium.

Services associated with Stages 4 and 5 emerged in parallel because the improvements and integration of business processes are often only made possible through system integration processes, first through web-enabling the existing enterprise and database systems, later through ambitions, mostly overtly optimistic, to build overall Internet-based infrastructures.

Stages 1, 2 and 3 gave rise to autonomous innovations (Teece, 1988) with no significant repercussions on business functions other than those in which the innovations were implemented. They were product or service innovations from the perspective of the firms developing software and services, but process innovations from the corporate customers' perspective. Stages 4 and 5 triggered systemic innovations whereby the autonomous innovations of earlier stages became inter-linked or complementary (cf. Stieglitz's typology of industrial convergence, Chapter 7 in this book).

The model depicted in Table 8.1 reflects the historically evolving opportunities emanating from Internet technologies since the early 1990s. Today, new companies face the full repertoire of opportunities from the start and hence do not necessarily follow the specific sequencing of stages outlined in the table.

The shifts in generations of services have resulted in major transformations in the ways of servicing OECs. Thus, each new generation of services has dramatically increased the *complexity* and *scale* of OECs' Internet investment projects. Services linked to Stages 3, 4 and 5 are organizationally, managerially, and technologically much more complex than the services linked to Stages 1 and 2, because Internet services become increasingly technologically sophisticated and increasingly interlinked with the customers' back-end systems, and require the co-ordination of an increasing number of employees across virtually all business processes. Moreover, the interaction between service providers and their clients has become increasingly extensive and complex. Whereas Stage 1 services tend only to require fairly brief interaction with the OECs' marketing staff,[5] services in later stages typically require involvement of general management. By implication, the creation of trust between service provider and customer becomes increasingly crucial.

3. THE STRATEGIC GROUPS ENTERING THE INTERNET SERVICES SCENE

In the very short life of the IS industry, five strategic groups[6] have surfaced in a context of the evolving user needs and proliferating and maturing Internet technologies. The groups differ with respect to competence profile, the type of services they provide, and the timing of entry into the industry. In Figure 8.1, the strategic groups are mapped according to their predominant competence area (communication, technology and business management) and the timing of their entry. In the following outline of the different strategic groups we focus primarily on the most important players (the pioneers and the large firms). However, it is important to stress that within all groups there is a vast number of small non-innovative firms serving the 'low end' markets by providing less complex and less sophisticated services for small and medium-sized firms.

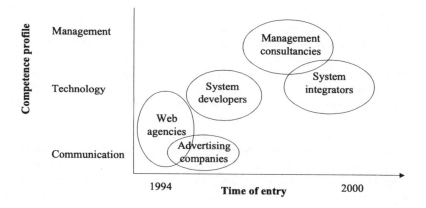

Figure 8.1 The strategic groups of Internet services

Three strategic groups of actors entered the industry in its early stages, providing first generation services: Web agencies, advertising agencies and system developers. The fourth strategic group of management consultants was attracted by the industry as the user needs for business process integration evolved, while the fifth strategic group of system integrators was prompted to enter by the increasing demand for technical system integration. Only the Web agencies who pioneered the industry were *de novo* entrants. The other entering groups consisted primarily of incumbents from other industries.

The first strategic group of IS actors encompass the pioneering *Web agencies*. These are the innovators of Web design services creatively combining knowledge of the World Wide Web and hypertext markup language (HTML) with knowledge of marketing and communication. The Web agencies initially targeted a national or local market base of OECs, dot.com startups and public institutions, and the most ambitious of these firms had venture capital fuelling the growth process. In experimenting with Internet technology, they primarily took advantage of the Internet's communication possibilities as related to marketing and communication strategies (Stage 1) or intranet and extranet solutions (Stage 2) (Computerworld, 2000).

These entrepreneurial ventures in fact created the IS industry and some of them for some time gained strong footholds or even temporary monopoly status on their respective national or regional markets.[7] Thousands of small Web agencies raided the Internet scene at a time when the New Economy hype was gaining momentum. Many of these firms, originating from a communication or media background, were successful in proliferating themselves as the very incarnation of the New Economy and in convincing their corporate clients that these Web services were business-critical and that early moving clients would reap significant first-mover advantages. Furthermore, since most of these clients were themselves experiencing booming markets and high profitability, the most creative and aggressive of the Web agencies experienced rapid growth in assets, revenue and profitability. In the very early phases, some of them were able to combine excessive charges with highly experimental approaches to design, exploiting the fact that many OECs were eager to jump on the Internet bandwagon without having much idea of what the Web agencies were doing for them.

However, the temporary monopoly positions that some Web agencies exploited in national markets did not last long. Shortly after they attained recognition and commercial success, two new groups of competitors entered the industry by expanding their service portfolios to include Internet-related services to OECs. These groups consisted of *advertising companies* and *system developers*. The entering advertising companies regarded the Internet solely as a communication medium and provided Internet-related services with a focus on branding and marketing management (external communication). For a time, a few of these gained some market position, but they never came to play any significant role within the IS industry. Advertising companies such as Grey, Young & Rubicam and Ogilvy established separate 'interactive departments' to deal with the new Internet-based opportunities, but most of these have since been closed or integrated into the companies' normal activities.

The entering system developers considered the Internet as a technical opportunity for designing internal communication systems based on software expertise. They entered the industry as the second and third phases of Internet use (Internal Communication and E-commerce) emerged, and, in contrast to the Web agencies, they possessed strong competencies in software (and some of them also in hardware) development and system programming.[8] These actors primarily dealt with the possibilities for enhancing intranets, extranets and e-commerce systems in OECs. They built their own service units or established alliances with service firms not only to gain a share of the IS market, but more importantly, to establish a spearhead for selling their standard software systems and platforms. The large system developers had a strong international market presence and substantial experience with long-term client relationships, two strongholds that Web agencies could not contest. Moreover, they could provide the basic technical infrastructure on which all Internet services are based.

The system developers did not engage in direct competitive confrontation with the Web agencies. Rather, they tended to challenge 'traditional' information systems providers with new Internet solutions dedicated to internal communication and e-commerce, and their services were underpinned by their proprietary software tools. However, system developers have in a more indirect sense imposed a severe competitive challenge on the Web agencies – namely by developing systems which have made updating and redesign of Web sites cheaper and easier to conduct in-house by non-professionals. This has implied that the market segment for Web design has declined, at least in relative terms. Thus, today only the higher end of this market segment is left to be commercially exploited by IS providers. Likewise, standard software has increasingly come to reduce the scope for 'manual' consulting and implementation of systems for internal communication and e-commerce. In other words, software vendors have created product innovations that for the corporate clients are process innovations, making it possible to 'automate' previously 'manual' services and to insource what were previously consulting services. Thus, standard software providers have gradually come to erode parts of the market for previous generations of Internet services.

The complexity of the industrial dynamics further increased with the entry of two more strategic groups, management consultancies and system integrators, responding to the emerging integrative service requirements. Numerous *management consultancies* entered at the peak, just prior to the burst, of the dot.com bubble, when OECs' needs for Internet services expanded in two directions. First, towards needs for assistance in establishing e-commerce systems. Among the existing actors, many Web agencies and system developers in particular learned to provide such systems. Secondly, towards needs for more systemic services in which Internet-specific services are aligned with more traditional management consulting and system integration services. Especially the large incumbent management consultancies possessed the former of these complementary competencies, and several of those who entered the IS industry massively invested in building Internet-specific capabilities as well (Saloner and Spence, 2002, p. 267ff.).[9]

There are numerous reasons why several of the global management consultancies entered at this particular stage around the turn of the millennium. The overriding reason is that the market for Internet services was rapidly expanding to become a new mega-market within consulting. Moreover, Internet services gradually extended their scope, implying strong overlaps with the traditional core services of the management consultancies. Finally, a section of the Web agencies increasingly represented a direct threat towards the large management consultancies. Not only had the most expansive of the Web agencies established strong footholds among the traditional clients of management consultancies; they also demonstrated an aggressive commitment to expand into new territories of services that were strongly overlapping with the classical domains of management consultancies. Thus, many Web agencies were successfully headhunting consultants from the management consultancies not only because these Web agencies were, up to the burst of the Internet bubble, able to pay higher salaries and offer attractive stock options, but also because they were gaining a reputation as the dynamic agents of the 'new economy' in contrast to the comparatively 'old economy' image of the traditional management consultancies.

Despite their late entry, the management consultancies proved most capable of responding to the new, more integrative needs of the OECs. Their competitive advantage within this business segment for on- and off-line business integration was based on their superior experience within the traditional fields of management and strategy consulting, their deep industry expertise from existing client relationships, and their competencies in managing large and complex projects. Furthermore, their strong international presence and their long-term knowledge of and solid reputation among large OECs certainly eased their entry into the industry.[10] This 'old' reputation seems to have become revitalized as many Web agencies experienced great difficulties in catching up with the rapidly changing competitive context for new generations of services and, thus, in establishing proper quality controls. In other words, the revitalization of the reputation of the management consultancies at least partly reflected the deteriorating reputation of many Web agencies. Finally it proved to be a distinct advantage to the management consultancies that they entered around the time when the 'Internet depression' (Mandel, 2000) paralysed the ambitious Web agencies in their efforts to provide leverage to their consulting competencies.

The system integrators entered the industry around the same time, or slightly later, responding to the expanding needs to implement overall Internet-based infrastructures.[11] System integrators hold specialist competencies in connecting corporate control systems, administrative databases, software and systems. Such competencies became vitally important when implementing Web-based or Web-enabled system integration. By 2002, this group of actors seemed to have gained a solid position in the IS industry, although exclusively within the market segment for technical system integration. The most advanced system integrators possess the backbone of Internet services, a technologically sophisticated and specialized competence. None of the other strategic groups has as yet been able to offer these types of services at a technically advanced level, probably because the competencies are both highly complex and systemic in nature and hence difficult to assimilate by 'outsiders' (Winter, 1987). The system developers, the other technology-intensive strategic group, have their competitive strength in standard software systems and their services tend to link up closely with their own systems, while the system integrators tend to make a point of being independent of specific software platforms.

4. THE DYNAMICS OF POSITIONING WITHIN THE IS INDUSTRY

Since the 'Internet depression' dried up the 'easy-going' expansion, companies in all the strategic groups of the industry, even those with full-service ambitions, have increasingly come to acknowledge that some of their competitors can be their complementors or partners as well. The term 'co-opetition' captures this co-existence of co-operation and competition in the industry (Shapiro and Varian, 1999, p. 228). By 2000, many IS companies still claimed that they were full-service providers and could offer all generations of services. However as the scope and complexity of Internet services have amplified in parallel to the 'Internet depression', very few firms, if any, in practice entail the full range of capabilities and co-coordinative capacity in-house to provide the whole spectrum of services.

Since around 1999, three types of positioning dynamics have characterized the IS industry: (1) An explosive growth in mergers and acquisitions (M&As) during the last phase of the dot.com boom; (2) a wave of divestments and downsizing leading many firms into bankruptcy and others 'back to basics' as the 'Internet depression' aggravated in the second half of 2000 and onwards; (3) a partnering game as the complementarities between the core services of different types of service providers became better specified and acknowledged in second and third generation services.

From around 1999 to mid-2000, numerous Web agencies in particular engaged in a frenetic M&As race. High and increasing stock prices made it possible for some Web agencies to pay for the acquired firms with stocks. For others, venture capital financed the expansion. The rapid extension of user needs for Internet services and the entry of new powerful competitors (such as the management consultants) forced many of the Web agencies out of their first-mover positions and into catch-up positions. Those who engaged in M&As did so in order to achieve critical size nationally or internationally, to get access to and control over new capabilities required to extend the scope of services, and to accommodate many clients' wishes to have Internet services provided by one sole vendor (Saloner and Spence, 2002, p. 88, Christensen et al., 2003).

As the financial drivers of the Web agencies' expansion eroded in 2000, the M&A wave faded out and was transformed into a massive wave of divestments and exits, on the one hand, and alliance formations, on the other hand.[12] The rapidly accelerating debt and liquidity problems forced the hitherto expanding Web agencies to combine dramatic divestments of no-longer viable business units (most of which had been acquired in the previous phase of expansion) with attempts of partnering up with complementors.[13] Most of them died in these attempts.

The combined fading of the M&A wave and the take-off of a partnering wave can probably be attributed to factors other than the blocking of easy finance. As the different categories of Internet services have matured, interfaces between complementary services have tended to become more standardized, hence more prone to co-ordination through partnership or market relations. But the partnering wave is also likely to have been stimulated by the experience-based acknowledgement of the severe failures associated with the previous M&A strategies. As pointed to in Saloner and Spence (2002), '... many felt that these firms were too busy and immature to integrate so many disparate pieces smoothfully' (p. 373). The Swedish Web agency Framfab was by the end of the M&A wave a collection of autonomous firms with only weak connections rather than a coherent corporation exploiting and exploring synergies and complementarities among its parts.[14]

The partnering web within the IS industry is highly complex and constantly changing. In particular, partnering tends to involve vertical or complementary relationships in a continuum from exclusive strategic alliances to ad hoc alliances, which in practice often do not involve more, or much more, mutual commitment than pure market relationships. There has been particularly hectic partnering activity between the powerful system developers (e.g. Oracle and IBM) providing enterprise software systems and platforms, and Web agencies and management consultancies respectively.[15] Especially in the relationships between large system developers and the smaller Internet consultancies, the former obviously possess superior bargaining power. To become certified by a well-reputed system developer may, however, provide the smaller Web agency with some market reputation and access to a particular IT architecture. But it may also lead to lock-in problems and the loss of independence in the provision of Internet consulting, reflecting the fact that the system developers perceive the Web agencies and management consultancies as an important channel for their proprietary products.

5. ANALYSING THE INDUSTRIAL DYNAMICS OF INTERNET SERVICES

Most existing models and frameworks of industry dynamics are based on empirical studies of manufacturing industries. When trying to come to grips with the underlying dynamics of Internet services, an obvious way to proceed is first to answer the question of whether, or to what extent, the observed development of Internet services can be explained by such 'old' models. This section compares the empirical outline of Internet services with three established frameworks in industrial dynamics: life cycle theory, organizational economics theory on vertical integration and specialization, and appropriability theory. In the concluding section we shortly discuss what cannot be easily explained by established theories and some reasons why.

5.1 Life Cycle Dynamics

Most industry studies have dealt with manufacturing industries whose evolutionary dynamics tend to be in broad accordance with life cycle models in which the early phase, characterized by radical technological innovation, waves of new entries, experimental and rivalling approaches to design and technological trajectories, is followed by a phase of shake-out, technological stabilization, possibly convergence around a dominant design, and the consolidation of a concentrated oligopoly structure (Klepper, 1996; Utterback, 1996). For most conventional manufacturing industries the evolution from embryonic to consolidated states has taken several decades (e.g. the automobile industry, the radio industry, the hearing instrument industry).

Internet services have witnessed a very similar evolution, although the speed of change has been much higher than what is typical of manufacturing industries. From the mid-1990s to around 2000, Internet-related technologies and service requirements have changed from being highly experimental to becoming much more well-defined and mature. Business dynamics have likewise changed from the early phases of massive Schumpeterian entrepreneurial waves of entry and fairly radical innovation, through a phase of shake-out to consolidation in which fewer large companies have come to dominate the competitive game along with more incremental, modular and systemic innovation (Henderson and Clark, 1990; Teece, 1988). However, even if the entry of powerful incumbents from neighbouring industries (software, management consulting and systems integration) and the massive shake-out of early start-up firms have reflected a movement towards a more consolidated, mature sector, an oligopoly structure has not emerged. No single company or small group of companies has so far been able to establish dominant positions across the different segments of Internet services, either at a global level or in most national markets in Europe and North America. This could be associated with some special characteristics that D'Aveni (1994) assigned to so-called hyper-competitive industries, namely that frequent and aggressive competitive moves by industry actors shape conditions of quasi-permanent disequilibrium and radical redefinition of industry boundaries. In this particular case the characteristics are strongly linked to the underlying technological and innovative developments related to the Internet.

Up until late 2000 or perhaps early 2001 it was possible to view the different groups of IS firms as being part of the same overall industry. First because the expansive Web agencies were still determined to contest the newcoming strategic players, and secondly because the most aggressive latecomers also invaded the segment of first generation services. However, what during the earlier years aspired to become a unitary IS industry later became compartmentalized into specialized, vertically related industries reflecting the different generations of services and their respective roles in the emergent overall value system of Internet services. Thus, as the competitive game evolved, the pioneering Web agencies that eventually survived the 'Internet depression' had to give up any ambitions of becoming full-service providers and accept being retrenched to niche positions associated with the first generation services that had not, in the meantime, been insourced by the customers due to the availability of user-friendly pre-packaged software. Moreover, as the market for Web design lost its 'magic', the advertising companies, management consultancies and system integrators also tended to pull out of this market.

What we so far have termed industry dynamics should more properly be characterized as value system formation. The formation of a value system of Internet services started out with front-end (downstream) user-application services, followed by increasingly back-end (upstream) and systemic services aligning Internet solutions with business integration and systems integration of the back-end technologies (see Figure 8.2). The tasks associated with each of the steps of the value system are more or less interdependent and can, in principle, be supplied and coordinated by different agents or constellations of agents. The early pioneers were *de novo* entrants of small firms and teams envisioning and creating Web services at the front-end of the evolving value system. At this early stage these services were perceived as stand-alone solutions, that is, they were not integrated with the conventional processes and tasks of the customer firms' value chains. However, requirements for such integration quickly emerged, and the later entrants were well-established incumbents from other industries with *ex ante* possession of the adequate complementary and systemic competencies. They developed the parts of the IS value system that became increasingly critical for customers in providing coherence between Internet-related processes and other value chain processes in their companies. Moreover, system developers engaged in software devel-

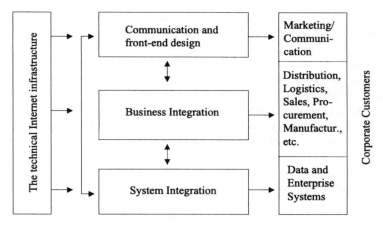

Figure 8.2 The value system of Internet-related business services

opment of Internet-based infrastructures and systems. As long as the front-end market was still booming and profitable, a number of these new players also expanded into first generation services.

In other words, earlier tendencies towards establishing a unified industry based on vertical integration strategies have been replaced by strong tendencies towards vertical disintegration. How can well-established theories of organizational economics, such as the resource- or competence-based theory and transaction cost theory, hitherto mostly applied to manufacturing industries, explain these dynamics of vertical integration and disintegration or specialization?

5.2 Dynamics of Vertical Integration and Specialization

Even if the different tasks of the IS value system can be provided by specialized firms, it is of critical importance for the customers that the individual services and systems are mutually compatible and can work together without too much friction. But who can assure that this co-ordination takes place when the customers do not possess the required competencies? According to transaction cost theory, firms will tend to integrate tasks, the co-ordination of which requires ongoing dialogue and exchange of tacit knowledge (Monteverde, 1995) reflecting a high level of inter-asset specificity (Christensen, 1996) and a substantial risk of opportunistic behaviour in market relations (Williamson, 1975), and they will tend to outsource tasks that require little co-ordination, due to, for instance, widely accepted standard interfaces. From a competence-based view firms will prefer to integrate tasks based on competencies that are similar or related to the firm's existing competencies, while firms will have difficulties integrating highly unrelated or 'alien' competencies (Richardson, 1972). How do the empirical realities of the IS firms fit these propositions?

Despite some overlap in knowledge profiles among the different strategic groups, the general pattern is that the main players in each group possess very different core capabilities and competencies (Figure 8.3). They not only differ in terms of the dominant functional fields of their capabilities (e.g. IT or communication expertise) but also in terms of the nature of their know-how (specialized capabilities or integrative competencies).[16]

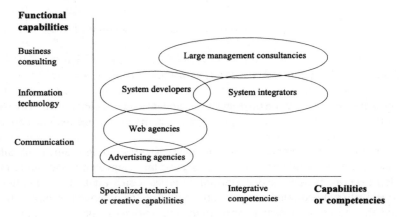

Figure 8.3 Core capabilities and competencies among the main players in Internet services

We have witnessed a strong move away from the early tendencies before and around the turn of the millennium towards extensive vertical integration as the financial markets surrounding Internet-related business have normalized. A likely explanation, which is in accordance with the competence view, is that the different tasks in the value system are based on fundamentally different types of capabilities that are difficult to align within a firm context. Or rather, firms have had serious difficulties not only in developing and maintaining front edge knowledge positions within more of the core capabilities required to be a full-service provider, but also in creating competitive advantage from mobilizing synergies across these capabilities, or creating integrative competencies.

However, the specialization dynamics may also reflect a tendency for coordination requirements and transaction costs to have decreased due to increasing standardization of interfaces, making it easier to manage these interfaces through partnership relations. A combination of both dynamics seems to have taken place. Hence both competence and transaction cost considerations may contribute to explain the tendency for the IS industry to become increasingly undermined as a unitary industry and replaced by vertically interdependent industries. The very quick maturing of Internet-related technologies and the parallel broad-scoped exploration of entrepreneurial and innovative opportunities are the main drivers behind these frequent redefinitions of industry boundaries. As has been the case in computer and consumer electronics and other manufacturing industries heavily influenced by digital technologies (see Ernst's contribution, Chapter 6, this volume), Internet services have evolved to become a distributed value system based on a large array of specialized services and systems suppliers possessing specialized capabilities. These specialized services are kept together by system integrators, defined more broadly than just IT system integrators, who possess the integrative competencies to align the different parts of the value system (cf. Pavitt, Chapter 4, this volume).

5.3 First-Mover Advantages and Appropriability

One remaining question concerning the particular dynamics of Internet services is why the early pioneers, the Web agencies, were not able to mobilize first-mover advantages to the extent that they could remain ahead of the competition into the new and more integrative generations of services. After all, the most successful of these firms became very large (e.g. Framfab employed about 3,000 employees and MarchFirst almost 9,000 people in early 2000), had a strong international presence, and were, contrary to their dot.com counterparts, earning rents.

According to the appropriability framework which has prominently been articulated by David Teece (1986), the winning companies of new innovation-led industries tend to be the ones who are best able (or positioned) to capture the rents from innovations through mobilizing a tight regime of appropriability which can keep imitators, whether new entrants or incumbents, at bay. A strong appropriability regime may accrue from one or more sources: high complexity or tacitness of the knowledge base underlying the innovation (Winter, 1987), the ability to keep the critical knowledge secret or to protect the innovation through the means of intellectual property rights, or the ability to control complementary assets (such as manufacturing and distribution assets) required to commercialize the innovation. According to Teece (1986), early pioneers of radical innovations often fail because they are unable to protect their innovations from imitation and/or they are not able to, or are not sufficiently aware of the need to, mobilize the proper complementary assets to commercialize the innovation.

Even though this framework has been applied primarily to manufacturing industries, it also seems able to contribute to explaining the short-lived first-mover advantages of the pioneering Web agencies. Their entry was based on (sometimes great) ideas and concepts rather than on difficult-to-replicate capabilities and competencies. Moreover, no intellectual property rights were able to protect these concepts from easy imitation. Thus, the innovative ventures were not protected by tight appropriability regimes. The complementary assets necessary to implement these Web services were owned by the suppliers of the technical infrastructure and software systems associated with the Internet and these assets are subject to much tighter appropriability regimes due to the complexities of the underlying knowledge and to better possibilities for patent protection (especially in the US where software can be patent protected). Moreover, when economic entry barriers (due for example to capital expenditures or scale advantages) are low, it becomes clear why first-mover advantages for Web agencies tended to be short-lived with weak opportunities to appropriate sustainable (not to mention above-normal) rents from their innovative ideas.

6. CONCLUSION

This chapter has analysed the evolution of one of the new business formations in the wake of the Internet revolution: the Internet-related business services. We have penetrated the historical sequences through which customer needs have evolved, service generations have been innovated, and strategic groups have been formed. The industrial dynamics of Internet services have been analysed from three different perspectives: From a life cycle perspective, an economic organization perspective, and an appropriability perspective. This analysis shows that these 'old' frameworks, which have in particular been applied to and developed on the basis of studies of manufacturing industries, also have substantial explanatory power in relation to a service sector such as Internet services.

However, contrary to most manufacturing sectors, this sector has, like other Internet-related business sectors, been subject to a much more rapid and turbulent development process reflecting the enormously wide applicability of Internet technology, its rapid diffusion, due among other things to the innovation of the World Wide Web, the pre-existence of a huge installed base of PCs, and the enormous potential for innovation and entrepreneurial venturing. The specific form of industry turbulence can be viewed through the lenses of industry convergence. This is not a new phenomenon, but in the new digital economy, industry convergence has become a much more prevalent aspect of industrial dynamics. Stieglitz in this volume (Chapter 7) proposes a taxonomy of four categories of industry convergence. In Internet services several of these forms of convergence have been operating more or less simultaneously.

First of all, the emergence of Internet services can be conceived as a process of convergence through technology substitution, or what Rosenberg (1976) terms technology convergence. A completely new industry, Internet services, emerged in the shape of specialized suppliers of new external communication media, new internal communication systems, and new transaction systems for corporate customers. In the user context these services functioned as process innovations (in part) replacing existing systems of marketing, communication and commerce. This type of industry convergence is well-known from the manufacturing sector and prominently illustrated in Rosenberg's (1963) study of the early emergence of a machine tool industry in USA consisting of specialized suppliers of mechanical machine tools. However, even if the market scope for specialized machine tool suppliers was large, it was still only some sectors, especially manufacturing industries, that would adopt these machine tools. In contrast, the growth of Internet services firms in the early years was staggering because virtually all firms and other organizations began to install these new Internet-related systems.

A second process of industry convergence emerged as firms from established industries (advertising, software, management consulting and systems integration) began to compete with the pioneering firms constituting the embryonic Internet services industry. On the one hand, firms in these other industries began to develop and expand their existing products and services by integrating Internet-related features. On the other hand, the specialized suppliers of the Internet services industry likewise began to expand their services to comprise for instance features of management consultancy and systems integration. Thus, we see different industries converging and engaging in both competition and co-operation.

This process of inter-industry convergence also involves what Stieglitz in this volume calls convergence through the creation of product complementarity. This process translates into two implications. First, the different Internet-related service innovations, which originally were stand-alone innovations, become inter-linked so that they can be used together (e.g. the home page can 'speak' to the e-commerce system). Secondly, these Internet-related systems become integrated with other business functions or processes. While IT system integrators take on the first task, management consultancies take on the second. This process of product complementarity has the consequence that specialized suppliers and 'integrator' firms become interdependent, possibly in network relations placing the 'integrators' in the dominating and organizing roles as suggested by Pavitt and Ernst in this volume (Chapters 4 and 6). Underlying these processes are also dynamics of technology integration implying that Internet-related as well as other digital and non-digital technologies gradually become 'fused' or inter-linked in ways that make product or service substitution and complementarity possible.

The complex and dramatic prevalence of convergence dynamics seems to be an inherent characteristic associated with digitization. However, this does not mean that all industries eventually end up as one big inter-linked industry. Rather it means a much more frequent and ongoing process of redefinition of industry boundaries. Returning to Internet services we have seen that most of the early 'pure play' pioneers were not able to adapt to the new conditions of the 'post hype' era, but the most successful of them are still alive, even if they have dramatically decreased capacity since mid-2000. It may very well be that a distinct IS industry will remain based on further elaboration of first genera-tion services. Since customers are involved in an ongoing learning process with system developers in applying the increasingly user-friendly software for Web design, the firms who are likely to survive will be those who will be able to engage in increasingly upmarket innovation of creative solutions. The com-panies representing the rest of the IS value system will probably in the future become much less identified with Internet-specific services. For the larger companies the Internet-related activities will most likely tend to become just one element of their main activities.

NOTES

1.   Helpful comments from Jill Archer, Jonas Sorth Kjær, Peter Maskell, Michael Holm Olesen and Nils Stieglitz are gratefully acknowledged. Much of the empirical information underly-ing the chapter has been collected by Marie Louise Schmidt and Mette Rønberg Larsen together with this author.
2.   The analytical question of whether Internet services in fact can be considered an industry in a strict sense will be left for discussion in the analytical part of the chapter (section 5). Until then we assume the existence of an industry.
3.   The study reported in sections 2, 3 and 4 is based on two categories of empirical data and insights. One is the type of information on firms and industry events that is available on the Internet and in the business press (the Web sites of relevant firms, notes and articles on the Web sites of IT-oriented research consultancies, in particular IDC, the business and IT press, particularly in Denmark). Another is knowledge and interpretations based on interviews with 27 specialists from Denmark and Sweden holding privileged inside or outside positions for understanding the dynamics of the industry. The interviews were conducted between May 2000 and May 2002. The nature of the empirical sources implies a bias in focus towards pio-neering and somewhat larger firms in the European, and especially the Danish and Swedish IS context. For a more comprehensive report of the study see Christensen et al. (2003).
4.   Front-end technology implies designing and programming the Web site, responding to the company's objectives as to how clients should be serviced. Such objectives can, for instance, be product descriptions, technical support, order status information, and on-line processing, which enables the company to deliver satisfactory customer service. Back-end technology targets the coupling of business systems like the controlling of stores, deliverance and distri-bution channels, and sales (Srivastava and Dutta, 2001).
5.   Exceptions can especially be found among large consumer companies with high branding profile (e.g. Nike, Coca-Cola or Lego). Such companies have made Web-based external marketing and communication a major strategic investment area.

6. Strategic groups are clusters of firms, whose services appear to be similar and to serve the same group of clients or market segments within a common industry. Within each strategic group, firms may operate in different ways, and these differences can play a substantial role in forming overall industry dynamics (Oster, 1999, p. 83).

7. Examples of Web agencies from the US with considerable commercial success during the latter half of the 1990s are, Agency.com, Organic Online, Proxicom, Razorfish, USWeb (which merged with Whitman-Hart into MarchFirst in 2000), and Viant. European examples are: Adcore (Sweden), Ahead (Denmark), Cell Networks (Sweden), Framfab (Sweden), IconMedialab (Sweden), Mindfact (Germany), Pixelpark (Germany), Syzygy (UK), and Wcube (France).

8. Among the globally high-profiled system developers entering the IS industry were Ariba, Cisco, Hewlett Packard, IBM, Intel, Oracle, Siebel, and Sun – all from the US.

9. This was the case with, among others, the both nationally and internationally positioned companies like Accenture, Deloitte Consulting, Gemini Consulting, KPMG, PA Consulting and PriceWaterhouseCoopers, who primarily saw their business opportunities in strategic consulting related to e-business strategies, business process improvements and change management.

10. Accenture was perhaps the most successful new entrant within this group. A likely reason is that Accenture, prior to entry, had made both IT and business strategy core products. While many other consulting firms saw strategy, change management and information technology in isolation, Accenture already in the mid-1990s made IT and business integration a strategic focus (Wooldridge, 1997).

11. Examples of national and international system integrators entering the IS industry are Aston Group (Denmark), Cambridge Technology Partners (USA), CSC (USA), Mandator (Sweden), Sapient (USA), and Valtech (France).

12. The sequentiality of these waves should not be overemphasized. Thus, of course, alliance formations also took place during the acquisition wave, and downsizing and exits also occurred during the grand waves of acquisitions and alliance formations. In using the term 'waves' we only want to stress the relative strength of the different categories of positioning dynamics.

13. Adcore's, Framfab's and MarchFirst's divestment measures appear to be symptomatic of the largest Web agencies. During the summer of 2001, Adcore liquidated all foreign activities in 11 countries, cutting down staff by almost 700, and rationalized extensively the remaining Swedish offices by 800 employees (Computerworld, 2001a). MarchFirst's liquidity problems in 2001 made it divest its European offices and sell off 19 American offices to the software incubator Divine, implying a 50 percent cut in total employment to 5,000 (Computerworld Online, 2001; Computerworld, 2001b). Shortly after, in April 2001, MarchFirst filed for bankruptcy protection (Computerworld, 2001c), and since then, MarchFirst has completely vanished from the Internet scene. System integrators, however, have also been hit by the new competitive and financial terms of Internet services. Cambridge Technology Partners disclosed three rounds of significant layoffs (800 employees) in the first half of 2001, leaving the company with a staff of 3,000. By July 2001, the software company Novell took over ownership of the entire systems integration company (Computerworld, 2001d).

14. On the issue of corporate coherence, see Christensen and Foss (1997), and Christensen (2000).

15. IBM, for example, has entered what it terms ad hoc partnerships with Web agencies such as Framfab and Ahead (*ITBranchen*, 2000), and Cisco has created temporary ties with IBM and the management consultancies Cap Gemini and Ernest & Young to offer various sorts of Internet solutions (Rangan and Adner, 2001, p. 49).

16. A capability is defined as a specialized team- or firm-specific functional or technical set of know-how associated with creating value from a given knowledge domain. A competence (or integrative competence) is defined as a team- or firm-specific set of know-how associated with creating value from co-ordinating different knowledge domains (Christensen, 1996, 2000).

REFERENCES

BRIE-IGCC E-Economy Project (eds) (2001), *Tracking a Transformation. E-commerce and the Terms of Competition in Industries*, Washington, DC, US: Brookings Institution Press.

Brousseau, E. (2002), 'The Governance of Transactions by Commercial Intermediaries: An Analysis of the Re-engineering of Intermediation by Electronic Commerce', *International Journal of the Economics of Business*, 9 (3), 353-74.

Brynjolfsson E. and B. Kahin (eds) (2000), *Understanding the Digital Economy – Data, Tools and Research*, Cambridge, Massachusetts: The Massachusetts Institute of Technology (MIT) Press.

Christensen, J.F. (1996), 'Innovative Assets and Inter-Asset Linkages – A Resource-Based Approach to Innovation', *Economics of Innovation and New Technology*, 4, 193-209.

Christensen, J.F. (2000), 'Building Innovative Assets and Dynamic Coherence in Multi-technology Companies', in N.J. Foss and P.L. Robertson (eds), *Resources, Technology and Strategy*, London and New York: Routledge, pp. 123-52.

Christensen, J.F. and N.J. Foss (1997), 'Dynamic Corporate Coherence and Competence-Based Competition: Theoretical Foundations and Practical Implications', in A. Heene and R. Sanchez (eds), *Competence-Based Strategic Management*, Chichester, UK: John Wiley and Sons.

Christensen, J.F., M.L. Schmidt and M.R. Larsen (2003), 'Turbulence and Competitive Dynamics of the Internet Services Industry', *Industry and Innovation*, 10 (2): 117-43.

ComputerResellerNews (2000), 'Nye tider for webbureauer', 4 October.

Computerworld (2000), 'Flere satser 100 procent på Internet teknologi', 27 June.

Computerworld (2001a), 'Adcore begaeres konkurs af to ex-chefer', 6 September.

Computerworld (2001b), 'Divine to buy bulk of MarchFirst's assets', 2 April.

Computerworld (2001c), 'MarchFirst files for bankruptcy protection', 13 April.

Computerworld (2001d), 'Novell to buy consulting firm', 13 March.

Computerworld Online (2001), 'Divine koeber MarchFirst aktiver', 2 April.

D'Aveni, R.A. (1994), *Hypercompetition*, New York: The Free Press.

Earl, M.J. (2000), 'Evolving the E-business', *Business Strategy Review*, 11 (2), 33-8.

Hagel, J. and A. Armstrong (1997), *Net Gain – Expanding Markets through Virtual Communities*, Boston, US: Harvard Business School Press.

Henderson, R.M. and K.B. Clark (1990), 'Architectural Innovation: The Reconfiguration of Existing Product Technologies and the Failure of Established Firms', *Administrative Science Quarterly*, 35, 9-30.

IDC (2001), *Worldwide Internet Services Market Forecast and Analysis, 2000-2005*, International Data Corporation.

ITBranchen (2000), 'Konsulenthusene breder sig', September.

Kenney M. and Curry J. (1999), 'E-commerce: Implications for Firm-strategy and Industry Configuration', *Industry and Innovation*, 6, 131-51.

Klepper, S. (1996), 'Entry, Exit, Growth, and Innovation over the Product Life Cycle', *American Economic Review*, 86, 562-83.

Mandel M. J. (2000), *The coming Internet Depression*, London, UK: Financial Times/Prentice Hall.

Monteverde, K. (1995), 'Technical Dialog as an Incentive for Vertical Integration in the Semiconductor Industry', *Management Science*, 41, 1624-38.

Mowery, D. C. and T. Simcoe (2002), 'Is the Internet a US invention? – an Economic and Technological History of Computer Networking', *Research Policy*, 31, 1369-87.

OECD (1999), *Strategic Business Services*, Paris: OECD.

OECD (2000), *A New Economy? The Changing Role of Innovation and Information Technology in Growth*, Paris: OECD.

Oster M. S. (1999), *Modern Competitive Analysis*, Oxford, UK: Oxford University Press.

Porter M. E. (2001), 'Strategy and the Internet', *Harvard Business Review*, 79 (3), 63-78.

Rangan S. and R. Adner (2001), 'Profits and the Internet: Seven Misconceptions', *MIT Sloan Management Review*, 42 (4), 44-53.

Richardson, G. (1972), 'The Organisation of Industry', *Economic Journal*, 82, 883-96.

Rosenberg, Nathan (1963), 'Technological Change in the Machine Tool Industry', 1840-1910, *The Journal of Economic History*, XXIII (4), 414-43.

Rosenberg, Nathan (1976), *Perspectives on Technology*, Cambridge, UK: Cambridge University Press.

Saloner, G. and A.M. Spence (2002), *Creating and Capturing Value. Perspectives and Cases on Electronic Commerce*, New York: John Wiley & Sons.

Shapiro C. and Varian H. (1999), *Information Rules*, Cambridge, US: Harvard Business School Press.

Smith, M.D., J. Bailey and E. Brynjolfsson (2000), 'Understanding Digital Markets: Review and Assessment', in E. Brynjolfsson and B. Kahin (eds), *Understanding the Digital Economy – Data, Tools and Research*,

Cambridge, Massachusetts: The Massachusetts Institute of Technology (MIT) Press.

Sonderegger P., J.C. McCarthy and A. Armstrong (1998), 'The Age of Netpragmatism', *Forrester Research*, 3 (3), 2-12.

Srivastava S. and S. Dutta (2001), *Embracing the Net – get.competitive*, London, UK: Financial Times/Prentice Hall.

Teece D. J. (1986), 'Profiting from Technological Innovation: Implications for Integration, Collaboration, Licensing and Public Policy', *Research Policy*, 15, 285-307.

Teece (1988), 'Technological Change and the Nature of the Firm', in G. Dosi et al. (eds), *Technical Change and Economic Theory*, London, UK: Pinter Publishers.

Utterback, J. M. (1996), *Mastering the Dynamics of Innovation*, Boston, US: Harvard Business School Press.

von Hippel, E. (1988), *The Sources of Innovation*, New York: Oxford University Press.

Williamson, O.E. (1975), *Markets and Hierarchies: Analysis and Antitrust Implications*, New York: The Free Press.

Winter, S. (1987), 'Knowledge and Competence as Strategic Assets', in D.J. Teece (ed.), The *Competitive Challenge, Strategies for Industrial Innovation and Renewal*, New York, US: Harper & Row.

Wooldridge, A. (1997), 'Survey of Management Consulting (7): Doing it this way – successes old and new (1248)', *The Economist*, 342 (8009).

9. Assessing European Developments in Electronic Customer Relations Management in the Wake of the Dot.Com Bust

W. Edward Steinmueller

1. INTRODUCTION

This chapter assesses the current state of development of customer relations management (CRM) in the context of the emerging Information Society in Europe based upon in-depth interviews with 69 European companies drawn from the financial, travel and retail sectors as well as a 'mixed' sector collection of companies regarded as having developed successful electronic customer relations management (e-CRM) systems.[1]

Before presenting the key findings and implications of this study with regard to business and policy strategy, it is helpful to put the concept of customer relations management into a historical perspective (section 2) and to examine the issues that are involved in implementing e-CRM (section 3). Within the historical and implementation context, the method of this study is briefly described in section 4. Section 5 is devoted to key results and a final section (section 6) highlights key conclusions and specific recommendations arising from this study.

2. MOTIVES

That a company has a relationship with its customers that extends beyond the negotiation and fulfilment of sales transactions is both an old and a new idea. The traditional part of the idea is that companies have a valuable intangible asset in the goodwill of customers based upon their accumulated experience with the company. This traditional view of customer relations had everything to do with what companies delivered in terms of products and services and very little to do with individual customers. A company that chose the appropriate policies in the provision of goods and services, that delivered its products and services consistently and reliably, and that managed its payment and credit policies in a sensible and forthright manner, could expect to accumulate customer goodwill. In this traditional context, the date of establishment of the company signalled to potential customers that the company had been successful, at least compared to its rivals, in meeting the needs of customers, often for several generations.

The 'new' meanings being applied to companies' relationships with their customers are the consequence of two trends. The first is the extent of personalization required by customers. The second is the opportunities that companies have to achieve higher revenues by more effectively meeting individual customer needs. These two trends are leading in the same direction. There are a growing number of personalized product and service offerings as well as a stronger degree of personalization in all company interactions with customers – i.e. pre-sales consultation, sales and delivery, and post-sales support.

A variety of reasons have been offered for why customers are becoming more interested in the 'personalization' of the sales and service relationship offered by companies. The rise of a time-impoverished professional class, the growth of an 'individualist' ethos or 'me' generation, an increase in 'consumerist' values that equate personal identity with consumption choices, and an unwillingness to follow the consumption patterns of parents, are among those that have been put forward in recent years.[2] It is also possible that the desire for more personal services has been 'latent' and, with higher income, demand has simply increased. Although it is possible to *associate* any or all of these developments with the growing preference for personalization and customization, it is difficult to systematically translate any of these reasons into *causes*. The near universality of the preference for greater personalization and customization within industrialized countries such as the EU member states makes these reasons equally plausible as explanatory factors. One might argue that over the past two decades a growing number of people have simply woken up in the morning with a different attitude to their consumption habits – one that favours an increasing degree of personalization and customization.

Whatever the source of these changes in customers' preferences might be, they are changes to which companies must respond if they are to retain and enhance customer goodwill and their competitiveness in the market. At a superficial level, this involves producing goods and services that are more precisely tailored to customers and in particular to demographic groups, such as young singles, urban residents, or parents of young children. At a deeper level, however, companies are being asked to recognize and fulfil individual customer preferences with an increasing degree of precision (Peppers and Rogers,

1997). These preferences extend not only to the goods and services themselves, for which ever more information is required, but also to the convenience and efficiency with which they are purchased, delivered and supported after the sales transaction (Seybold and Marschak, 1998). A central tenet of thinking about customer relations management is that in order for companies to respond to these preferences, they must gather increasingly sophisticated and detailed information about individual customers (Dyché, 2001).

The need to collect customer information is, however, not only a consequence of a greater preference of customers for personalization and customization, it is also a consequence of the capacity that companies now have to record and manage customer-related information. Over the period of a hundred years (the late 19th to the late 20th century), personalized relationships between many businesses and customers were 'disrupted' by the emergence of mass production and consumption (see Beniger, 1986). As Beniger makes clear, the 'disruptive' features of mass production and consumption created the necessity for an entirely new 'control' system for the flow of goods and services, a system that was applicable to both service and manufacturing operations.

This controlled mass production and consumption system produced an enormous gain in the efficiency with which companies could make sales. It contributed to the growth of very large companies which have become the familiar 'brand names' in retailing, personal insurance, retail banking and many activities in which individual transactions occur in volume. The 'control technologies' available to manage this growth, however, were limited in their applicability to individual transactions. They were designed to optimize the 'throughput' of goods and services, and individual customers were treated as 'parameters' rather than as people. The extension of the 'business model' of mass production and consumption continued throughout the 20th century. For better and worse, it entered domains as varied as convenience foods (MacDonalds), pharmacies (Boots), and resort holidays (Club Med). Of course the spread of these methods was not uniform. For example, while hairstyling was 'mass produced' in the United States by the 'Supercuts' chain, similar developments failed to materialize in Europe.

The maturation of this trend was apparent long before it became a focus for criticism and before the search began for alternatives. However, the technologies and business reforms needed to create new methods for 'controlling' (or managing) the customer relationship took a long time to establish.

Two industries that pioneered these new developments were airline travel and retail banking. In airline travel, the creation of computer reservation systems during the 1960s provided a means to customize travel arrangements for individual customers while preserving a controlled mass production system – in this case, an international transportation network. It is important to note that these developments began through the use of an extensive network of travel agent intermediaries. These intermediaries have persisted despite ever more slender margins on their services.

Somewhat later, in the 1970s, retail banking provided customers with access to their accounts through automated teller machines (ATM). Although these services were rarely more, and in many cases less, 'personalized' than interactions with bank clerks, they provided customers with an unprecedented degree of control as to when they could deposit and withdraw funds from their accounts. They also provided current account balance information directly to the customer without the intervention of the bank clerk. These early changes in the capabilities to personalize services highlight that the models that deliver personalization may differ substantially depending upon what products or services are involved.

The contemporary context is one in which the Internet technologies appear to offer a universal solution to all of the hopes that companies might have with regard to managing their relations with customers. In principle, these technologies provide a channel for eliciting information about customers from the customers themselves. This may be done directly, by asking individuals about their preferences and experiences with a company. Or it may be accomplished indirectly, by monitoring the activities of individuals who are using the Internet or other information technologies to gather 'profiles' from which conclusions may be drawn with regard to their desires and interests.

In addition to these forms of interaction with customers, a growing number of companies record transactions with individual customers with respect to their means of payment, loyalty cards, or by taking customer details at the point of sale or while the customer is engaging with the services. All of these means of personalized data collection are subject to re-processing and re-combination in ways that, in principle, allow companies to create detailed models of individual customer preferences and habits. They are apparent in practices such as the retail receipt that provides 'discount coupons', custom-produced for the individual based upon his or her recent buying patterns. Personalized data collection is also a feature of systems that provide 'agents' with a recapitulation of past choices and preferences, such as the travel agency that records a customer's seating and dietary preferences.

In recent years, call centres have become a powerful adjunct to the capture of information from customers using Internet technologies and to the use of other customer databases such as those employed by retailers or travel agencies. Call centres extend sales and customer servicing activities by providing a means to centralize the collection of information and the delivery of sales and support resources to agents employed directly by companies or 'outsourced' to specialized companies. Call centres are also a means to provide direct services such as retail banking and credit services, holiday planning and, increasingly, practical information and problem solving services such as those related to the provision of medical consultations and treatment.

These examples provide a basis for the working definition of e-CRM which will be employed in this chapter.

e-CRM (or electronic customer relations management) is the collection of techniques that are employed, or that might be employed, to capture, retain, analyse, and productively utilize information about customers (or potential customers) for the purposes of marketing, pre-sales support, making sales and arranging delivery, and providing post-sales support to individual customers as well as in marketing and other business planning functions.

With some care in the further elaboration of what is meant by 'analyse and productively use' information, this definition encompasses virtually all of the functions that might be expected to support customer relations. For example, the productive use of information should include the goals of finding new customers and retaining the loyalty of customers. In principle, such information should also prove useful in the modification of products, negotiations with suppliers, and other aspects of business. As this chapter makes clear, however, the companies that were examined in the STAR research study (see Appendix) have not yet exploited these more far-reaching implications of e-CRM.

Although the working definition is consistent with discussions in the e-CRM literature and industry, there are three very important limitations to this working definition that must be considered in evaluating current and prospective developments in e-CRM. These limitations are:

1. The omission in the definition of any basis for evaluating the effectiveness or value of these techniques;

   The absence of criteria of effectiveness or performance in common definitions of e-CRM is not accidental but reflects an implicit perspective that e-CRM techniques are inherently superior to alternatives in delivering value, without explicitly identifying how this value will be delivered except by creating 'more satisfied' and therefore, presumably more numerous, customers. Empirical examination of e-CRM must begin by questioning whether this assumption is true, and if not true in all contexts, what are its limitations? Issues of customer identification, adding value to the services provided to customers, and retaining their loyalty, interest and enthusiasm are all aims for the *use* of e-CRM methods and therefore starting points for examining its effectiveness. These issues, many of which involve customer expectations, experience and engagement, are also central tenets in the implementation of the e-CRM paradigm and are critically examined in the next section (section 3).

2. The absence of clues about what practical problems might be encountered in realizing the functions mentioned in the definition;

The definition obscures the practical problems involved in realizing the range of functions that are mentioned. It does not provide a basis for identifying the likely practical issues that will be encountered in implementation or what should be done if limited resources or scepticism about value lead to a less than complete implementation of e-CRM methods. It is therefore important to consider what may be necessary in terms of human interaction and intervention to make such systems work effectively to deliver added value to customer relationships. These issues, which are central to the implementation of e-CRM systems have produced another set of ideas that are central tenets in thinking about e-CRM. In brief, these ideas centre on the value of comprehensiveness in the implementation of e-CRM systems and are examined critically in the next section (section 3).

3. The generic use of the term 'techniques' provides little guidance for assessing or identifying the methods that might be employed to further e-CRM;

This definition employs the term 'techniques' in a very broad sense. It provides little basis for evaluating the comparative significance of different technological developments. This imprecision in definition with respect to technology is intentional as is the imprecision with regard to value generation – it implicitly assumes that cost-effective technological solutions exist and only need to be installed to deliver effective outcomes. Rather than focusing on specific techniques that might be used in relation to the implementation of e-systems such as Internet-based e-commerce or customer databases, the definition focuses attention on the collection and use of information resources to support customers' needs and preferences. The actual means by which this is done are rapidly evolving and strongly overlap with the central tenet that the implementation of e-CRM systems should be comprehensive.

This section has identified several sets of ideas as central tenets in thinking about e-CRM. First, in order for companies to respond to these preferences, they must gather increasingly sophisticated and detailed information about individual customers. Second, customer identification, adding value to the services provided to the customer, and retaining their loyalty, interest and enthusiasm are all aims for the *use* of e-CRM methods that are a starting point for examining e-CRM effectiveness, an examination that must take into account customer expectations, experience and engagement. Third, the previous two sets of tenets suggest the need for comprehensiveness in the implementation of e-CRM systems. This comprehensiveness may involve different degrees of human intervention in the implementation and operation of such systems. At one extreme, human intervention is seen as a temporary expedient that is likely to give way to automated methods and at the other e-CRM may be seen as a source of further demand for continuing human involvement in delivering e-CRM services. Which extreme is closer to reality is a matter for empirical investigation, as is the extent to which information gathering and processing are necessary for successful implementation (the basic ideas comprising the first two tenets).

3. IMPLEMENTATION OF E-CRM: VISION VERSUS EXPERIENCE

The aim of CRM is to identify, secure and retain customers by offering them meaningful and valuable services in relation to their purchases of a company's products and services. The characteristics of the 'infrastructure' of CRM, the central feature of the definition offered in section 2, provides little understanding of how these goals may be met. To develop this understanding it is necessary to analyse more deeply the nature of the 'relationship' that is to be managed.

The contention that customers value their interactions with companies more highly when they are convinced that the company has a specific concern to serve their interests is closely related to the basic tenet that extensive data gathering and processing are a necessary feature of e-CRM, and to questions about how much human intervention is needed in this process. Establishing this customer conviction or belief is not a straightforward task and there is little guarantee that extensive data gathering, processing or human intervention will effect this. It clearly is not likely to be achieved through inexpensive and simplistic personalization techniques such as addressing the customer by name in telephone or World Wide Web interactions. Instead, it involves convincing customers that they have, at least to some degree, a one-to-one relationship with the company, i.e. that they are recognized as a person rather than as a generic 'customer' (or to use the rather derisive UK term, as a 'punter'). Some of the characteristics that CRM methods need to convince the customer that this is the case include (Peppers and Rogers, 1997; Cotterill, 2001; Dyché, 2001):

- Awareness of the customer's previous dealings with the company.
- Ability to address a customer's issues in a consistent way regardless of how the customer interacts with the company (e.g. by telephone, electronic communication, or post).

- Providing information that is directly relevant to customer needs.
- Putting the customer in control at every stage of interactions with the company rather than 'scripting' or 'directing' the interaction in ways that confine or constrain the interaction of the customer with the company. A corollary of this principle is that the various communication 'channels' that customers have access to must offer similar capacities. Post-sales support should be smoothly integrated with pre-sales information and the capacity to make sales.
- A capacity to set evaluation criteria for the success of CRM activities, to monitor the meeting of these criteria, and to adapt activities after evaluation.

These examples make it clear that the process of building effective e-CRM systems involves far more than an information gathering and processing infrastructure. It also involves deep organizational and procedural changes within the company, many of which involve 'integrating' functions that might otherwise be developed independently and with little relationship to one another.

The importance of 'connected up' strategies is a central theme in the literature on e-CRM. Many authors conclude that implementing e-CRM systems in one department of the company is useless (Seybold and Marschak, 1998; Gummesson, 2000). This is because such systems are unable to deliver to customers a 'full range' of services encompassing all of their potential interactions with the company. When e-CRM systems are incomplete, they may even have a negative effect because of customers' desires for an integrated and coherent approach to addressing their needs. The shortcomings of partial solutions, as well as the complexities of delivering the characteristics outlined above, are central to the practical issues of implementing comprehensive e-CRM systems, discussed further in section 3.1.

It is also commonly emphasized that a 'connected up' strategy implies an analytical capacity, i.e. the capacity to set evaluation criteria for the success of CRM activities, to monitor whether these criteria are being met, and to adapt the company's activities after evaluation as indicated in the list above. This analytical capability is important not only for meeting customers' expectations about the qualities of a 'one-to-one' relationship with the company, but also for the company to decide which customers should receive the greatest attention and, therefore, a disproportionate share of company resources. The contribution of individual customers – their 'value' – to the revenues and profitability of a company differs between industries. At the extreme, all customers are of similar value to the company and it makes little sense to distinguish between them in efforts to develop CRM tools and resources. More commonly, however, the most valuable customers produce revenues and profits several times greater than those of the average customer. This suggests a strategy of 'segmentation' with disproportionate investment in finding and retaining the customers that will produce higher revenues and profits. It is also possible that a company may wish to move towards a situation in which 'high value' customers are selectively recruited and retained. These strategies suggest that companies must take specific actions that are based upon an analysis of the effectiveness of their actions in relation to the 'target' segment. Such actions may be different from those that are required for generalized improvement of e-CRM capabilities.

The preceding discussion has focused upon the 'dyadic' relationship between the customer and the company. It presupposes that it is the individual customer that is of central concern and that this customer is disconnected from a social context. An alternative, and often complementary, strategy is to identify customer 'segments' that represent communities of common interest within the company's customer base and to encourage interaction within these customer 'communities' (Hagel III and Armstrong, 1997). This strategy carries the risk that negative impressions of the company may spread quickly among customers. It is not clear whether acute problems can be averted if serious customer opposition materializes. The DIVX (DIgital Video eXpress, a usage-sensitive format for DVDs (digital video – originally versatile – discs) used to implement pay-per-view business practices, is an example. DIVX encountered heavy resistance from many customers, eventually leading to the failure of the standard and the withdrawal from the market of DIVX DVD players and media, see Mansell and Steinmueller (2000: 322-3). Consumer action WWW sites featured prominently in the resistance campaign to DIVX. This experience raises the spectre that companies that do not provide opportunities for dissension (as well as for approval) will find that they have little or no opportunity to intervene in the discourse between customers, that is, no 'natural' forum for product supporters to confront critics.

Customer interaction at company WWW sites is particularly useful in the case of consumer electronics, computer retailing, and related software and services where supporting the product is costly due to its complexity and interaction with other features of user systems, see Teuber (2002). It is likely that many other areas of business could benefit from the capacity of users to interact with one another. User comments, reviews and reader favourites lists play an important role at Amazon.com, the leading e-commerce site for books.[3] By providing a means to review the comments of others, the electronic medium offers opportunities for inter-customer communication that are potentially greater than customer interaction in other contexts. For example, customers encounter one another in stores without a social context in which to initiate conversation. They have little or no opportunity to exchange, let alone to 'broadcast' their comments, advice and ideas for improvement.

In summing up this review of the implications of the central tenets of the e-CRM vision, several key questions are worth highlighting as a basis for building an evaluative framework for examining e-CRM practice and experience. These questions are:

1. How will integration between company functions occur and what are the expected returns compared to the costs of making this integration?
2. What strategies will be chosen to personalize customer services and to empower the customer? While some of these issues are matters of good design and best practice, the generality of such rules is limited. In practice, companies must develop analytical capabilities to understand what is an effective strategy for *their* customers – a requirement that becomes more demanding if the company chooses to focus on customer segments that may produce higher revenues and profitability.
3. Will the company choose to develop a customer 'communities' approach in which customers (or the general public) may interact with one another to augment, complement or even substitute for other efforts at CRM?[4]

Creating the enabling conditions for realizing the basic beliefs of the e-CRM vision is by no means straightforward, as the following sub-section (3.1) makes clear.

3.1 Practical Issues of e-CRM Implementation

While it is straightforward to state the *possibilities* for the utilization of e-CRM techniques, understanding implementation practices in actual applications is a far more difficult matter. In this, as in many other emerging technologies, there is a tendency towards 'cognitive presbyopia' (seeing the distant future with a clear focus, while seeing the intervening events in a hazy or indistinct manner).[5] Cognitive presbyopia should provoke caution and scepticism since it is likely to lead to snags and spills in the headlong rush towards the future. It is, however, often accompanied by a high degree of optimism that the intermediate and intervening requirements for reaching the future are mere 'details'. 'After all,' the promoters respond, 'the opportunities and possibilities are clearly apparent' in the long-term 'visions' for the application of these technologies. The findings from the STAR research project provide a basis for scepticism about the rate at which these visions are becoming reality.

The dangers of cognitive presbyopia, as well as of the magnification of this tendency as a result of the self-interest of technology 'promoters' such as software and specialized consultancy companies, make it particularly important to identify the problems in achieving long term 'visions' for the application of new technologies. Technological history is replete with examples of the technologies whose eventual use and value were enormously different from the ideas of their inventors or those who were the first to apply them commercially.

In the case of e-CRM, the central implementation problem is the extent to which the company must effectively integrate information and knowledge about its customers across different departments. Doing so allows customers to perceive the company as coherent and engaged in a consistent way with their needs and interests. Failing to achieve effective integration implies that companies' e-CRM efforts will be futile, or, worse, counter-productive.

The question remains, however, as to what 'effective integration' actually means in the experience of companies that are having a degree of success in implementing e-CRM solutions. The main *tenets* of e-CRM suggest that all of a company's business functions related to the customer must be sufficiently integrated so that customers will perceive the company as relating to them on a one-to-one basis. It also suggests that this perception must hold, regardless of which part of the company the customer is dealing with. Few companies have been able to achieve this standard of 'effectiveness'. It is clear from the company experiences reported in the empirically-grounded trade and consulting literature that relatively few companies believe that they will achieve this goal in the near future: see for example Samuel (2002); Sweet (2002); Teuber (2002).[6]

Given the gap between the imperative tone of the consultancy literature which sets out the tenets of the e-CRM vision and the reality of company experience, it is important to ask companies how they are managing to achieve a degree of success *without* total integration of all of their customer-related business processes. A large number of companies do appear to view themselves as having been reasonably successful without having achieved a high degree of integration.

This raises further questions about the extent of specialization in the ways companies are actually employing e-CRM techniques. There may be gains to be made in the short run, in terms of recruiting and retaining customers (principal goals of e-CRM), which can be achieved without complete implementation of the full e-CRM vision; a vision which may be subject to 'cognitive presbyopia' as suggested above.

The European companies that are examined in this chapter are achieving a measure of success in their e-CRM activities by pursuing strategies involving a degree of specialization and focus. They are not undertaking a wholesale 're-engineering' of their organizations to conform to the tenets of e-CRM. This does not make these tenets irrelevant; it suggests only that some degree of success, at least in the view of the company respondents to the STAR survey, is achievable using a more limited strategy. It is important to note, however, that as shown in section 5, many companies do not have an explicit strategy for evaluating the effectiveness of their e-CRM strategy. Because of this, it seems that some firms are violating another tenet of e-CRM, perhaps with more serious consequences given the costs of these operations.

In summary, the practical problems of implementing the degree of integration suggested by the visionary proponents of e-CRM are greater than most companies are willing to tackle at present. Our investigation of European companies that are successfully engaged in specialized activities involving e-CRM indicates the possibility of success without total integration.

4. THE METHOD EMPLOYED IN EXAMINING E-CRM

The STAR research project on e-CRM was based upon two-part in-depth interviews with appropriate company personnel. The first part of the interview involved gathering key factual information about the company and describing recent experience in the use of e-business and e-CRM techniques (a 'company profile', see below).

The 'company profile' was used to gather information concerning company activities, ownership structure, target markets, number of employees and revenues (both worldwide and at the national level). Questions were also asked to ascertain whether the company was at an early, medium or advanced stage in the adoption of e-business. The interviewer often completed this part of the questionnaire before the in-depth interview based on desk and Internet research.

The second part of the interview was structured according to an Interview Guide, and included questions exploring the use of e-business in CRM and related organizational changes. It was divided into five sections:

- *Functional change:* identification of major changes in business functions (finding, acquiring and retaining customers) related to the use of e-CRM.
- *Organizational change:* locating the effects associated with the use of e-CRM in the way companies organize their businesses and in their relationships with suppliers and distributors.
- *Impacts of change:* evaluating the positive or negative impacts of e-CRM on company competitive performance and relationships with customers.
- *Assessment of employment and skills impacts:* assessing the impacts of e-CRM on the number and characteristics of jobs, the skills required and the implications for teleworker and mobile worker employment.
- *Drivers, barriers and perspectives:* the reasons for company adoption of e-CRM techniques, the problems they encountered and their plans for the future in terms of exploitation or extension of e-CRM.

4.1 Selecting the Companies

In order to select the companies, several 'activity areas' were chosen, three of which roughly correspond to NACE sectors, travel services, financial services and retail trade. In addition, companies making innovative use of e-CRM techniques for customer service functions across a variety of sectors were selected as a fourth activity area. Interviews with representatives of the companies required that the companies be selected from the home countries of STAR Project Consortium participants, i.e. France, Germany, Greece, Italy and the United Kingdom.

The sample size of the study was 69 companies (see Table 9.1). These companies were selected according to the following criteria:

- size: generally medium and large organizations (firms with more than 200 employees) except in those sectors where a few small organizations were identified as being exemplary;
- presence of an e-business activity in the core business; and
- ownership of a Web site for at least one year prior to Spring 2002.

The sample could not be statistically representative of the population of firms in each sector or country given the variety of the responses that were requested and the need to develop detailed case studies to capture ongoing development of e-CRM practices.

Table 9.1 Companies interviewed by country and by industry

	France	Germany	Greece	Italy	UK	Total
Retail services	4	2	4	4	4	18
Financial services	4	3	2	4	4	17
Travel services	4	3	2	4	5	18
Customer service and e-CRM Innovators	4	3	1	4	4	16
Total	16	11	9	16	17	69

5. KEY RESULTS

The principal findings of STAR research on e-CRM developments are that:

1. a diversity of models is being successfully employed by companies, contradicting the widespread belief that there is one clear path or prescription for implementing e-CRM systems
2. there are systematic differences between sectors in the use of e-CRM techniques including differences in the priority assigned to database integration, WWW site development, call centre sophistication, and linkages with suppliers
3. issues surrounding integration of existing databases are a dominant and constraining influence on e-CRM implementation
4. call centre operations rather than WWW-based applications lie at the centre of company strategy and user activity in the firms that were surveyed
5. WWW-based applications of e-CRM are dominated by satisfying users' needs for information rather than interaction or transactions between companies and customers.

These findings suggest that there is no single 'best practice' model for the implementation of e-CRM applications. Differences in the interactions with customers across different sectors lead to e-CRM implementation based on strategies comprising several distinct elements. Within sectors, companies appear to choose different configurations of the elements of the dominant sector strategy.

The advent of a 'virtual' e-CRM relationship that is dominated by the use of WWW and Internet resources lies beyond the planning horizon of almost all the companies interviewed. Only very specialized customer service firms are emulating companies like Amazon or EasyJet in their principal reliance on WWW customer interactions. In part, this is due to the continuing hesitance of customers to make final purchase commitments or other primary transactions through the use of WWW interfaces alone. Rather, customers are utilizing the Internet to inform themselves about payment terms, service, and other options connected with their purchase of goods and services. This makes the 'call centre,' i.e. telephonic connection with humans, a central component of almost all WWW-based e-CRM strategies and enhances the importance of establishing call centre and WWW site linkages.

The innovations required to make e-CRM successful are primarily organizational rather than technological. With a few exceptions, the main challenge that the companies interviewed were addressing was the selective integration of their customer databases. Accomplishing this integration was seen as an organizational rather than a technological issue, although adaptation to existing tools and techniques is often required to achieve the goals sought in organizational change.

The role of e-CRM applications in supporting customer needs for information suggests a further development of the trend towards a 'self-service' economy observed 20 years ago by Gershuny and Miles (1983). From a business perspective, encouraging customers to meet their own information needs through the use of Internet resources is, in principle, an excellent way to raise the productivity of company personnel. Assuming that these informational requirements can be met as effectively through customer-based Internet interactions as by company employees would permit a re-deployment of personnel to higher value-added activities. Experience with this strategy is mixed. Many companies are reporting that improved access is leading to higher levels of customer information requests and that there are major costs involved in implementing and promoting these new channels. However, companies continue to be convinced that there is value in this approach and that it offers further opportunities for 'segmenting' customer groups so that customers producing the highest revenue and profitability for the company receive the best possible service.

The following sub-sections highlight the findings for individual sectors.

5.1 Financial Services

The financial services sector, which sometimes is taken to include insurance, has historically been a leader in the use of information and communication technologies. Extensive information about customers flows through the information systems of financial service companies. The use of this information for customer relations management, however, has traditionally been of lower priority than the established uses of these systems for tasks such as account settlement, accountancy and the preparation of statements.

Strategies for the application of e-CRM techniques in financial services are emerging. STAR research on the sector identified a broad or 'model' strategy employed in various configurations by almost all of the companies interviewed. This model strategy comprises three elements:

1. The extension of the 'self-service' banking model originally developed with the aid of ATMs. The aim of this strategic element is to shift a significant share of 'low value-added' functions from the bank to the customer. Examples include account balance and recent transaction enquiries, information on standard service rates, etc. While this feature is most conspicuous in the financial services sector, it plays an important role in all of the sectors examined.

2. The development of information-rich services that allow the customer to 'research' potential services and financial product offerings at their convenience. This feature is shared with other sectors and only a few financial services sector companies (mostly those offering personal portfolio management services) are at the forefront of these developments.
3. The augmentation of customer loyalty by providing customers with a convenient means to access their account information while at the same time helping them to become more accustomed to the financial institution's user interface (e.g. security procedures, information displays, ordering methods, etc.). Banks appear to be taking a leading position in developing this e-CRM feature.

Some of the respondents speculated about the possibility of a fourth theme involving the customization of services to individual customers. This, however, is rarely an active area of development. In other words, one of the key elements of the e-CRM consulting literature remains a speculative possibility for financial services companies.

Financial services companies believe that they can make productivity gains by encouraging customers to service their own needs with regard to account balance and transaction enquiries or finding information about service rates and availability. A higher quality of service and, potentially, higher customer loyalty can be obtained by the financial service company personnel being freed up to answer more complex queries and to complete transactions that customers are often unwilling to make over the Internet. In practice, however, experience is mixed, with financial services companies reporting that the costs of installing and promoting such systems delay the realization of positive financial returns. This experience is similar to the history of ATMs, where many of the expected gains were eroded by competitive service rate reductions.

The same technologies that make it possible for banks to extend telephone service and ATM banking to customers is available to new financial services companies (e.g. online stock brokers), and to companies engaged in other businesses with extensive customer interactions (such as supermarkets, post offices or department stores). In this respect, the improved convenience for customers not only offers the prospect of productivity increases but also is becoming a necessary component of financial services provision.

The use of Internet-related technologies for providing information about financial services extends beyond banking account services to a much broader range of financially-related services that banks may choose to offer. In this respect, the development of effective means for explaining service offerings, enrolment procedures and rates and rules are a second element of the strategy that banks are employing in the use of e-CRM. While the transactions that lead to commitment to these services will most often be done through personal or call centre contact with customers, customers using these services appear to need to make fewer contacts and are generally well informed about their transactions. The spread of Internet access to larger numbers of people puts an important constraint on the receipt of the full benefits from this feature of e-CRM. The problems involved in customer support are increased when some customers are poorly informed while others hold a lot of information as a result of their use of the Internet resources.

For firms whose customers do employ the Internet for access to financial services there are new opportunities for establishing customer loyalty. Much as users become accustomed to a particular word processing or e-mail software interface, customers' use of online financial services software (including the manipulation of the WWW interface of their particular bank) provides banks with the ability to engage more deeply with these customers. As yet, the banks employing online access appear to be most concerned with issues of security, reliability and speed of access. For many financial services companies, these aspects have quite recently become more satisfactory to customers, allowing these companies to contemplate the development of a higher degree of user customization and service. For these reasons, the financial services industry is likely to reproduce in e-CRM services the lead that it demonstrated in earlier generations of information and communication technologies and services.

5.2 Retail Trade

Many of the dot.com companies targeted the retail trade sector, attempting to create a new form of retail intermediation. Existing retail companies did not, in general, rush headlong into making a competitive response to these 'challenges', most of which evaporated along with the companies that sponsored them. Incumbent retail companies are, however, engaged in important experimentation with e-CRM techniques. A key feature in the use of the e-CRM medium by the companies interviewed is the relatively minor importance attached to customizing the 'flow' of interaction with customers who are repeat purchasers, a key tenet in much of the consultancy literature on e-CRM applications. (Customer loyalty cards, however, are a central part of the strategy of many companies.) Instead, two strategic elements are identifiable in the retail sector's use of e-CRM techniques:

1. The use of the 'information-rich' Web sites to satisfy customers' needs for more detailed information about the products they are contemplating buying or after-sales support for products. The omission of the purchase transaction itself is conspicuous, with most retailers focusing on directing the

potential customer to call centres or retail outlets to complete their transaction.

2. The incorporation of e-CRM in wider strategies of creating integrated databases of retail operations. The amount of information gained through electronic business-to-consumer exchanges is relatively small in terms of total
information flow (e.g. from the general use of customer loyalty cards at
points of sale) and does not appear to have major independent value.
However, it is a useful complement to other information flows within the
company and provides further impetus for improving data storage and
analysis techniques within the company.

Together, these strategic elements indicate a relatively conservative approach
to e-CRM implementation by retailers which is based upon their traditional
sophistication in advertising with only minor application of the more recent
techniques for developing customer loyalty.

Like the financial services sector, retailers believe that information-rich
Web sites offer the potential for gains. The model of how such gains are to be
realized, however, differs in the case of the retail services sector, largely due to
the nature of the product. The relatively small share of revenue that retail companies receive from Internet purchases has discouraged most companies from
making major investments in online purchasing systems. Several companies
had been disappointed about the realization of expectations from online sales
and other retail companies that were identified as leaders in the CRM area had
not developed this channel intensively. Instead, a principal purpose of the
Internet component of the business is to enhance customer loyalty. The traditional medium of the retailer credit or payment card, combined with the more
recent development of loyalty systems based on volume of purchases, provide
a focus for retail promotion efforts. Despite the apparent potentials offered by
customization and direct customer identification, however, retailers have
focused on customer loyalty and retention largely through provision of useful
information resources on their WWW sites. For some retailers, the use of the
Internet has become another 'advertising' medium that is particularly useful in
notifying those of its customers that are Internet users, of the sales and promo-
tions that are generally advertised through direct mail or telephone contact. A
few companies are undertaking more ambitious experiments with customer
interaction including the novel use by at least one French company of IP-
telephony.

The major technological and organizational issue facing retailers in
improving the use of e-CRM techniques is the integration of company databases. Unlike the financial services sector in which a significant degree of
integration was required to exploit information systems, the application of
information systems in retailing is more often organized by 'stovepipe' func-

tionality in which distinct and unconnected tasks are augmented by automated methods according to the immediate returns that they offer. For example, point-of-sale terminals were deployed first, with later adoption of automated inventory and ordering systems that often were not integrated with the point-of-sale terminals. In recent years, retailers have been struggling to fulfil the promise offered by combining the databases generated by these systems into data warehousing and analysis systems. The vastness of the retail transaction volumes makes this a difficult task and the particular contribution of the 'customer specific' content of these data (generated through customer loyalty or credit cards) is only one of many possible methods for understanding customer buying behaviour.

Much of the conservatism in the retail sector arises from uncertainty about the added value that will accrue from e-CRM techniques directly related to customer tracking. The behaviour of aggregate groups of customers rather than individual customers has been the traditional means of analysing retail spending behaviour. Thus, while the retail companies that were interviewed were optimistic that e-CRM techniques would eventually be more fully articulated, and found discussions about e-CRM useful in supporting the general aim of improving data integration and the accompanying organizational changes required for such integration, they did not regard implementation of customer-specific e-CRM techniques as their highest priority.

Some of the companies interviewed in the 'customer service' portion of the study (considered below) were specialized retailers who have adopted a specific e-CRM implementation strategy.

5.3 Travel Services

The use by the travel services sector of e-CRM techniques most closely reflects several of the advantages of e-CRM portrayed in the consultancy literature. The travel industry is engaged in a protracted struggle for horizontal and vertical control which has been underway since the development of computerized reservation systems (CRS), a radical information and communication technology innovation. This struggle is apparent in two distinct strategic elements employed by travel service companies:

1. Increases in vertical control can be achieved by bypassing (or dis-intermediating) parts of the supply chain along which travel services are provided. This process involves both upstream and downstream bids for further control – thus airline companies attempt to engage customers directly through e-ticketing, and holiday companies provide greater flexibility and options for their customers by engaging a wide variety of suppliers of the travel services that their customers want. This strategy has implications for

horizontal concentration, providing larger companies with new opportunities for achieving competitive advantage.

2. At the same time, many travel services are information-rich and complex. Customer requirements are becoming more complex as travellers become more experienced and require a more complex mix of standardized and low-cost service offerings (e.g. air travel to their chosen destination) with customized and higher value-added components (e.g. eco-tourism, sports tourism and specialized itineraries). Supporting the information and planning needs of individual customers is thus an opportunity to apply e-CRM techniques.

These two strategic elements are largely distinct and require different approaches to the implementation of e-CRM systems. While the first focuses on the transaction, the second focuses on the provision of information resources and the travel planning process.

A major share of the business and pleasure market is occupied by customers who want travel services to be a low-cost 'means to an end' – the desired travel destination. This portion of the travel services market, centring on passenger transportation and routine hotel booking services, has become ever more competitive with slender and shrinking margins for intermediaries such as travel agencies. The possibility of bypassing intermediaries, a rationale of the business-to-consumer e-commerce model, is one of the principal axes around which the competitive struggle has been organized.

The use of e-commerce type techniques involving direct customer transactions such as electronic reservation and ticketing furthers the competitive aims of transport and hotel service companies and has both economic and control effects. The economic effect is to reduce the price customers pay for transport and accommodation services (reducing the two-level effects of market power), which leads to higher revenues for the final service providers at the expense of intermediaries. The other, and more important, effect of these methods is to link customers more strongly to transport and accommodation service providers and thereby support the use and effects of customer loyalty schemes such as air miles rewards. This latter effect is the consequence of increasing competition in the market for transport and accommodation services, a trend that seems likely to continue.

The travel services market (fortunately) is not solely composed of standardized transport and hotel service packages. Individuals with more complex and demanding requirements account for a growing share of holiday and some business travel. The sophistication and experience of Europeans in travel greatly increased in the latter half of the 20th century. Serving these customers' needs involves an entirely different e-CRM strategy. In this part of the travel services market, the focus is not on transactions, which are likely to be completed face-to-face, as this provides a degree of reassurance with regard to the risks of travel. Instead, the planning of more complex holiday and business travel involves the development of information-rich WWW resources to complement the traditional advertising medium of 'glossy' travel brochures and catalogues. In addition, the development of customized services offering complex combinations of transport, tour and hotel services offers travel agencies and other industry participants a profitable addition to their more standardized travel arrangements business.

The use of Internet-based resources for promoting and planning more complex travel arrangements requires careful attention to the customer's information and interaction needs. It also creates challenges in linking the planning process to the personal transaction. To meet these challenges travel agencies, particularly those companies offering 'bundles' of services, will eventually need to link their online presence with their in-house data booking systems. At present there are severe problems in achieving this objective due to the variety of the information systems that must be linked and the absence of widely accepted standards. The transfer of information from e-CRM interactions into the booking systems of travel agencies and transport, tour and accommodation service companies adds another impetus to such developments, but only one of several that have so far failed to overcome the competitive incentives that fostered the original divergence in these information systems.

5.4 Interim Summary and Comparison

The sector studies from the STAR research project on e-CRM reveal that the historical processes of accumulating capabilities and structuring data resources dominate the implementation of e-CRM strategies. These strategies are further shaped by the nature of the competition within the sector. Financial services companies hope that e-CRM systems will reinforce customer loyalty in the face of new competition, but expect quicker returns from enhancement of self-service banking and customer account access. Retail service companies are generally not persuaded that the 'customization' offered by e-CRM will have a remarkable effect on their business, but appreciate the complementary value of the additional stream of data that e-CRM produces for promoting their information system integration strategies. Depending on their position in the industry, travel services companies are attempting to benefit from or to survive the emergence of business-to-customer model e-commerce, but see new opportunities in complex and customized travel service arrangements. While data integration issues figure prominently in each of the sectors, the means of achieving this integration differ and none primarily depends upon customer interaction with Internet-based services. These interactions are, in turn, influenced by the nature of competition in each of the sectors, one of the influences that draws companies together in their strategies for e-CRM implementation.

The data integration issues are prominent in existing academic and consultancy literature on e-CRM. What distinguishes the experience of the companies interviewed from the idealization in this literature is that data integration is a goal that is approached incrementally rather than being a 'prerequisite' to enhancing customer relations through the use of Information Society technologies.

The experience of companies also raises important questions about the specific role of these Information Society technologies. The predominant use of Internet-based applications is to provide information resources for customers, not as a means of completing transactions. Transactions are made in person or, with growing frequency, through interaction with call centres. The role of call centres is extremely important, and suggests the need for renewed attention to organizational, technological and regulatory issues influencing call centre development and viability. Call centres and Internet-based applications are very closely related – progress in one area is likely to stimulate service demands in the other.

This finding strongly contests the viewpoints that the Internet will become a gigantic shopping mall or that virtual interactions are likely to replace personal exchanges. Instead it suggests that a principal value of the Internet is to extend and further articulate trends towards the 'self service' economy in which customers produce services for themselves, principally the services involved in the informing and planning stages that occur prior to committing to a purchase transaction.

Finally, the experience of the companies interviewed raises important questions about whether visions of e-CRM services as a means of extending and strengthening customer tracking and individualization of services will be realized. The vision and the reality are clearly most out of line in the case of retail services where the primary interest lies in capturing customer data as an input into a larger agenda of data aggregation and integration. In both financial and travel services, customization *is* sought, but in very different ways. In financial services the principal strategy involves developing robust systems to support customers in servicing their own information needs while the individualization strategy of travel services companies focuses on single, albeit complex, planning processes with little attention to future interactions.

Collectively, these divergences from any 'standard' model for e-CRM expansion do not suggest that what is happening is only a process of early development. If this were true, convergence might be foreseen at some time in the future. Instead, the striking feature of these developments is the implausibility that they would lead to convergence in a dominant model of e-CRM application relevant to a broad range of service industries.

To test this non-convergence proposition further, the next section examines a heterogeneous collection of companies (and activities) involving customer service and e-CRM innovations.

5.5 Customer Services

As noted earlier, the process of identifying companies as customer service and e-CRM innovators sought to exclude companies that were just getting started or that were pioneering radically new techniques that had not been market tested. The companies were drawn from diverse economic sectors, ranging from consultancy and insurance services to retailers of personal computer equipment and automotive parts.

The aim of identifying companies that had a well-developed customer relations specialization was not universally successful. One retail company, for example, saw little value in providing personalized information about their products or in acquiring information about customers through their online operations. A magazine publisher maintained that the principal purpose of its Web site was to advertise its call-centre number for subscription purposes. These companies, however, were the exceptions. An electronics retailer offering customers the capacity to assemble their own systems, and a brokerage firm seeking new ways to package financial research from other companies to support their clients' needs, were more characteristic of the companies interviewed. The companies identified as 'leaders' in the customer service area were generally employing some feature or aspect of e-CRM intensively. These companies focus on one, two or three aspects of e-CRM rather than developing the entire e-CRM model as described in the consultancy literature.

Despite the dramatic differences in their activities, the companies interviewed employed the same strategic model, which included three basic elements. These elements were combined in different ways depending on relationships with customers and the nature of the products or services being offered. The common strategic elements were:

1. Attempts to increase the intensity of customer involvement by providing a means for them to express preferences, keep up-to-date with new developments of individual interest and, in some cases, interact with other users.
2. Integrating data resources across the company so that at whatever point the customer might interact with the company, information about the customer is readily available (e.g. call centre, online, and promotional offerings by phone or direct mail).
3. Simultaneous development of on-line and call centre operations in which on-line reference information resources are available for learning about

product and service options with telephone support for ordering and responding to specialized questions.

A factor shaping the mix of these strategic elements in the different companies was the 'path' that they had followed in adopting or making incremental improvements in the use of e-CRM. In general, there were no 'comprehensive' or 'attack on all fronts' efforts to improve e-CRM in the customer service area. Companies had begun by translating their traditional strengths into the virtual environment (where this was appropriate) or by developing specific initiatives with a limited scope (for both investment and return) which would allow them to develop knowledge and competence in the use of e-CRM.

The companies that had a close relationship with their customers in the traditional off-line environment sought mainly to reproduce this relationship in the on-line environment. These companies were most likely to pursue the first strategic element, providing a means for customers to express their preferences including their specific information needs. Nonetheless, the extent of personalization was modest and companies indicated that this was not, in general, a high development priority in the near term.

Despite the considerable attention in recent years devoted to on-line communities and the value of encouraging interactions between customers, few companies had made this a high priority. An important exception was an electronics retailer that provided a forum for users to exchange experience in the use of systems purchased from the company. In part, the disinterest in customer communities may reflect the risks of sponsoring a forum that could result in adverse publicity. The power of modern search engines, however, makes it likely that knowledgeable customers will be able to find reviews of companies and products or customer feedback from other locations.

The interviewed companies had a much more active interest in improving the integration of their databases so that their customer service operations could be consistent across all of the possible points of contact (on-line, call centre, postal communication and personal contact). A central feature of these integrating activities was the uniting of different physical locations through a common information infrastructure (often employing Internet technologies and software tools). Companies believed that the principal value of such initiatives was customer loyalty, arguing that the first step towards personalization is consistency in the company's ability to follow up on past interactions. There were, however, exceptions to this strategy. One major vehicle breakdown service and insurance company concluded that the value of knowing the history of past interactions with the company was of little help in resolving current problems or queries, even though this information was useful in rate setting and other contexts. The same company had established a major call centre employing sophisticated operator information terminals.

As in the financial and travel services sectors, call centres play a central role in customer services and e-CRM innovator companies. All but a few of these companies have call centres and view them as a focal component of their strategy in employing Information Society technologies. The distinguishing feature of these companies was the combination of the call centre operations with on-line resources available to call centre operators. Individual operator terminals are often networked and linked to the integrated databases that these companies are attempting to construct. This suggests a more general point about the implementation of e-CRM systems. In the context of companies whose customers are drawn from a cross-section of the population, a relatively small share will be on-line and a still smaller share will be on-line during their call centre interaction (due to the use of a single phone line for on-line access). Companies' responses to this issue focus on the development of the more traditional channel of call centre operations with on-line resources as an adjunct. This suggests that company strategies regarding innovation and data resource development are likely to originate in the call centre rather than in the on-line environment.

The experience of the customer service and e-CRM innovating companies confirms the specificity in e-CRM development and implementation processes observed in the financial, travel and retail service sector studies. The 'starting place', where e-CRM applications are developed, influences the next step in development. Since this next step often involves combining data resources from different parts of the company, database and system integration is a common priority for these companies. It must be stressed, however, that these integration activities are often pursued in steps rather than in a comprehensive fashion.

The unlikelihood of the near term emergence of a universal model for the application of e-CRM is confirmed by the experience of these companies. Specific development projects are far more likely to be pursued than broad development projects. Correspondingly, these companies are sceptical about 'powerful', 'general purpose' tools that claim to be designed to be useful in e-CRM applications, preferring to use applications constructed from more basic building blocks that often involve Internet-related software tools. By proceeding in this way, companies generate and solve a more limited range of implementation problems and avoid the problems of systems not being fully functional until all of their elements are in place.

6. RECOMMENDATIONS FOR POLICY AND RESEARCH

Policy recommendations from STAR research on e-CRM are relevant to both the private and public sectors.

With respect to private sector policy, i.e. business strategy, the following recommendations are of central importance:

- Companies should not expect to pursue e-CRM implementation as an all-encompassing goal requiring major transformations in every aspect of their organization and business practice – translating traditional strengths first provides a better foundation for identifying the returns and pitfalls.
- Implementation of e-CRM applications seems invariably to lead to perceptions of the need for data resource and system integration. Integration plans that offer a tangible near or medium term benefit seem to offer better prospects of success than the pursuit of 'grand architectures' that may remain only partially completed. Due to the nature of the sampling methodology, problems in implementing e-CRM are not well addressed by the STAR research project and remain to be further investigated. One possible source of such problems is efforts that are too ambitious, another is failure even to begin e-CRM development.
- Exploiting the development of on-line resources will require enhancement and enlargement of call centre operations. Achieving an effective link between on-line and call centre operations requires in-house development or a very close relationship with the firms selected for outsourcing.
- On-line resources are, in the first instance, tools that allow customers to explore and discover information. In many cases, this will produce some benefits from a reduction in simple queries. Customer loyalty and retention does seem to be higher as the result of these tools, although few companies were able to quantify exactly the extent of their benefits.
- On-line resources, however, will also generate a significant increase in more sophisticated queries and the expectation that company representatives (e.g. call-centre operators) will be aware of the on-line information resources, which suggests specific strategies for training such personnel and providing them with appropriate on-line capabilities.
- Few companies are reporting large gains from the deployment of e-CRM techniques but most companies are convinced that it is important to begin developing such techniques now so that experience can be accumulated. The priorities appear to be enhancement of call centre operations, enhancement of data integration to present customers with a consistent experience regardless of their means of interacting with the company, and development of on-line information resources that allow customers to widen their knowledge of product and service offerings.
- Despite academic and consultancy interest in on-line customer communities, relatively few companies are assigning a high priority to such developments at present. Successful employment of this strategy appears to require a specialized customer base with a high degree of computer literacy.

- Similarly, users remain resistant to the use of on-line payment systems or other forms of commitment that are not intermediated by a human being. This resistance is stronger among customers in Southern Europe, but is also observable by companies operating in the UK and Germany.

STAR research on e-CRM has also highlighted the importance of public policy actions including those undertaken in recent years and those being considered for future implementation.

- The actions taken in recent years to enhance the reliability and security of on-line transactions, i.e. the e-commerce policy framework sought in Action Plans developed in recent years, are clearly addressing a major problem. Customers continue to be sceptical about on-line purchase commitments, particularly for complex or costly transactions.
- Concerns about call-centre development, including the difficult tradeoffs between their positive feature of job creation and the potentially negative feature of the creation of a more casual labour force, are clearly warranted given the increasing centrality of call-centre operations in e-CRM strategies.
- Policy concerns and actions regarding privacy are important in building the trust needed to increase interactivity and customized services. There was, however, little evidence in the companies interviewed of an existing capacity to systematically use customer-specific information to discriminate either positively or negatively between specific groups of customers. Many companies did, however, suggest that developing this capability was a future aim, once more basic issues had been resolved.
- Increasing the utilization of Information Society technologies is clearly a necessary step towards realizing the opportunities offered by e-CRM techniques. Delays in participation and inadequacies in access appear likely to lead to a development path along which call centre intermediation (with a higher level of access for the operators) continues to gain strength at the expense of direct access to information resources by customers. While in some activities (e.g. on-line payment) this may be preferred by customers, in others it is clearly a disadvantage for those who have or can acquire the skills to make use of on-line resources.

The most fundamental finding of this research that is relevant to both public policy and business strategy is that 'best practice' in e-CRM development and implementation is sector specific. This means that the existing research foundations for both public policy and business strategy, which are based on a convergent and universal model of e-CRM, are entirely inadequate. What is clearly needed, and what the STAR project has endeavoured to produce in part, is knowledge about the drivers and barriers to e-CRM implementation and how they *differ* between sectors. Systematic differences arising from a competitive structure and the nature of customer relationships with companies dictate different company strategies depending upon the sector in which the company operates. In formulating public policy, the further successful development of e-CRM is likely to depend on more targeted and focused policy initiatives that take specific sector differences into account.

NOTES

1. See Appendix for further details concerning the nature and availability of the reports produced by the STAR research project.
2. See, for example, Peppers and Rogers (1997); Seybold and Marschak (1998); Tapscot (1999).
3. Amazon.com offers other items for sale in markets where it is not the dominant competitor.
4. Although this question is one of the means for empowering customers, its requirements and consequences are distinct from those of the strategies discussed in the previous point.
5. See David (1986) for a closely related use of this term in the context of policy decision-making.
6. The first two sources report on reasonably extensive surveys of company experience in the UK and France. The third highlights the specific UK experience in attempting to support DSL service installation through 'help desks' and Web sites rather than through on-site engineer installation (a service that is available in the UK at a higher cost).

REFERENCES

Beniger, J.R. (1986), *The Control Revolution: Technological and Economic Origins of the Information Society*, Cambridge MA: Harvard University Press.

Cotterill, D. (2001), 'New Channels, New Challenges', *Consultants' Advisory Journal*, September, 6.

David, P.A. (1986), 'Narrow Windows, Blind Giants and Angry Orphans: The Dynamics of Systems Rivalries and Dilemmas of Technology Policy', CEPR Paper No. 10, Stanford University, March.

Dyché, J. (2001), *The CRM Handbook: A Business Guide to Customer Relationship Management*, Boston MA: Addison-Wesley.

Gershuny, J. and I. Miles (1983), *The New Service Economy*, London: Pinter.

Gummesson, E. (2000), *Total Relationship Marketing: From the 4Ps – Product, Price, Promotion, Place – of Traditional Marketing Management – to the 30Rs – The Thirty Relationships – of the New Marketing Paradigm*, Oxford: Butterworth-Heinemann.

Hagel III, J. and A.G. Armstrong (1997), *Net.gain – Expanding Markets through Virtual Communities*, Boston, MA: Harvard Business School Press.

Mansell, R. and W.E. Steinmueller (2000), *Mobilizing the Information Society: Strategies for Growth and Opportunity*, Oxford: Oxford University Press.

Peppers, D. and M. Rogers (1997), *The One to One Future: Building Relationships One Customer at a Time*, New York: Currency/Doubleday.

Samuel, A. (2002), '"La France S.A." has the same problem … ', CRM Forum (last accessed: 4 September 2002).

Seybold, P. and R. Marschak (1998), *Customers.com: How to Create a Profitable Business Strategy for the Internet & Beyond*, New York: Times Books.

Sweet, P. (2002), 'CRM Hangover', *Consultants' Advisory Journal*, June 2-5.

Tapscot, D. (1999), *Growing Up Digital: The Rise of the Net Generation*, New York: McGraw-Hill.

Teuber, B. (2002), 'Analysis: Support Fails Broadband Customers', CRM Forum, http://www.crm-forum.com/cgi-bin/item.cgi?id=76146 (last accessed: 5 September 2002).

APPENDIX

The STAR (Socio-economic Trends Assessment for the digital Revolution) project is co-ordinated by Gabriella Cattaneo of Databank Consulting, Milan, Italy and involves the partnership of other organizations, Department of Economics, Management and Social Sciences, Ecole Nationale Supérieure des Télécommunications (ENST), Paris; empirica, Germany; SPRU – Science and Technology Policy Research, University of Sussex, UK; and the Laboratory of Industrial and Energy Economics, National Technical University of Athens.

Further elaboration of the details of this project are available on request from star@dbcons.it; please enter 'Methodology Request' in the subject field of your e-mail. The sector report titles and partner responsible follow:

Retail by Ecole Nationale Supérieure des Télécommunications (ENST), Issue Report No. 20 'Emerging Trends in Customer Relation Management Using ICT: the Retail Trade Industry'.

Financial Services by Databank Consulting, Issue Report No. 21 'Emerging Trends in Customer Relations Management Using ICT: the Financial Services'.

Travel by National Technical University of Athens, Issue Report No. 22 'Emerging Trends in Customer Relation Management Using ICT: the Travel Industry'.

Customer Services by Science and Technology Policy Research, Issue Report No. 23 'Customer Relations in the Information Society'.

These reports are available at the World Wide Web site of STAR – http://www.databank.it/star/ where a report on employment implications by empirica is also available, Issue Report No. 24 'Employment Implications of Electronic Customer Relationship Management'.

Index